The Philosophy of Social Research
Second Edition

ASPECTS OF MODERN SOCIOLOGY

General Editor: Professor Maurice Craft, Foundation Dean of Humanities and Social Science, Hong Kong University of Science and Technology.

SOCIAL RESEARCH

THE LIMITATIONS OF SOCIAL RESEARCH
Marten Shipman

DATA COLLECTION IN CONTEXT
Stephen Ackroyd & John Hughes

THE PHILOSOPHY OF SOCIAL RESEARCH
2nd edition
John A. Hughes

FORTHCOMING:

SOCIAL RESEARCH AND SOCIAL POLICY
Roger Burrows

READING ETHNOGRAPHIC RESEARCH
Martyn Hammersley

ETHICS IN SOCIAL RESEARCH
Roger Homan

The Philosophy of Social Research

Second Edition

John A. Hughes

LONGMAN
London and New York

Longman Group UK Limited,
Longman House, Burnt Mill, Harlow,
Essex CM20 2JE, England
and Associated Companies throughout the world.

Published in the United States of America
by Longman Inc., New York

First published 1980
Second Edition 1990

British Library Cataloguing in Publication Data
Hughes, John A. (John Anthony), *1941–*
   The philosophy of social research.— 2nd ed.
   1. Social sciences. Research
   I. Title
   300.72

ISBN 0-582-04563-0

Library of Congress Cataloging in Publication Data
Hughes, J.A., 1941–
   The philosophy of social research/by John A. Hughes.— 2nd ed.
     p.   cm. — (Aspects of modern sociology. Social research)
   Includes bibliographical references.
   ISBN 0–582–04563–0: £7.95 (est.)
   1. Social science—Research—Methodology. I. Title. II. Series.
H61.H88 1990
300'.72—dc20   90–5764
                                                                                      CIP

Set in 10/11 Times

Produced by Longman Group (FE) Limited
Printed in Hong Kong

CONTENTS

Editor's Preface   vi

Preface   vii

1. The philosophy of social research   1

2. The positivist orthodoxy   16

3. Positivism and the language of social research   35

4. Positivism, theory and science   69

5. The interpretative alternative   89

6. Meanings and social research   115

7. Concluding remarks   148

Index   165

EDITOR'S PREFACE

The first series in Longman's *Aspects of Modern Sociology* library was concerned with the social structure of modern Britain, and was intended for students following professional and other courses in universities, polytechnics, colleges of education, and elsewhere in further and higher education, as well as for those members of a wider public wishing to pursue an interest in the nature and structure of British society.

This further series sets out to examine the history, aims, techniques and limitations of social research, and it is hoped that it will be of interest to the same readership. It will seek to offer an informative but not uncritical introduction to some of the methodologies of social science.

Maurice Craft

PREFACE

This second and enlarged edition tries to bring up to date some of the major issues and debates in the philosophy of social research. A new chapter has been added on the philosophy of science more generally, largely because it has something new to say about the relationship of philosophy to research, and the conclusion is completely rewritten. Changes to other chapters have often been extensive, though occasionally minor. Another important change is one of tone, mainly in the conclusion, though it does depend a great deal upon what has gone before about the relevance of philosophy for social science, which ought to be a great deal less than it has been in the past. However, as always, this is a debatable and, certainly, contentious issue and not one to be concluded dismissively. The problem is to find a place for philosophy rather than ignore it altogether. There is much, of course, that is missing from the discussion, mainly any reasonably full treatment of structuralism – Foucault, post-modernism, and the rest – partly for reasons of space, partly because I lack the confidence to say anything very much about them, and partly because it is not clear just what implications they might have for the nature of social research beyond the kind of remarks already raised in the book.

There are many people to thank for their help, encouragement and sympathy. Wes Sharrock and Bob Anderson (and they are in that order because the former always complains about being last in the list of authors!), with whom I have been working for many years, have influenced me so much that it is pointless for me to try to specify what is theirs and what is not. As will be apparent from the references, in significant respects they are the co-authors of some of what appears here, although it would be wrong to hold them responsible for the form in which they appear here. My indebtedness to them is total. Dan Shapiro's unflagging intelligence, intellectual integrity, calm and control under computer 'failure', makes me forgive his cycling clothes. Richard Harper, Val Prince, Keith Soothill, Corinne Wattam, Steve Ackroyd have all proved themselves generous colleagues to work with. As usual, none of them could be held responsible for what is in these pages, except perhaps for some of the better bits.

CHAPTER 1

The philosophy of
social research

INTRODUCTION

The relationship between philosophy and what we now refer to as
the social sciences has a long history bearing some resemblance
to the parable of the prodigal son. Like petulant adolescents,
the social sciences, having been born and nurtured within the
familial fold of philosophy, reject their parentage, squander
their inheritance, only to return for refuge and succour when
the 'going gets tough'. Since developing as relatively autonomous
disciplines, the social sciences have tended to re-examine, and seek
support from, their philosophical foundations only during periods
of crisis; when tried and hitherto trusted methods no longer seem
to justify the faith originally invested in them, when researchers
lose confidence in the significance of their findings, and when
obvious and taken-for-granted principles no longer seem quite
so clear and obvious. It is in such periods that warnings about
the 'coming crisis' go out, or pleas for a re-examination of
basic principles are voiced. Such periods – and, for many, the
social sciences seem to consist almost entirely of these lacunae
– force scholars to look again at fundamentals and especially the
philosophical bases of their disciplines.

Although philosophical issues perhaps become more salient in
periods of intellectual crisis, this is not to say that philosophical
matters are relevant only at such times. Indeed, as far as sociology
is concerned, the founding trinity of Marx, Weber and Durkheim
spent a considerable amount of intellectual effort, the result of
which still massively affect styles of sociological thinking, in
establishing and refining the philosophical bases of their more
substantive enquiries. Though Weber, for one, was less than
enthusiastic about methodological disputations, regarding them
as a 'pestilence', much of his early writing was devoted to taking
to methodological task some of the scholars of his day.[1] For them,
and this is perhaps more typical of the European traditions of social
science than it is of the British and the American, philosophical
questions had to be settled in advance of empirical enquiries.

What, then, is the relationship between philosophy and the
social sciences? Why do the prodigals return when times are bad?
What does philosophy offer that the social sciences, seemingly,

cannot provide out of their own resources? Obviously, these questions, however they may be phrased, are beyond simple answer and are still unclear. And nor, it is necessary to add, need there be only *one* answer to this question. Nonetheless, it is necessary to sketch out some of the issues involved before discussing some facets of the relationship between philosophy and the social sciences in more detail.

The relationship between philosophy and the social sciences involves historical as well as logical and conceptual dimensions. Indeed, historically speaking, it is only relatively recently that the relationship has come under scrutiny in ways that make it articulable as an issue. A long period of intellectual development is presupposed and it is only at the end of this that the very idea of a social science becomes conceivable. Plato, for obvious example, spoke of society, of the relationship between the collective and its individual members, of stratification, of ways of designing and reconstructing society so that it better exemplified certain values, and so on, but had different aims and spoke under different auspices, than did Marx, Weber and Durkheim and later social theorists. Between Plato and the major theorists of the late nineteenth and early twentieth centuries have been the major successes of the natural sciences that have had a portentous influence on the ways in which we now think about and study human social life. We can no longer think about society, about human behaviour, as if the natural sciences had never existed. This is true not only of sociology, of course, but of economics, psychology, political science, anthropology, and even history. Indeed, most of these disciplines – the exception being history, but even this was not immune from the ensuing debates – owe their origins to the desire to create *sciences* of human behaviour. This is not to say that these disciplines have slavishly followed the method of the natural sciences; far from it. It is simply to point out that they have the natural sciences as an inevitable feature of their intellectual background and one to which they feel it necessary to respond either by rejection of the natural science model or by embracing it. Neutrality is not, seemingly, an option.

The question of whether the study of social life could be like the scientific study of nature was the outcome of a long philosophical debate; a debate that is of continuing importance. But, then, we might ask, what is it about philosophy that gives it this seemingly vital role in human intellectual affairs? Is this simply a contingent fact of our intellectual history, or is there something distinctive about philosophy itself which gives it this authoritative place?

THE NATURE OF PHILOSOPHY

There have been many definitions of philosophy and as many different philosophical styles as definitions; and, from the point of view of securing a definition of philosophy, matters are made worse by the fact that there are special difficulties about defining philosophy that we shall not be in a position to understand until we examine philosophical problems about definition in general.[2] This is not untypical of the way in which philosophical questions start to assume an interminably circular quality by depending upon so many other matters before we can even begin to see what an answer to what looked like an inoffensive and straightforward question could be like. 'What is reality?', 'Are there other minds?' rarely get answers of the form, 'Reality is such-and-such' or 'Yes, there are other minds – sometimes'. More often than not such questions will invite other questions: 'What is meant by . . .? 'How could we determine whether or not there are other minds?', 'What criteria could we use to distinguish the real from the unreal?', and so on.

It is this indirectness which is no doubt responsible for much of the sense of wonder we feel when faced with philosophical questions for, though they can look simple enough, it becomes very hard just to know quite what kind of answer is required. In addition, there is the feeling that they are about the most fundamental and general kinds of things: Reality, Other Minds, the Nature of Knowledge, Matter, Truth, and more. They are, of course, about these things, but in a special way. Philosophical questions about the nature of matter are not the kind of questions physicists, say, can answer. Philosophical questions about 'other minds' are not the kind of questions on which psychologists might devise experiments to explore. Philosophical questions about truth are not reducible to the manipulation of logical formulae or to the advice of lawyers. It is this style of questioning and the almost childlike and innocent way it has of producing confusion in our established and taken-for-granted ideas about the world that seem special about philosophy. Not that there is any clear and unambiguous answer to what makes a question a philosophical one. It is not so much its form *as a question*; not all questions are philosophical, after all. It is more, as said earlier, a matter of the uncertainty about whether a serious question is being asked at all that helps make questions philosophical. With most queries, such as 'what is a gearbox?', we generally know what form an answer might take even if we ourselves are incapable of providing a satisfactory one. With philosophical questions, on the other hand, we are not sure what kind of answer will suffice which, in turn, makes us doubtful about the character of the question itself. The other features I have mentioned, like a sense of wonder, a feeling that philosophical questions are about the most general kinds of things, about fundamentals, seem to hang upon this quality. Let me try to illustrate these points from a mundane example.

Occasionally, when driving around the British countryside, one comes across lorries with the word 'Milk' painted on their rear and sides. A fairly obvious conclusion to draw on seeing such a lorry is that this is a vehicle designed to carry milk going about its business picking up milk from the farms to be delivered to the dairy. But what is the basis of this inference? The fact that 'Milk' appears on the lorry? More than likely, but what does this presumption depend on? It depends, for one thing, on presuming that 'Milk' refers to what the lorry carries. Yet, as we well know, lorries can have names or words on them which do not refer to what they carry. Sometimes the name of the firm or owner is blazoned on the side, or the name of some product. So, how do I know that the lorry referred to carries milk? 'Milk' may have been the owner of the lorry, or a firm, or even the make of a lorry. How can I be sure about my claim? What kind of claim is it? Is it a claim about what I believe or about what I know? There are, of course, lots of reasons I could provide to substantiate my claim: it was a tanker lorry; 'Milk' is not a usual surname; it is not, as far as I know, the name of a firm, and it would be strange to use it as a petname, etc. And, perhaps, an accumulation of such reasons might 'add up' to a conviction that I am right: this lorry does carry milk. But why?

The reasons just adduced include reference to my personal experience, my personal knowledge, the practices of vehicle manufacturers, lorry drivers, and more. How far do I need to go before the link between the sign 'Milk' and the function of the lorry is established beyond doubt? It could be argued that no amount of personal beliefs and reasons are sufficient; what I need to do is look inside the lorry. Again, what makes looking any more certain or corroborative than the reasons I have already offered? I may still be deceived. What should I conclude if the lorry was full of whisky instead of milk? Accuse the driver of smuggling? Conclude that I had misunderstood the label all along and that milk refers to a bright brownish liquid that comes from Scotland and not to a white thick liquid that comes from cows?

But whatever conclusion I came to, the point is that I would be embroiled in questions about the nature of evidence – how we know certain things, believe others, how we know things to be true or false, what inferences can legitimately be made from various kinds of experiences, what inferences consist in, and so on. Of course, in doing so we begin to lose something of our sense of direction; familiar experiences become doubtful and even the most self-evident, certain, commonsensically true features of our everyday world begin to take on a puzzling air.

Note that these questions arose out of an everyday ability of human beings. No esoteric knowledge is required to make the sort of connection between the label on the lorry and its function of carrying milk. We make such connections routinely as part and parcel of our daily lives. The ability to read road signs, labels on packets or bottles, headlines, street names, and so on, is an essential part of our everyday competence. In which case, why raise philosophical questions about it? Of course, at one level there is no reason whatsoever why we should do so. Certainly it is unlikely that philosophical discussion of this ability will have very much bearing upon the way in which it enters and affects our lives. However, at another level, philosophical questions are important and this has to be with questions of intellectual authority.

ONTOLOGY, EPISTEMOLOGY AND INTELLECTUAL AUTHORITY

The above kind of philosophical probing, albeit of a very modest kind, stands as an example of a philosophical issue which has been dominant in Western philosophy for centuries, namely, 'What is the character of our knowledge of the world?': a question which motivates that aspect of philosophy known as epistemology. Related to this is the equally vital question, 'What kinds of things are there in the world?': a question of ontology. Epistemology is, to put it briefly, concerned with philosophical claims about the way in which the world is known to us or can be made known to us and, as such, clearly involves issues about the nature of knowledge itself. Such questions are not about techniques or matters of fact, such as 'How do you measure IQ?' or 'What was the suicide rate in the United Kingdom in 1973?' since such technical questions presume, it can be argued, philosophically justified epistemological positions. In short, epistemological questions are questions, among other things, about *what are to count as facts*.

Quite clearly ontological and epistemological issues are not unconnected. Claims about what exists in the world almost inevitably lead to questions about how what exists is made known. It is important to emphasise, however, that ontological and epistemological questions are not to be answered by empirical enquiry since they are concerned with, among other things, the nature and significance of empirical inquiry. We cannot empirically inquire into the question of whether or not there are empirical facts. We can do so in respect of particular facts but not whether the world is factual or not. The latter is not an empirical question but one requiring philosophical and logical argument and debate in which the very presuppositions of knowledge, as a general issue, are of concern. Philosophical questions are to be resolved by reason, not by empirical inquiry.

Philosophical issues are not resolved by citing evidence since much of the argument is about what is to be allowed to stand as evidence or stand as fact. Instead, what is required to resolve a philosophical dispute is an argument which shows how a set of conclusions follow, step by step, from some agreed-upon premises. If the premises are agreed and the steps consistently and rigorously followed, then the conclusions must follow *as a matter of logical argument*, no matter how outrageous they may seem commonsensically.[3] Of course, securing agreed-upon premises, following the steps strictly through to their conclusions, are neither easy nor straightforward.

In making a knowledge claim, whatever it may be, one is also indicating a preparedness to justify that claim by pointing to the ways in which one knows. Such ways may include reference to experimental methods, correct procedures of analysis, authoritative sources, spiritual inspiration, age, experience, and so on: that is, by reference to those procedures collectively accredited as, in general, good reasons for knowing. It is this public collective licensing from which the intellectual authority of our knowledge derives.[4] Receiving such a licence is not, of course, always a sufficient guarantee that one does know. What is being stressed here is the reasoned nature of our knowledge claims and the way in which particular reasons have an authoritative status, but, like all reasons, they are defeasible. To put it another way, there may be, in the case of a particular knowledge claim, reasons why normally 'good reasons' are not acceptable or, alternatively, it may simply turn out to be wrong. Nevertheless, seeing if our 'good reasons' are, ultimately, good is one of the aims of philosophical inquiry.

But why, if we recall the example of the milk tanker, should there be any doubt about the facts of the matter, that it carried milk, or doubts about how we could find out what the facts are? In the practical sense already mentioned, there is no reason at all, except in the cases where, for example, there is suspicion of smuggling, deceit or whatever – cases which are, again, also very practical ones. Of course, from a philosophical point of view, cases like these can only be resolved, one way or the other, within a framework which allows them to be dealt with in terms of factual evidence and such like. Claims, it is true, which require the assemblage of evidence, argument, and so on, to establish, but claims and evidence, nonetheless, only articulable once there is in place some framework for underpinning them as claims and evidence and about which it is reasonable to ask, 'Why this framework and not others?' and, further, 'What is the nature of this framework?'

In an important practical sense, we learn frameworks as we learn about the world. Philosophically, however, this really gets us nowhere because it is possible that what we learn may be wrong, and systematically so. We might be dreaming, deluded, blinded by personal prejudice or have learned cultural practices and beliefs that are false. In other words, it is reasonably possible to be sceptical about whether what we learn about the world is, in fact, the way the world is. One can simply point to the variety of views and conceptions held by various historical societies about the world – beliefs in witchcraft, gods sitting on mountain tops, procreation as the result of jumping over fires, magic, crossed fingers as inducing luck, and much more – to suggest that the way the world is underdetermines human conceptions of it. In which case, then, questions arise about the manner in which discriminations can be made between the way the world is and the way in which we might believe it is. Moreover, such a distinction would have to be secured by other than empirical evidence since appeal to this would not escape the arguments of that crucial philosophical character, the persistent sceptic. After all, the gods of ancient Greece, or whatever, were real, facts if you like, to the members of those societies, who might well regard the facts of our world, such as the internal combustion engine, television, or aircraft, as some species of magic. But, just what this difference might imply for the essential character of knowledge is by no means clear. Were the ancient Greeks deluded, and if they were, on what grounds can we secure our claim that gods on mountain tops do not exist? What entitles us to assert against the ancient Greeks given that, to all intents and purposes, the facticity of gods was, so to speak, something it was difficult for them to doubt? What secures our knowledge that they did not exist, against their equally fervent belief that they did?

Thus, epistemology is concerned to find arguments against persistent scepticism; an endeavour directed towards, to put it simply, finding arguments for the objectivity of certain forms of belief in order to better secure an authoritative distinction between knowledge and those beliefs which simply masquerade as knowledge. Indeed, one of the major activities of philosophical theories of knowledge has been, and still is, to give what Quinton calls, 'a critical account of the logical order of justification'.[5] This has often taken the form of a search for the indisputable foundations of human knowledge; that is, a search for those beliefs upon which other sets of beliefs rest and are justified by. If such beliefs, which it would be impossible to doubt, could be formulated then all beliefs could be arranged in a hierarchical order at the bottom of which are those which, while justifying those above, do not themselves require support. These beliefs, those of absolute epistemological priority, would be the foundations of human knowledge and, hence, the source of intellectual authority.

Unfortunately, and as we shall see, candidates for such beliefs have not received universal assent and the philosophical search goes on. Moreover, as said before, conceptions of the world have changed historically. Anyone with even a cursory knowledge of history and anthropology quickly realises, as said earlier, that in many respects our forefathers had ideas about the world very different to our own, and these have influenced philosophy itself.

What this means is that we need, perhaps, to heed Toulmin's advice not to treat epistemology as if it were without roots in the thought of a period, or unrelated to the practical procedures and problems of historically conceived disciplines.[6] For example, the methodological debates within the social sciences cannot be understood independently of the wider cultural setting of the findings produced by earlier research and based on different epistemological assumptions, and, as indicated earlier, such debates have been massively influenced by the rise of natural science. No epistemology can be composed of self-evident truths, firm for all time. Indeed, as we shall see, and have cause to criticise later, the present-day 'commonsense' conceptions of the nature of the world and the ways in which it is possible to know it themselves derive from seventeenth-century debates when they were extremely radical ideas.

Descartes and Locke, two of the major figures in Western philosophy, despite their genius, were men of their age and discussed the principles of human knowledge against the background of the then current ideas about the order of nature and man's place within it. According to Toulmin, they took three 'commonplaces' for granted, 'commonplaces' that were felt to be in need of philosophical justification: that nature was fixed and stable, to be known by principles of understanding equally fixed, stable and universal; that there was a dualism between mind and matter, the latter being inert, while the mind was the source of reason, motivation and other mental functions; and, finally, that the criterion of knowledge, of incorrigible certainty, was provided by geometry against which all other claims to knowledge were to be judged. We can see how such a conception provided both a basic ontological description of the world and epistemological prescriptions about how that world could be investigated. It directed scientists' and philosophers' attention and, through time, became established as the authoritative version of the world rather like a set of instructions about how the world should be sensibly assembled. This arose because it became a view, a conception, widely held by scientists and philosophers. More detailed theoretical work within various disciplines was given intellectual validity by the extent to which it was seen as consistent with this conception, and, at the same time, reflexively established its own validity. There were many different theoretical schools, even within a single discipline – rationalists, empiricists, corpuscularians, vorticists – taken as consistent with the ontological and epistemological principles put forward. Nonetheless, these principles set the context of debate within which the different schools fought their disagreements and their selected versions of the world. In short, it was these principles which had intellectual authority.

An awareness of the social and historical contexts of claims to knowledge does raise a problem, again one that will be addressed more fully later, which has to do with the relativity of knowledge arising, as one might say, from its social determination. Although the 'commonplaces' of the seventeenth-century view of the world – a view, incidentally, that was specific to learned groups in Europe – retained a strong influence throughout the succeeding two centuries, none of them has the same meaning, or is held with the same conviction, today. The ideas of evolution and a changing universe no longer support the conception of a fixed and unalterable universe in quite the same way. Similarly, the distinction between mind and matter, so 'commonsensically' true, no longer has the clear bright force it once had. The invention of new non-Euclidian geometries, too, went a long way towards questioning the geometrical ideal as the frame of the universe, allowing that discipline, paradoxically, more room as a human creation, useful and powerful for particular purposes but by no means the source of certainty as a universal standard of knowledge. But, if such 'evidently true' principles of our own culture and our past have come to be questioned, what is to take their place? Further, is this change a progression, an evolution of our knowledge towards better forms, or can systems of knowledge only be judged in their own terms as the product of particular social and historical societies? What are we to make of forms of knowledge alien to our own, such as beliefs in witchcraft, for example, or in medicines which rest on very different conceptions of disease and, yet, have a remarkable efficacy at least in the cultures they serve?

These examples, and there are many more, sharply pose the issue of the relativity of the criteria of knowledge or, to put it another way, the sources of our intellectual authority. How do we judge between different systems of knowledge? Are there clear and unambiguous criteria, as Plato and Descartes felt geometry represented, by which we can determine whether or not what we know is true? Is there, in short, any universal source of intellectual authority, or is all our knowledge simply relative to the society and the period in which we happen to live? Questions such as these, abstract though they may seem, are important in helping us to understand what we are doing when, among other things, we engage in social research to produce knowledge.

This brings us to another feature of philosophy, namely, that it arises in that area of human thought where our ideas and concepts are stretched to their limits. I spoke earlier of the prodigal social sciences returning to philosophy when there arises a deep uncertainty about what they are about, when human thinking seems to be getting out of hand, when barely articulable questions seem to undermine our most cherished and securely based conceptions. It is at times like these that social scientists, or at least some of them, begin to speak of 'epistemological breaks' and 'paradigm shifts' or, more prosaically, developments in human thought.

PHILOSOPHY AND THE RESEARCH PROCESS

To round off this introductory chapter I want to try to relate these general remarks about the nature of philosophy to the process of social research.

Broadly speaking, research is carried out in order to discover something about the world, a world conceived, albeit loosely and tentatively, in terms of concepts that characterise a discipline, whatever it might be. The popular image of the researcher emphasises what one might term the manipulative aspects of the role, the tangible, the 'mucking about' with things, whether they be chemical compounds, test tubes, microscopes and slides, particle accelerators, wires and transistors, microchips, and so on. This imagery derives, in large part, from the salience of natural science within our culture, and if 'mucking about' were all that was necessary to research it would have little philosophical interest. Although many of the major discoveries of our age and others have been unintended, accidental even, they have been established and accredited as discoveries through the application of a method, a corpus of procedures vested with the power to produce knowledge we would call 'scientific' which are, in effect, collective agreements as to how specific versions of the world can be arrived at. How they relate to actual scientific practice is another matter.[7]

Having raised the epistemological issue it is less easy to say exactly what the procedures are. We could easily point to things like experiments, hypothesis-testing, the public scrutiny of method and so on, as composing at least some of the methods important in producing scientific knowledge. However, for any set of procedures it is open to us to ask 'Why these procedures and not others?' 'What sort of guarantees, if any, do these methods provide that others cannot?' To pose these questions in the context of social science, it is necessary to ask what it is about the procedures and methods used by social researchers, of whatever social science discipline, that makes them superior (and gives them greater intellectual authority) to those used by, say, the man or woman in the street, the journalist, the racial bigot, the politician, the revolutionary, or a Trobriand Islander. Or, to put it even more fundamentally, what is the basis of their claim to intellectual authority?

It will be no surprise to find that answers to these questions are not straightforward. The difficulties grow if we take even a cursory look at what social researchers do when they say they are engaged in research. The training of a social researcher will normally consist in his or her being required to master questionnaire techniques, the principles of survey design and analysis, the intricacies of statistics, maybe even computer programming and modelling, and so on. Of course, the emphasis given to different techniques would depend on the discipline involved: the sociological researcher might also have to know about participant observation as well as statistical techniques, the economist about even more sophisticated mathematical and statistical tools, while the historian would probably be more concerned with developing skills in the interpretation of various kinds of documentary evidence. The point is that these skills can be learned and used as if they were the skills of a craft. Researching a problem is a matter of using the skills and techniques appropriate to do the job required within the limits set: a matter of finely judging the ability of a particular research tool to provide the data required. In short, it is to treat research methods as a technology; and, make no mistake, without this attitude 'normal science', to borrow Kuhn's phrase, would not be possible.[8]

The relevance of the philosophical issues mentioned arises from the fact that every research tool or procedure is inextricably embedded in commitments to particular versions of the world and to knowing that world. To use a questionnaire, to use an attitude scale, to take the role of a participant observer, to select a random sample, to measure rates of population growth, and so on, is to be involved in conceptions of the world which allow these instruments to be used for the purposes conceived. No technique or method of investigation (and this is as true of the natural sciences as it is of the social) is self-validating: its effectiveness, i.e. its very status as a research instrument making the world tractable to investigation, is, from a philosophical point of view, ultimately dependent on epistemological justifications. Whether they may be treated as such or not, research instruments and methods cannot be divorced from theory; as research tools they operate only within a given set of assumptions about the nature of society, the nature of human beings, the relationship between the two and how they may be known. It is at this level that one begins to meet the philosophical questions and issues mentioned earlier.

However, what is not so clear despite the kind of account given earlier of philosophy being concerned with providing intellectual authority is whether, indeed, philosophy *can* provide such authority and, even so, what *its* basis of authority is. What is true is that for most researchers, be they in the natural or the human sciences, philosophical inquiry is largely an irrelevance to their activities, and it can be suggested that the extent to which they are concerned about what philosophy has to say, is motivated more by a search for security, like Linus and his blanket, than it is for practical guidance.[9] Moreover, the kind of status that philosophy has had in our own culture for a very long time as *the* learned pursuit, may well be a reflection of the contingencies of our culture rather than due to any intrinsic and necessary feature of the character of philosophy itself as a form of knowledge. Not surprisingly, the nature and status of philosophical knowledge has been, and still is, a contentious issue in philosophy itself. Locke, for example, held to a modest 'underlabourer' conception of the philosophical task, as one concerned to clear up confusions, muddled thinking, unclarities, and the like, in knowledge. For him the new and developing science was of much greater significance. The great metaphysicians, on the other hand, such as Descartes, Kant, Hegel and, more recently, the Phenomenologists, Husserl and Heidegger, propounded much mightier views on the nature of philosophy as the arbiter of knowledge itself; a role also embraced by the Logical Positivists but without the systemic earnestness of the great metaphysicians to build great systems of philosophical rumination. Yet other philosophers, and here perhaps Wittgenstein is the most salient figure, questioned whether metaphysics said anything at all and, in doing so, challenged the very notion that has motivated much of Western philosophy, namely, that knowledge needed philosophical foundations.[10]

There is, of course, no reason why there should be only one valid conception of the relationship between philosophy and social research, especially since the nature of philosophy, and its relationship to other forms of knowledge, is itself contentious within philosophy. What can be acknowledged, however, is the fact that philosophy had, and still does have, a strong relationship to social science and, through this, to social research even though this may be unclear and arguable. We can also accept that philosophical issues can arise from within any activity, though not with equal virility at all times. Professional philosophers are not the only ones capable of raising philosophical issues although they may be rather better at it than those not so trained.

My concern here is with philosophical issues arising from social research. Inevitably many of the issues to be discussed will be of a wider concern than simply social research methods. Accordingly much of the discussion will cover the ground of the philosophy of science. There is no avoiding this, but I shall try to point more directly to questions about the nature of social research practice itself. This is more than just of technical interest, as it might be in an underlabourer conception of philosophy. The lack of consensus within and between the various social sciences, reaching chronic proportions in some of them, as to whether they are sciences, pseudo-sciences, immature sciences, multiparadigm sciences, moral sciences, or whatever, makes the issues all the more important, if still difficult to resolve. Since their appearance on the intellectual scene, the social sciences have been accompanied by a continual sense of failure over their inability to produce analyses of social life as convincing as those produced by the natural sciences of the natural world. In spite of Economics we still have economic crises, a fact sometimes blamed on politicians for not listening to their economic advisors who, in any event, speak with very different voices. In turn, politicians blame social scientists for not dealing with the 'problems of our time', and so it goes. The status of the social sciences is not settled. Within sociology, for example, debates range over whether it can be scientific in the manner of the natural sciences which has led, in its turn, to an examination of what natural science is as a form of knowledge. There is a disquiet, too, about whether the optimism of a decade or so back was really justified, as many eminent methodologists begin to question the direction of social research.[11] Whether philosophical rumination on these and other problems will resolve them is doubtful, since the problems are so widespread and multifarious. Nevertheless, what can be said is that some effort at clearing some of the philosophical ground would not go amiss.

It could be said that my concern is with the methodology of social research; that is, with an examination of the means of obtaining knowledge of the social world. As far as methods of research are concerned, I shall endeavour to approach them through what claims can be made about the knowledge they produce. This involves looking at the theories of knowledge on which they are based and coming to some conclusions about their philosophical plausibility. I shall begin, in the next two chapters, by discussing what I have termed the 'positivist orthodoxy' since, as a theory of knowledge, it has been, and still is, a major influence in the social sciences. I shall then go on to examine an alternative view which implies rather different conclusions about the nature of the social sciences and the forms of knowledge to which they can, or ought, to aspire.

One final word. By training I am a sociologist so, on the principle that an author should write according to his strengths, such as they are, most of the examples and ideas are derived from this particular social science. However, it should not be thought that other social sciences do not experience the issues I shall discuss; on the contrary. Throughout, unless accurate exposition dictates otherwise, I have used the term 'social science' for convenience, and would remind the reader that the scientific status of these disciplines is an issue in what follows.

REFERENCES

1. See his 'Knies and the problem of irrationality' in *Roscher and Knies: The Logical Problem of Historical Economics,* trans. Oakes, G., New York. Free Press, 1975, pp. 93–207.
2. Hospers, J., *An Introduction to Philosophical Analysis.* Englewood Cliffs. Prentice Hall, 1967, p. 1; Honderich, T. and Burnyeat, M. (eds), *Philosophy As It Is,* Harmondsworth, Penguin, 1979, is a good introduction to current philosophy.
3. Of course, logical entailment is no guarantee that what is concluded is true *except* as a matter of logic. This sort of problem, namely, the relationship between logical truth and, for convenience, what we might call empirical truth is, itself, a philosophical issue. The strong sense in which we seem to be constrained by logical procedures, no matter how ludicrous the conclusion might be, is a crucial matter in philosophical logic.
4. Toulmin, S., *Human Understanding,* Vol. 1, Oxford, Oxford University Press, 1972, p. 10.
5. Quinton, A., *The Nature of Things,* London, Routledge and Kegan Paul, 1973, p. 115.
6. Toulmin, S., *Op. cit.,* pp. 13–14.
7. This is one of the concerns of the new sociology of science. See Chapter 4. See also Yearley, S., *Science and Sociological Practice.* Milton Keynes, Open University Press, 1984.
8. Kuhn, T., *The Structure of Scientific Revolutions,* 2nd edn, enl., Chicago, University of Chicago Press, 1970.
9. As hinted at earlier, the issue of philosophy's own intellectual authority has recently come under attack from scholars who argue for the social construction of knowledge, a form of relativism in which philosophy, too, is culturally shaped and, hence, no more absolute than any other form of knowledge, including that of science. See, for example, Bloor, D., *Knowledge and Social Imagery,* London, Routledge and Kegan Paul, 1976. Hazelrigg, L., *Social Science and the Challenge of Relativism.* Vol. 1: A Wilderness of Mirrors: On Practices of Theory in a Gray Age, Gainsville, Florida State University Press, 1989, is an extensive review of the issue of relativism.
10. See Wittgenstein, L., *Philosophical Investigations,* Oxford, Blackwell, 1958, and for a summary, Anderson, R. J. *et al.,*

Philosophy and the Human Sciences, London, Croom Helm, 1986, ch. 8.
11. See, for example, Lieberson, S., *Making It Count: The Improvement of Social Research and Theory,* Berkeley, University of California Press, 1985.

CHAPTER 2
The positivist orthodoxy

A word of caution is in order about the title of this chapter. The critics of positivist social science, among whom I wish to be counted, like all critics have a tendency to present a picture of the opposition as if it were not only stupid but without subtlety and variety. Although it is necessary to give a summary picture of positivism, the reader is warned that it is neither a stupid position, though it is more than possible to argue that it is wrong, nor some monolithic school of thought. It also needs to be pointed out that what I am referring to as 'positivism' also goes by other names, 'empiricism', 'behaviourism', 'naturalism', even 'science', some of which, to make matters worse, are labels used on occasion to refer to anti-positivist viewpoints. It is also a term, as mentioned, associated with a number of rather disparate philosophical schools. Nevertheless, on the admittedly hazardous rose principle that it would be the same by any other name, I shall use the label I have chosen since it is the most common, and shall draw attention to differences as and when necessary.

I refer to positivism as the orthodoxy because, in some of its versions, it is the philosophical epistemology that currently holds intellectual sway within the domain of social research though, these days, this hold is weakening, sometimes significantly. Further, since it has been attacked most vehemently in the last decade or so, there are few brave enough to now embrace the label with any gusto. Nevertheless, despite this ebbing of positivism, its influence has inspired much of social research's most used research instruments, such as the survey, the questionnaire, statistical models, the idea of research as hypothesis-testing and theory corroboration, to mention but a few. As one commentator says of the relationship between positivism and sociology, 'even if in its simpler philosophical forms it is dead, the spirit of those earlier formulations continues to haunt sociology, in a full range of guises . . .'[1] Also, while in some social sciences, such as sociology, its authority is less than absolute and probably always has been so, in economics it is not seriously challenged. Political science had its 'behavioural movement' rather later than its compatriot disciplines and it still holds a strong position in various branches of that subject. In psychology, too, its hold is weakening but is still immensely strong. History is beginning to make more use of statistical methods classically associated with social research and, to this extent, developing what could be described as a more positivistic orientation. The growth of such fields as educational research, management studies, marketing – as endeavours within higher education institutions, and closely associated with the human sciences – have revived positivism's fortunes in some ways.[2] So, it is still worth looking at the philosophical character of positivism not out of some archaeological interest in a decayed civilisation but because it is very much alive.[3]

However, the authority of positivism did not arise overnight, but grew out of an intellectual debate spanning many years.

AN INTELLECTUAL BACKGROUND

Although it is customary to trace philosophical ancestors back to some early Greek philosopher, the more proximate origins of positivist epistemology lie in that blooming of European thought in the sixteenth and seventeenth centuries. Even though the Renaissance and Enlightenment picture of the intellectual darkness of the Middle Ages was overdrawn, even caricatured, later centuries did see tremendous changes in ways of thinking, particularly in what we would recognise as the beginnings of modern science and also in social and political thought. In brief, European thought was gradually freed from the theological cage erected by an alliance between political Absolutism and the Roman Catholic Church. Although 'natural philosophers', and Newton is a good example of this, often saw their endeavours as primarily religious rather than narrowly scientific, as a means of better understanding the mind of God and his creation, the allegorical world picture of medieval times was replaced by a scepticism over whether nature could so easily be explained by reference to the Bible or to religious dogma. Though religious elements were still strong, the groundwork was being laid for a secular vision of the traditional theological images of the natural and the social worlds.[4]

Two figures stand out sharply: Bacon (1561–1626) and Descartes (1596–1650). The former represented the Aristotelian legacy of empiricism as the account of the foundations of human knowledge, while the latter continued the Platonic rationalist tradition. Both were looking for an intellectual method that would overcome scepticism and, in doing so, provide a new certainty for knowledge of the world. Bacon argued for the authority of experience, experiment, induction and painstaking observation as the way towards providing a reliable basis for scientific ideas rather than the *a priori* method of medieval scholasticism. For him, a theory of knowledge had to emphasise the methodical accumulation of experientially tested knowledge. True knowledge of nature required the scrupulous design and conduct of experiments, patiently working to the 'most general axioms, ridding the mind of false notions', opinions and received tradition. Descartes, on the other hand, placed his faith in the certainty of mathematics, especially geometry, as the fundamental instrument of scientific knowledge. For him, mathematical principles were timeless and unchanging and, therefore, the most suitable language for expressing the laws of nature. Though the doctrines each of these figures represented were in many respects very different, they did have in common the search for the foundations of human knowledge. Descartes, along with other rationalist philosophers, such as Spinoza and Leibnitz, while not denying the value of sensory experience, experiment and observation, stressed the role of logical deduction from self-evident premises, while Bacon, Locke, Hume and other empiricist philosophers gave pride of place to sensory experience, and it was this branch of the epistemological divide that was carried forward by positivist philosophy.

In the social sciences the first self-conscious voice proclaiming the positivist view was to be heard in the writings of Auguste Comte in the early nineteenth century. It was Comte who followed the optimistic impulses of Diderot and other **'philosophes'** in extending Bacon's conception of the study of nature to the social. It was Comte, too, who coined the term 'positivist philosophy' and, incidentally, 'social physics' or 'sociology'.[5] Comte's work was influenced by the major philosophical attacks on metaphysics made by Hume, and others, in the eighteenth century, and by the new ideas of progress and order emerging in and after the French Revolution. Indeed, Comte's positivism is also very much a theory of history in which progress in knowledge is the motor of history itself. Comte saw the task of philosophy as attempting to express the synthesis of scientific knowledge in which all the sciences would be integrated into a single system. His own theory of knowledge stressed that science consisted of precise and certain method, basing theoretical laws on sound empirical observation. For him the social sciences were kin to the natural sciences, sharing the same epistemological form and free from the speculative dross of metaphysics. Though Comte was sufficiently a child of the Enlightenment to reject religious criteria for knowledge, he also rejected much of traditional metaphysical philosophy's claim that knowledge could be derived by rational thought alone, and, instead, pressed the claim that knowledge is derived only from empirical evidence.

Though Comte's explicit doctrines have little more than historical interest these days, his spirit was carried forward in the work of J. S. Mill, Herbert Spencer and Emile Durkheim, and is diffusely represented in the style and manner of the social sciences today.[6] Of all Comte's claims, perhaps the most important is his assertion that society, including values and beliefs, could be studied using the same logic of inquiry as that employed by natural science. Comte's explicit espousal of a unity of method between the natural and the social sciences was both timely and fateful. For one thing it gave impetus and strength to the view that the explanation of social phenomena, and by this is meant all that is studied by the human sciences, was not, in principle, different from the explanation of natural events: a view endorsed by Mill. Indeed, for Comte, the development of all sciences followed from mathematics, through astronomy, the physical and the biological sciences, and reach their apogee in the rise of the social sciences.[7] Phenomena in both the human and the natural worlds were subject to invariant laws. Though there were differences between the human and the natural sciences arising from their respective subject matters, the development of appropriate research methods in the former would remove these irritants so that the social sciences could take their rightful place at the head of the hierarchy of human knowledge. As indicated earlier, Comte himself stressed the importance of indirect experimentation, observation, and the comparative method. More deeply than this, his view encouraged a deterministic conception of man and society by effectively underplaying those factors normally regarded as uniquely human: free will, choice, chance, morality, emotions and the like. Human social life was simply the result of a coalescence of forces interacting so as to produce a particular sequence of behaviour. History, too, was simply a theme with variations in which human and other factors combined to work themselves out through time.[8]

Throughout the nineteenth century this conception gained an authority continually reinforced by the seemingly amazing progress of the natural sciences and their applications. The landmarks of this progress are familiar, the most famous being the publication in 1859 of Darwin's, *The Origin of Species*, which gave the world a systematic statement of the idea that mankind was irretrievably part of nature and subject to the same laws of process, adaptation and change. It was not long before the social sciences began to use these insights to develop theories of human society. Herbert Spencer, for example, explicitly borrowed from Darwin's work as a vindication of his own theory and method.[9] By the end of the century the scientific-deterministic view of positivism was firmly entrenched as the ambition of the social sciences. However, although, as far as the human sciences were concerned, it was positivist systems which became dominant, there were rivals. There was, in philosophy, towards the end of the nineteenth century, a revolt against positivist thought and a resurgence of idealism and romanticism, a movement particularly strong in Germany.[10] More recently, positivist thought has come to be associated with statistics as the manipulation of quantified social facts: a tradition, by the way, to which Comte was strongly opposed.

The questions to address now are 'What did this view of science and knowledge involve in practice for the social sciences as opposed to exhorting an overarching ambition?' 'What procedures and rules of investigation did it justify and authorise?' 'What kind of knowledge did it claim was the proper goal of social science?'

THE ELEMENTS OF POSITIVISM

According to Giddens, in its widest sense, 'positivist philosophy' refers to those perspectives that have made some or all of the following claims.[11] First, that reality consists in what is available to the senses. Second, philosophy, while a distinct discipline, is parasitic on the findings of science. Associated with this is an aversion to metaphysics as having any rightful place in philosophical inquiry proper. As a philosophy, therefore, it is as much concerned to establish the limits of knowledge as well as its character. Hume's petulant outburst against metaphysics captures this and its general spirit well:

If we take in our hand any volume; of divinity or school metaphysics, for instance; let us ask, Does it contain any abstract reasoning concerning quantity or number? No. Does it contain any experimental reasoning concerning matter of fact and existence? No. Commit it then to the flames: for it can contain nothing but sophistry and illusion.[12]

Third, that the natural and the human sciences share common logical and methodological foundations. This is not to say that they share precisely the same methods since their respective subject-matters require rather different methodological approaches, but this is a pragmatic not a logical or principled difference. Fourth, that there is a fundamental distinction to be made between fact and value, science dealing with the former while the latter belonging to an entirely different order of discourse beyond the remit of science. However, as we shall see later, this did not imply that all human qualities were beyond the reach of scientific understanding. While scientific knowledge has its limits these do not exclude knowledge of the mental or 'inner' life of human beings. What science is neutral about are the values to which human beings ought to aspire.

This resumé of the main elements of positivist thought as it applies to the human sciences cannot, obviously, do justice to the various and important nuances represented by its many schools.[13] From the perspective of social research the important questions turn on what positivism implies for the methods of studying society; what it claims about the proper knowledge to be gained from such study and, equally important, the criteria necessary to assess that knowledge and distinguish this from beliefs and understanding which cannot qualify as knowledge. These are wide–ranging questions, and there are many styles of social research consistent with the broad domain precepts reviewed earlier. However, as a system of thought with pretensions to authorising particular versions of the world, both the natural and the social (and positivism is particularly strident, not to say intolerant, in its views of what knowledge is), we need to look closer at its various postures.

The revulsion against metaphysics was bound up with a strong commitment to knowledge which dealt with facts, systematically discovered, rigorously supported and which could serve to ground adequate theories. In order to make and maintain the distinction between empirically grounded knowledge and mere speculation, demarcation criteria were needed. Positivism recognised only two forms of knowledge as having any claims to the status of knowledge, the empirical and the logical: the former represented by natural science and the latter by logic and mathematics. By far the greater importance was attached to the empirical. In this it took its inspiration from that philosophical tradition which claimed that all our ideas come in one way or another from our sensory experience of the world; any idea that cannot be shown to be derived from this was not a genuine idea. Clearly, such a view is dependent on a presumption that the external world acts on our senses and, in this way, is made known to us at least in a 'brute' form. The knower contributes very little to this experience and the knowledge it provides and what organisation there is to this knowledge is itself provided by experience. This view served as a criterion by which to determine what was knowledge and what was mere speculative dross; ideas only deserved the appellate of knowledge if they could be put to the test of empirical experience. There was no knowledge *a priori* of experience which, at the same time, was informative about the world. As we shall see later, mathematics was a problem for this view.

Though this view of the source of knowledge had some plausibility as an account underpinning natural scientific know-ledge, there were difficulties in applying it to human life. The notion of fact, especially when posed in opposition to value and the kind of entities conjured up by metaphysicians, had strong connotations of the material world, the world of fixed, tangible, permanent *matter*. To this extent, positivism had to overcome a distinction expressed in a number of ways between 'things material' and 'things human'; a distinction massively important in the history of thought involving, as it did, legal, religious and ethical as well as political implications. Given the imperial ambitions of positivism, one position it had to invalidate was that the human and the material world were different orders of phenomena and had to be understood differently. Some positivists denied the distinction altogether by reducing what we would regard as human to manifestations of material nature. Reducing, that is, human activities to the outcome of physiology, chemistry or a particularly behaviouristic psychology. Others, however, were not reductionists in this sense claiming instead that human and material phenomena were both real, if different in important respects, but could be made knowable by using the same methods of scientific inquiry.

The difficulties of showing the latter were manifold. For one thing phenomena in the material world, as a matter of commonsense alone – which, in effect, provided positivism with the problem in the first place – seemed to have a nature and character independent of the observer, while so much of human phenomena seemed entirely the product of human beings. How could one reach an understanding of beliefs, systems of magic, emotion, morality, legal codes, legends, public opinion, and the like, in the same way that one could of the moon, the stars, skeletons, gases, chemical compounds, and so on? Do they possess the same attributes of permanence, durability, independence of human volition and perception as phenomena of the external material world? These were the questions that had to be answered before positivism could successfully claim that the human world, like the physical, operated according to natural laws which could be discovered by a scientific method taken from the natural sciences.

So, the questions were: 'What in the human world corresponded to the "hard facts" of nature?' 'What procedures were appropriate for discovering and studying these facts?' And, assuming these questions were satisfactorily answered, 'What were the laws corresponding to the laws of nature?' By the early nineteenth century there were some hopeful straws in the wind. Some scholars were beginning to take seriously the observation, now a rather self-evident one, that human action is not random but conforms to certain predictable patterns. One of the great insights, late in the eighteenth century, was Adam Smith's formulation that individuals acting on their own self-interested preferences could, as if controlled by an 'invisible hand', produce large-scale social regularities.[14] The very notion of society, it was realised, strongly implies a set of phenomena which, though involving individuals with all their uniqueness, whims and fancies, nevertheless, exhibits large-scale regularities in some sense as real and as predictable as individuals are unique and different. In short, there were ideas around which made it plausible to conceive of society as a level of reality *sui generis*. The problem was to say how.

There were, and still are, many puzzles here and it is opportune at this juncture to look in more detail at one attempted answer to these and related questions, that of Durkheim, one which illustrates some of the major issues confronted by a positivist social science and which was profoundly influential in setting the terms of such an approach. This is not to argue that Durkheim's work is without its problems let alone provided all the answers. It was enough that he did at least do much towards identifying many of the issues. As is perhaps inevitable, the corpus of Durkheim's work displays many contradictions, inconsistencies, doubtful reasonings and other difficulties, but he does exemplify well the spirit of positivist social science.[15]

DURKHEIM'S POSITIVISM

Durkheim was the first sociologist since Comte, to whom he owed a considerable intellectual debt, and in a serious sense carried on Comte's vision in French sociology, zealously to justify sociology as an autonomous discipline characterised by the application of the scientific method. Durkheim shared Comte's empiricism, his views on the unity of science, his devotion to rational social reform, and his distrust of psychology, but rejected as bordering on the metaphysical many of Comte's pronouncements about the historical progress of knowledge. Durkheim's own work encompassed philosophical discussions on the nature of sociology as well as his more substantive enquiries into the division of labour, suicide, religion and education. In significant respects his work is a bridge between the nineteenth century and the twentieth. Many of his ideas – including the centrality of the division of labour for social organisation, the recognition that society represented a level of reality in its own right, that society was fundamentally a moral order – had their roots in Comte and his contemporaries. Other scholars, too, particularly J. S. Mill, Spencer, Tönnies, had their influence on Durkheim's ideas. However, although Durkheim was very much a child of nineteenth-century thought, he was to modify that tradition in consequential ways, and none more so than in his stress on social science as dealing with quantifiable data.

Durkheim insisted that society was a moral phenomenon in that collective ways of thinking, perceiving, acting, included elements of constraint and obligation and, therefore, constituted a collective moral consciousness. This, he held, was expressed in religion, in law, in the division of labour, in institutionalisation itself. Yet, like a true child of positivism, he wanted to show how the methods of science were provably superior to other methods of conjecture and speculation, including those of social philosophy, for studying the moral association of society; an endeavour that tried to forge a new unity between idealism and materialism. The former group of philosophies argued for a strict duality between nature and human life rejecting, in other words and among other things, the positivistic idea of a unity of method between the natural and the social, or human, sciences. For his part, Durkheim wished to retain a distinctive, and moral, conception of humankind but to study this by using the methods of natural science without their materialistic implications which, unfortunately in his view, leads to a reduction of the distinctively human to the material. Herein lies the importance of his efforts to establish sociology as an autonomous discipline defined by its object of study and to avoid the tendency in much of nineteenth-century thought to reduce the moral and the social to an epiphenomenon of material forces; a tendency most marked, though not simply so, in Marx. Moral phenomena, such as law, religion, morality itself, and so on, could be the object of a natural science of man if they were studied in the correct way. 'The aim is to bring the ideal, in various forms, into the sphere of nature, with its distinctive attributes unimpaired.'[16] These aspirations left Durkheim with two related problems to solve and to do so within the framework of positivism: first, to establish the reality of the social and, second, to discover ways in which it may be scientifically investigated.

Science, for Durkheim, was the study of 'things' and was concerned, in the first instance, to describe and classify these accurately, and, in the second, to explain the ways in which they were connected. The notion of 'things' is contrasted with ideas:

Things include all objects of knowledge that cannot be conceived by purely mental activity, those that require for their conceptions data from outside the mind, from observations and experiments, those which are built up from the more external and immediately accessible characteristics to the less visible and more profound.[17]

A most important characteristic of 'things' is that they are not subject to our will, but resist our subjective attempts to change them, proving, according to Durkheim, that their existence is independent of our ideas about them; they belong, in brief, to the external world.

Sciences deal with 'things' and sociology and the social sciences should be no exception to this. So, turning from the properties of 'things' in general we must now examine the way in which Durkheim tries to establish the facticity, the 'thingness', of the social. 'Social facts' take on properties of 'things' in general: they are external to us, are resistant to our will, and constrain us. By way of illustration he cites the French language, moral rules, economic organisations, laws, customs: all social phenomena but which are independent of and constrain individuals.

Here, then, is a category of facts with very distinctive characteristics: it consists of ways of acting, thinking, and feeling, external to the individual, and endowed with a power of coercion, by reason of which they control him . . . the term 'social' applies to them exclusively, for it has a distinct meaning only if it designates exclusively the phenomena which are not included in any of the categories of facts that have already been established and classified. These ways of thinking and acting therefore constitute the proper domain of sociology.[18]

These facts are not reducible to other disciplines, for example, to biology or to psychology, which have their own order of facts. 'Social facts', nonetheless, are 'things' in that they possess externality, constraint, diffuseness and generality, and are distinctive to sociology belonging to no other discipline or science. This, in sum, is his argument for the autonomy of sociology.

Durkheim's conception of society is a realist one claiming that there exists, within the realm of nature, an entity defined in terms of a system of relations responsible for generating collectively shared norms and beliefs. Society is a reality 'in itself' and 'social facts' exist 'in their own right' quite apart from manifestations of them in and by individuals. It is individuals who commit suicide but the suicide rate indicates a 'social fact' independent of individual suicides. It is the interaction and association of individuals which gives rise to the emergent phenomena of the social, and which is not reducible to psychology (a fate Durkheim particularly wanted to avoid) or biology. For Durkheim this means that the explanation of 'social facts' has to be in terms of other social facts.

Society is not a mere sum of individuals . . . the system formed by their association represents a specific reality which has its own characteristics . . . It is, then, in the nature of this collective individuality . . . that one must seek the immediate and determining causes of the facts appearing therein.[19]

The task of the sociologist, according to Durkheim, is to describe the essential characteristics of social facts, demonstrate how they come into being, enter into relationships with one another, act on each other, and function together to form social wholes.

In this way Durkheim attempted to reject the dualism between ideas and matter, but in a way that would preserve the qualities of ideas and not reduce them to merely material productions. Social relations and the phenomena engendered by them are facts, they possess a reality though not a material one. They exist neither apart from individuals nor in any single individual, but in and among associated individuals. By acting together individuals produce linguistic symbols, religious beliefs, moral codes, laws and the like, shared by most members of a particular society or group. Accordingly, when individuals think and act on these shared ideas or 'representations' they do so not as isolated individuals but as members of a larger cultural whole. Moreover, in doing so they produce a structure or pattern which gives that group or society its characteristic morphology. Social life consists of 'representations' which are states of the 'conscience collective' distinct from the individual consciousness of its members and conforming to different and non-psychological laws.

Having established, to his own satisfaction at least, the reality of the social, Durkheim's next task was to show how it may be made known by a social science. To this end he devoted one of his most famous studies to elucidating the procedures for a definitive study and explanation of 'social facts'. The broad outlines of such an endeavour were already there in the notion of 'social facts' as 'things' but there were essential details of method and methodology arising out of the particular nature of the social. His conception of 'social facts' as external to the individual led him to reject the view that a satisfactory explanation of a social fact was to describe its present use in society and, as a corollary, to explain it by saying that it had purposely been brought into being to fulfil those uses. In short, he eschews any form of teleological explanation: 'social facts' require explanation by causes that are deterministic rather than purposive.

Earlier it was remarked that Durkheim, in his efforts to establish an intellectual warrant for sociology, had to overcome the dualist view which sharply distinguished between 'ideas' and 'matter'. This step was necessary in order to bring the world of 'ideas' under the inquiring eye of science. Science, for Durkheim, dealt with that which is 'subject to observation'.[20] Each science is concerned with a distinct species of reality which is its exclusive domain, so making each science autonomous. Scientific observation was, however, and as Durkheim realised, no straightforward matter. 'Things', or in the specific case of sociology 'social facts,' did not just appear to our senses. On the contrary, what appears directly to our senses is often mistaken, even illusory. For Durkheim, the members of society – though subject to or bearers of 'social facts' – more often than not are deluded about the nature of social reality. They are more likely to substitute the 'representations' of 'social facts' for the real thing. These *notiones vulgares* or *idola* are illusions which distort the perception of real social processes and are entirely the products of the mind 'like a veil drawn between the thing and ourselves'.[21] To build firm foundations sociology, like any science, must break away from these mental illusions to uncover the real. The scientist must, then, be prepared to approach the social world as if he/she were looking at it for the first time: 'He must feel himself in the presence of facts whose laws are as unsuspected as were those of life before the era of biology; he must be prepared for discoveries which will surprise and disturb him.'[22] Thus, Durkheim draws a firm contrast between what we might term 'commonsense knowledge of society', the knowledge that the members of society use to describe and explain the world as it appears to them, and 'scientific knowledge' produced by the correct application of the rules or method of science.

The point that Durkheim is making here is an important one. In saying that the members of society do not know what 'social facts' are scientifically, he is not saying that they have no idea of them; simply that they are vague and confused as to their real nature. Especially revealing in this connection are his remarks on defining 'suicide' as a scientific construct:

We must inquire whether, among the different varieties of death, some have common qualities objective enough to be recognisable by all honest observers, specific enough not to be found elsewhere and also sufficiently kin to those commonly called suicides for us to retain the same term without breaking with common usage.[23]

However, what is also clear from this quotation is that the social scientist cannot ignore common conceptions despite the fact that they are vague, often unclear, ambiguous, rough and in need of clarification. On the contrary, the concepts of ordinary life are a source of social scientific concepts and the task of the social scientist is to transform them into scientific ones by dealing with the phenomena they denote as 'things' and try to rid him/herself of the prejudices and other preconceptions commonsense knowledge contains and which, for Durkheim, are impediments to scientific knowledge. 'Social facts' must be observed from the 'outside', as it were, objectively discovered as one would discover physical facts.

Durkheim is making more than the point that science comes about because the scientist adopts a particular *attitude* to the world, as his dictum 'social facts must be regarded as things' might seem to imply. Important as this posture is, he is also claiming that it is efficacious is making the real nature of the world known. However attitude and stance are not enough; other methods are required to enable the sociologist recognise 'social facts'. What these are are already provided in his notion of a 'thing', and its embodiment in the concept of 'social fact', which provides some criteria for identifying phenomena that are 'social facts' and those that are not; 'social facts' are general, external, collective and constraining. So, beginning with what might be the appearances of 'social facts', the 'illusions' – which are all that is available to start with, not the direct apprehension of 'social facts' – the social scientist must be rid of preconceptions. The second task is to look for the phenomena that display the characteristics of 'things' and, third, define them scientifically. Definition is an essential procedure in Durkheim's epistemology since it is the means by which the scientist establishes 'contact with things'.[24] Up to this point the investigator is dealing only with the appearances given to perception as the only available clues as to the reality underlying them.

A scientific definition of a phenomenon is constructed by grouping together common external and 'objective' characteristics and, once having formulated a definition, including in the investigation all those phenomena that conform to it. To define crime, for example, it is first observed that crime can be recognised by particular external signs and that what distinguishes crime from other social phenomena is that it provokes a societal reaction, namely, punishment. Punishment is not an individual act though individuals are its operative agents. It is a societal matter embodied in legal and moral codes and, as such, a sign that the 'collective conscience' is involved in some manner. Similarly, 'suicide' is defined as 'all cases of death resulting directly or indirectly from a positive or negative act of the victim himself which he knows will produce this result'.[25] This definition, according to Durkheim, denotes a homogeneous group, distinguishable from others, and delimits a phenomenon for investigation as a 'social fact'.

To effect the move from external appearances to the real phenomenon Durkheim invokes the principle of causation, an axiom essential to his epistemology. Durkheim had closely attended to J. S. Mill's methodological writings and agreed with him on the difficulties faced by the social sciences in devising suitable experiments to test their theories. Yet, since Durkheim insisted that the hallmark of science was that it dealt with causes, then this must also be a normal procedure for sociology. The explanation of social facts should be tested on the assumption that a given effect always proceeds from a single cause despite the fact that, in actuality, causal relationships were entangled in complex ways. Thus, once a category of social fact has been defined, it will be possible to find a single explanatory factor for it. Or, as in his study of suicide, identify subspecies or types of suicide in terms of their different subspecies of causes.

Since direct experiment to establish cause was not possible for the social sciences, resort must be made to the comparative method. For Durkheim this meant, effectively, 'concomitant variation' or, as we know it now, correlation; that is, the parallel movement of the series of values presented by two phenomena. This alone, provided that the relationship has been shown in a sufficient number and variety of cases, is proof that a causal relationship exists. The constant concomitance of two factors is sufficient to establish a law.[26] By itself the discovery of a lawlike relationship was not sufficient for any profound understanding, but only to indicate that a connection of some causal kind existed. A third factor might be responsible for the correlation between the original facts and further investigation would need to deal with this possibility. But, through successive refinements, a closer and closer approximation could be effected towards uncovering the true relationship between 'social facts'.

One point that needs to be repeated and stressed here is Durkheim's insistence that the causes of 'social facts' must be sought among other 'social facts'. This is one of the conditions on which the very existence of sociology as an autonomous discipline depends; it must not be reducible to the phenomena which belong to the domain of another discipline, such as psychology or biology. Each science deals with its own domain and cannot look beyond itself for explanatory causes.

One of the important aspects of Durkheim's work was that he was not content to rest with programmatics, but was also deeply concerned to apply his methodological 'rules' to substantive problems not only of sociological theory but of society itself. This latter concern maintains the moralistic and reforming tradition of Comte, and other positivists, and its interest in intervening in society in a rational and ameliorative way. The knowledge provided by social science was an essential prelude to understanding the origins, and possible prevention, of the various pathologies society was heir to. To take a slightly narrower focus, Durkheim's ideas offered an enormously interesting, and influential, set of justifications for using various forms of data to test sociological theories. His 'rules of sociological method' were intended to go beyond the merely illustrative use of historical and social materials, with which he claimed Comte, Spencer, and others had been content, but instead to ground such materials systematically within a rationally conceived social science.

Of particular interest is Durkheim's study of suicide, which impressively displays the relationship between his philosophical ideas about science, the nature of sociology and their application to the investigation of a substantive phenomenon. The decision to study suicide was a particularly courageous one given Durkheim's assertions about the nature of social facts. Of all human acts, suicide seemed so personal, so much a product of individual will – a point of view he fully recognises in his definition of suicide – that it is hard to see how it could be studied as a sociological rather than a psychological matter. Nonetheless, he strongly maintained that explanation in terms of individual psychology was insufficient. Concomitant variation shows that there is no relationship between the suicide rates in different populations and the rates of certain psychopathological states. For example, the proportion of neurotics and insane persons among Jews is relatively high, yet the frequency of suicide in the same religious group is low. In a similar fashion he disposes of explanations of suicide in terms of heredity and imitation. So, by the elimination of alternative explanations and by the assembly of other evidence he intends to demonstrate the social nature of suicide. Among the positive indices he points to is the constancy of the rate of suicide in various societies over significant periods, how the rates differed between societies, and how the rates varied in a constant manner with variations in certain social conditions. Thus, though the individual no doubt had private experiences connected with suicide, the rates were due to the associational conditions prevalent in the groups to which the individual belonged. Variations in these general conditions gave rise to different types of suicide, the altruistic, the egoistic and the anomic. In this way Durkheim was able to move towards a relationship of constant concomitance between a single cause, the degree of the social integration of social groups, and a single effect, the propensity towards suicide; the latter varying inversely with the former.

Although Durkheim contributed little, if anything, directly to the development of statistics, nevertheless, his use of descriptive statistics did help make possible ways of using such materials that went beyond mere numerical recording.[27] Suicide rates, population figures, and the like, were for Durkheim the observable sediments of the moral state of society, 'social life consolidated', making it possible to study social reality through these objective manifestations. He saw suicide rates, for example, as the product of the 'suicidogenic current', or those 'social facts' which establish that there will be, in particular groups, a certain number of voluntary deaths of one sort or another. By using these 'objective manifestations' according to the principle of correlation to establish causal connections, the sociologist was thereby able to penetrate beneath appearances to the real factors underlying social life.

LESSONS OF DURKHEIM'S POSITIVISM

It is impossible here to present a full appreciation of the many subtleties of Durkheim's thought, or rail against many of its crudities. He is important for our purposes because he confronted many of the issues that positivist social science had to solve if it was to be successful in establishing itself as *the* way forward for social science. It should go without saying that Durkheim is not the only figure of importance within this tradition. His debts to Comte and J. S. Mill have already been noted. Nor was his influence in subsequent years to remain unmodified and undistorted, as scholars read in his work what they wanted to read in order to justify their own ideas. Founding fathers always run the risk of misrepresentation as their authority is sought to lend credence to less impressive productions, but, as far as the philosophy of social research is concerned, what is Durkheim's importance?

The first feature to note is what his work implies about the relationship between social science and philosophy. Though rejecting, like Comte, the metaphysical tendencies of much of nineteenth-century social thought, Durkheim did see fit to justify his own conception of what empirical social science should be like in philosophical terms. The picture of science he proposed was very much a philosophical one. Similarly, as he argued, the problem for sociology is to reconcile idealism and materialism in order to identify its own distinctive domain of inquiry. In this respect, his concern was to establish the social, the collective, as a reality in its own right that was not reducible to phenomena at some other level and belonging to some other discipline, such as psychology or biology. He endeavoured to show how 'social facts' were every bit a part of nature as biological, chemical and physical facts. This 'social relational realism' enabled him to argue that the social could be studied with the same scientific methods used in the natural sciences, with suitable modifications, without, as said earlier, reducing social phenomena to material 'things'. Thus, ontologically speaking, natural and social realities were of the same order – 'thing-like' – and being so could be studied using the same epistemological principles. Once he had established the independent reality of the social and the unity of method he was able to argue that social life could be studied objectively by means of the method of science.

A second feature of his work caused him rather more difficulty though his solution is both ingenious and consequential. Science dealt with the objects of sensation; it was this which effectively marked it off from metaphysics and established it as a valid and superior form of knowledge. In espousing this view and claiming that 'social facts' were 'things' – though not material things like rocks, tissues, cells, or whatever, but taking on the characteristics of 'thingness' as objects in an 'external world' beyond ideas – Durkheim had to deal with the fact that the social world, as experienced by those who live within it, did not appear as 'thing-like' in this sense. On the contrary, though much of the social world is constraining, much of it was not only amenable to human will and choice, but seemingly dependent upon human conceptions. Consequently, he had to undermine this commonsense view of society as illusory, while retaining the conception of science as dealing with 'objects of sensation'. To this end, therefore, he had to develop a theory and method for relating the way society appears to its members and its real nature.

This he tried to do, not altogether clearly, in a number of ways. He urged the adoption of a particular attitude by the social scientist towards social phenomena: an attitude of objectivity, strangeness, surprise, shorn of prejudice and preconceptions. Further, the notion of 'thing' when applied to the social provided an ontological criterion by which the real processes in society could be identified. They were to be identified, using the principle of correlation, through their collective manifestations, the sediments and other traces they left behind them, and the effects that had on the world of appearances. In this way the laws of society were revealed by a properly constituted science. So, he retained the idea of science as dealing with observables but only as indices of deeper-lying causes. These deeper causes were not available either to direct observation or to the ordinary members of society, blinded as they were by their preconceptions and prejudices, but required the scientific method to make them visible and known. Thus, social scientific knowledge is special knowledge produced by persons trained in the method of science; in short, professionals.

Durkheim stands out in the recent history of social science because he tried to make legitimate a conception of social science consistent with the prevailing image of natural science, at least as he saw it. This image was to turn out to be profoundly misleading, as we shall see, but his stress on laws and causal explanation, objectivity, and rigorous method is important and gave authority to his own substantive investigations. His efforts to demonstrate that society was a reality *sui generis* as part and parcel of his wider commitment to demonstrate the scientificity of sociology did not escape criticism. It was claimed that it reified society by attributing properties to it that it simply could not possess. Certainly, much of what Durkheim had to say gave the strong impression that he did think in terms of group minds, or of society as an organism in more than just a figurative sense. Nevertheless, in spite of these and other criticisms he does represent what is the core of the positivist interpretation of social science. It should become apparent in succeeding chapters that this view is not without its difficulties.

REFERENCES

1. Halfpenny, P., *Positivism and Sociology,* London, Allen and Unwin, 1982, p. 120. More recently, Pawson echoes the same sentiments when he suggests that positivism lost the battles but won the war. See his *A Measure for Measures: A Manifesto for Empirical Sociology,* London, Routledge and Kegan Paul, 1989.
2. The position of marketing is an interesting irony since a number of the most commonly used social research

techniques, such as sampling, polling, questionnaires, were originally developed in this field and later taken over by social researchers.

3. See, for example, Phillips, D. C., The demise of positivism' in his *Philosophy, Science and Social Inquiry,* Oxford, Pergamon Press, 1987, who remarks that 'some of the most boisterous celebrants at positivism's wake are actually more positivistic than they realise . . .' (p. 44).

4. Becker, C. L., *The Heavenly City of the Eighteenth Century Philosophers,* Yale, Yale University Press, 1932, is still one of the best accounts of the intellectual consequences of these changes in European thought. See also Nisbet, R., *The Social Philosophers,* London, Heinemann, 1974.

5. Interestingly, in using these terms Comte was trying to distinguish his endeavour from the developing science of statistics under the guidance of Quetelet. Another curious irony given the major role statistics now plays in modern positivistic social science.

6. Halfpenny, *op. cit.,* ch. 1 and Simon, W. M., *European Positivism in the Nineteenth Century,* New York, Cornell University Press, 1963.

7. The one human science missing is psychology which Comte rejected as a species of metaphysics. He believed it would be replaced by 'cerebral physiology'.

8. See, on this, Toulmin, S. and Goodfield, J., *The Discovery of Time,* London, Hutchinson, 1965, esp. ch. 5.

9. It is claimed that Marx wished to dedicate *Capital* to Darwin, which attests to the importance of his work for nineteenth-century social thought.

10. See Hughes, H. S., *Consciousness and Society: The Reorientation of European Social Thought, 1890–1930,* London, MacGibbon and Kee, 1967.

11. Giddens, A., 'Positivism and its critics' in his *Studies in Social and Political Theory,* London, Hutchinson, 1977, pp. 28–9. Halfpenny, *op. cit.,* identifies 12 positivisms in an examination of this tradition in sociology.

12. Hume, D., *Enquiry Concerning Human Understanding,* London, Longman, 1875, Sec XII, Part III, ed. Green, T. H. and Grose, T. H.

13. Halfpenny, *op. cit.,* p. 8.

14. Smith, A., *The Wealth of Nations,* ed. Skinner, A., Harmondsworth, Penguin, 1970.

15. Apart from Durkheim's own writings, other useful accounts are Aron, R., *Main Currents of Sociological Thought, II,* Harmondsworth, Penguin, 1970; Lukes, S., *Emile Durkheim: His Life and Work,* London, Allen Lane, 1973; Tiryakian, E. A., 'Emile Durkheim' in Bottomore, T. and Nisbet, R. (eds),

History of Sociological Analysis, London, Heinemann, 1979, pp. 187–236.

16. Durkheim, E., *Sociology and Philosophy,* trans. Pocock, P. F., London, Cohen and West, 1953, p. 96.
17. Durkheim. E., *The Rules of Sociological Method,* ed. Catlin, G., New York. Free Press, 1966, p. xliii.
18. *Ibid.,* pp. 3–4.
19. *Ibid.,* pp. 103–4.
20. *Ibid.,* p. 27.
21. *Ibid.,* p. 15.
22. *Ibid.,* p. xiv.
23. Durkheim, E., *Suicide,* trans, Spaulding, J. and Simpson, G., London, Routledge and Kegan Paul, 1952, p. 42.
24. *Rules, op. cit.,* p. 42.
25. *Suicide, op. cit.,* p. 44.
26. *Rules, op. cit.,* pp. 130–1.
27. See Shaw, M. and Miles, I., 'The social role of statistical knowledge' in Irvine, J., Miles, I. and Evans, J. (eds), *Demystifying Social Statistics,* London, Pluto Press, 1979, pp. 27–38; Halfpenny, *op. cit.,* ch. 2.

CHAPTER 3

Positivism and the language of social research

The first half of this century saw the flowering of positivist philosophy as the orthodox philosophy underpinning empirical social science. This is not meant to imply that its doctrines were unanimously agreed; simply that it served to set the lines of debate, in so far as this took place, about the nature of the social sciences. It was positivist philosophy of social science that had to be argued against. It became the dominant methodological justification for what Kuhn referred to, though in another context, as 'normal science': a science practised without constant reference back to fundamental philosophical premises.[1] It is science characterised by 'puzzle solving' empirical research rather than debates about fundamental theories and approaches. Most social scientists agreed that the social sciences should model themselves on the natural sciences, especially physics, since it was these disciplines that represented the peak of achievement in human knowledge. Accepting this ambition, however was one thing, there was rather less agreement on the precise nature not only of the social sciences but of the physical sciences, too, and it is important to remember that although the social sciences took the natural sciences as their yardstick they did so with respect to particular *philosophical* interpretations of natural science of which positivism was the major one. What was rarely done, if ever, was compare social scientific *practice* with that of physical science. It was philosophy that was the interpreter and mediator of the method of science.

Within positivistically inspired social science there were debates, and still are, about, for example, the nature of scientific explanation, whether social science theories could attain the certainty of theories in natural science or had to be satisfied with probabilistic ones, whether falsification or verification was the fundamental criterion distinguishing scientific statements from non-scientific ones, and so on. These debates, among others, formed the core issues in the philosophy of social science.[2] The concern in this chapter, however, is mainly with philosophical issues arising out positivism's stress on the sovereignty of the empirical, and, in this respect, is focused rather closer to the research process itself. This is not to say that such issues are not unrelated to the wider issues of the philosophy of science, though such connections can be

d. However, in so far as one is dealing with questions
ie nature of knowledge, one cannot avoid them. As we
:he previous chapter's discussion of Durkheim's attempt
olish a social science of sociology, the explicit use of
wnat is regarded as the correct philosophical account of natural
science, namely, positivism, has been the traditional mode of
demonstrating that, despite their different subject-matters, the
social sciences use the same epistemological principles as the
natural sciences. However, some of these wider issues will be
dealt with in the following chapter. This division is somewhat
artificial but expedient in view of the nature of the issues and
the lengthy exposition required of a number of different if related
themes.

THE LANGUAGE OF OBSERVATION

One of the important features of positivist philosophies of science
was the pre-eminence accorded to empirical research in the
production of knowledge. All the major scientific advances, it
was claimed, had resulted from the patient accumulation of facts
about the world to produce the generalisations known as scientific
laws. Science, above all else, was an empirical pursuit and its
basis lay in the observation of what we can term 'brute data':
that is, data which are not the result of judgement, interpretation,
or other subjective mental operation.[3] In the same manner as
natural scientists describe and classify phenomena by noting such
observables as shape, size, motion, and so on, so should social
scientists define and chart their phenomena of interest.

Positivists argued, then, that the basis of science lies in a
theoretically neutral observation language which is both ontologically and epistemologically primary.[4] That is, statements made in
this privileged language are directly verifiable as true or false
simply by looking at the 'facts' of the world. In this it espoused
a correspondence theory of truth, namely, that the truth of a
statement is to be determined by its correspondence with the facts.
If it did correspond then it was true; if not, then false. Later this
would become, in modified form, a criterion of the meaningfulness
of a statement and a way, thereby, of distinguishing scientific
statements from non-scientific ones.

The clearest and most influential version of positivism in this
century was that propounded by a group known as the Logical
Positivists, which began in Vienna in the late 1920s under the
leadership of Mach, Schlick and Carnap.[5] They were to give
positivistic philosophy of science a shape and system which served
to make it the predominant view of the first half of this century.[6]

As in other forms of positivism they rejected metaphysics by recognising only two kinds of proposition: the analytic, e.g. those of mathematics and logic, and the synthetic, e.g. those verifiable by empirical observation. Statements belonging to neither kind were not propositions and were meaningless. Religious, moral and aesthetic statements along with metaphysical ones were consigned to the dustbin of meaninglessness or, a slightly better fate, statements about personal taste or preference, since they were verifiable neither by empirical observation nor by logical deduction. The principle of verification, as it was called, served as a criterion for deciding whether a statement was meaningful or not.

Logical Positivism also differed from nineteenth century versions of positivism by stressing the *logical* character of the scientific method as well as the empirical. Logic had always been a problem for positivist and empiricist philosophies given their emphasis on the empirical as the source of knowledge and, from this, their rejection of rationalist doctrines as little better than metaphysics. Some, J. S. Mill for one, put forward an empiricist interpretation of logic and mathematics. For him logic and pure mathematics consisted of propositions that were generalisations from experience: a view which rendered mathematical statements, such as 2 + 2 = 4, susceptible to empirical refutation. It was developments in formal logic from the middle of the nineteenth century onwards that offered a resolution of the suspicions with which empiricist philosophies held logic and mathematics. Logic, and mathematics as a branch of logic, came to be regarded as a collection of formal rules for constructing propositions and stipulating the conditions under which, within the formal system, they could be taken as true or false. Formal logic, in other words, elaborates the relational structure of terms within a symbolic system but is empty of empirical content. Thus, although beyond experience, logic and mathematics, unlike metaphysics, expressed *analytical* truths; that is, their statements were true or false by virtue of the rules for manipulating the symbols. Mathematical and logical truths are *a priori* not, as many rationalists thought, because they mirror the way in which the human mind works, but because they are analytic and tell us nothing about experience. As analytical truths they could be incorporated into science without fear of metaphysical contagion.

As far as Logical Positivism was concerned, these developments in the reconceptualisation of the nature of logic and mathematics spelt the end of traditional metaphysical philosophy. Logical analysis, as a method, could resolve philosophical problems and paradoxes by reconstructing philosophical statements in the language of formal logic. They also helped to reformulate the notion of empiricism. Since Hume, empirical knowledge had been conceived in terms of ideas, or concepts, which were the remains of sense impressions. These were the source, and the only source, of our knowledge of the external world. As said earlier, *contra* rationalists, such as Descartes, there were no innate ideas. However, the notion of a primary observation language as the bedrock of scientific knowledge was a troublesome if powerful one.

While many of the more extreme positions of the Logical Positivists were found to be untenable, there is little doubt that their influence was profound. Their view was taken by many philosophers, and by many scientists, as the philosophically authoritative version of science's epistemology. Though difficulties remained, these were not considered to be of such fundamental importance as to invalidate the positivist tradition itself.

THE LANGUAGE OF OBSERVATION AND SOCIAL SCIENCE

The idea that knowledge is based upon a primary, or 'protocol' language was intended to ground science as an empirical discipline, giving it an objective character by providing, in principle at any rate, a publicly available, emotionally, ideologically and theoretically neutral mode of expression, providing a clear criterion of truth independent of human whim and prejudice, and privileging its status as knowledge of the highest order. However, the very difficulties of formulating an adequate basic observation or protocol language suggested that observation was a complex matter. Indeed, there were radical empiricists, including Mach, who were suspicious of the powerful theoretical concepts of even physics such as 'atom' or 'absolute vacuum', since they were beyond experience. But for the more moderate empiricists the idea of a sensory experiential language proved, in the end, a difficult idea to establish. Facts did not just appear. They were not just lying around waiting to be picked up by some wandering scientist; they had to be discovered, assembled and made informative. All the 'facts' Darwin used as evidence for this theory of evolution were 'known' before he used them. Fossils had been noticed by other naturalists many years before Darwin, most of the flora and fauna, too, had been discovered or seen by other travellers. What Darwin contributed was a profoundly radical way of rearranging these materials.[7] There was, then, more to scientific observation than 'simply looking at the facts', however basic these so-called facts appeared to be. So as far as the Logical Positivist position was concerned while most members of the school saw this language as consisting of the direct non-inferential reports of experience, exactly what the 'protocol' terms in the observational language referred to was a matter of much inconclusive debate. Some argued for a sense data interpretation of the non-inferential reports of experience, others for 'physical objects', and yet others for 'atomic facts'. But, for our purpose, the point is that whatever the characterisation of these protocol terms, it was the observational language that was ontologically and epistemologically privileged as beyond reasonable doubt. So far as scientific practice was concerned, it was not suggested that all descriptive terms and concepts be couched in this basic observational language. All that was necessary was that if they were to be meaningful, then they should, in principle, be translatable into, or reducible to, statements in the observational language. As with the nature of the basic entities themselves, there was considerable debate as to how such a translation or reduction could be carried out.

So, while the formulation of a primary observation language proved philosophically elusive, if not illusory, other criteria or principles of observation for determining facts were required. To an extent these were already implicit in the positivist theory of knowledge. The world, whether natural or social, operated according to strict laws and therefore possessed a deterministic structure which it was the business of science to discover; a structure which could be described formally and quantitatively. Methodologically, then, empirical research, and here one might as well say scientific research, amounted to discovering those regular and invariant properties of the phenomena of the world and the relationships between them; the properties being described, as far as possible, in terms of what is rigorously observable. Thus, the physicist does not deal with billiard balls, falling feathers, crashing cars, boiling water, but with bodies of a particular shape, size, mass, motion, wavelength or whatever. Correlates among such attributes constitute the basic ingredients of scientific theories. Many such attributes may not be observable unaided by instrumentation, but the principle is there nonetheless.

Carried over into the human sciences this kind of conception faced a number of problems. One of these had to do with so-called 'mental states'. Human beings are not simply external shells of shape, size and motion: they have an inner life not accessible to observation in the normal way, unless private introspection is counted as a publicly available form of observation. Some argued that the inaccessibility of mental phenomena implied that they could not be dealt with objectively, that is, scientifically. Physical objects, physical events, physical processes could be described in more rigorous versions of the five senses and were, accordingly, publicly available. Mental states or states of consciousness, on the other hand, could only be experienced, and truly known, by one person, namely, the person undergoing the experience. Some Logical Positivists, Neurath's 'physicalism' being perhaps the most prominent of these, claimed that science could only deal with 'mind' in so far as its products could be described in the language of physics; that is, as spatio-temporal phenomena, such as speech, facial expressions, etc.[8] The social sciences were, in other words, the study of behaviour with this being construed extremely narrowly. Few were, however, quite prepared to go this far.

A more typical strategy was to argue that though mental states were not observable in any direct fashion, nonetheless particular mental states were associated with specific outward bodily displays. For example, we see a person clenching his fists, gnashing his teeth, glaring wide-eyed from a red face, and reasonably infer that the mental state the person is experiencing is that of anger; indeed, that the cause of all this dramatic posturing is the internal experience of anger and rage. Accordingly, the argument was adduced that all statements referring to mental states could be analysed into a further set of statements referring to overt bodily signs or displays. Mental phenomena, then, could be observed, for all intents and purposes, by studying the corresponding outward behavioural display, the latter being an index of the former.

This sort of account of the relationship between mental states and overt behaviour was comfortable to many empiricists since it, seemingly at least, brought the 'mind' into a scientific frame of reference in which its features could be publicly observed, charted, quantified and correlated. The epistemological principle of sensory experience as the foundation of scientific knowledge was preserved and no unsystematic introspection involved. However, though this account had some plausibility with reference to anger, pleasure or pain, human beings experience more sophisticated mental states, to call them that, than these. They can desire wealth, status or power, can believe in democracy or the divine right of kings, determine the moral worth of actions, admire the beauty of the Giaconda, despise Dynasty, fall in love, and many more. Could these emotions, beliefs, morality, judgements be interpreted in the same way? Do these mental states correlate with determinate bodily displays in the same way that it might be said of anger? For the positivists the answer was in the affirmative. The beliefs people hold, the values they subscribe to, the judgements they make, their tastes and their preferences, are all publicly verifiable since they issue in, or result in, publicly observable behaviour, artifacts of various kinds, and so on. Values are objective in the sense that they are held by persons who can report their values and beliefs. The social scientist does not have to agree or disagree with such expressions; he simply has to report on them or use them as primary data. In short, the values people hold are as factually brute as geological strata, atoms, gas flows, velocities and the like.

By using carefully constructed instruments, such as questionnaires, attitude scales or interviews, subjects can provide responses which are indicative of mental states and in this way provide objective access to important aspects of human mental life.

Developing a methodology for investigating the mental aspects of human life was itself part of a larger issue mentioned earlier of formulating principles of social scientific observation. It was felt that to conform to what natural scientists were able to achieve, the language of social science observation had to consist of terms objectively defined, and had to be generalisable and, if possible, quantifiable. Since the aim was, in effect, to achieve the Comtean vision of discovering general laws of social life, the basic terms of the scientific language had to express general rather than particular qualities. One of the important moves in this respect was the adoption of quasi-mathematical terms in which to talk about data, namely, the language of variables. This represented a way of talking about social phenomena within an apparently neutral framework in terms of their attributes and properties and how they varied between and among one another.

THE LANGUAGE OF VARIABLES

It is difficult today to recapture the revolutionary impact of this formulation of the character of social research and its phenomena, since the language of variables is so much taken for granted in empirical social research.[9] These developments owed much to the work of Paul F. Lazarsfeld (1901–76) – an occasional participant in the Vienna Circle prior to the Second World War – and his colleagues. His major efforts were devoted to developing research techniques and designs in the context of research on, for example, the effects of the mass media and on the determinants of voting choice; both areas in which he did pioneering work. His work was inspired by a particular, though not unique, conception of science and how this could be translated into making social research more scientific in its quest for adequate empirically based theories.

The notion of a variable has a long tradition in mathematics, statistics and, importantly, symbolic logic. It is essentially a simple idea. A variable as opposed to a constant can vary in value within a range of values, even if this is of the order of 0 or 1, where 0 indicates the absence of a variable and 1 its presence. The innovative move was to use this idea as the pivot around which a whole way of thinking about social research could revolve. 'No science', declared Lazarsfeld, 'deals with its objects of study in their full concreteness.' [10] Certain properties are selected as the special province of study of each science, among which each tries to discover empirical relationships, the ultimate being those of a lawlike character. Thus, physics is interested in its objects not in their full concreteness but in abstracted properties of them, such as their mass, length, force, velocity, molecular composition, and so on. Science's connection to the world is an abstracted one dealing with the properties or qualities of things, not with things in themselves. In this, Lazarsfeld is thoroughly Kantian espousing the position that empirical knowledge can never penetrate to the 'essence' of phenomena but deal only with their 'surface' appearances or indications. This means that the first task of any science is to identify those properties which are its concern: no simple task as the history of science attests to. It is particularly difficult for the social sciences where there is no standard terminology. Nevertheless, for Lazarsfeld this was not an insuperable problem nor, indeed, one that needed to be solved by epistemological or ontological rumination. What he proposed was an empirical strategy for pursuing this goal for social science by treating properties as variables; that is, using variables as 'devices by which we characterise the objects of empirical social investigations'.[11]

Briefly, Lazarsfeld saw the research process as one of translating concepts into empirical indicators; that is, indicators based upon what is observable, recordable, measurable in some objective way. The first step was the creation of a 'vague image', or construct, that results from the immersion of a reseacher in a theoretical problem. The real work begins by 'specifying' its components, aspects or dimensions, and selecting 'indicators' which can 'stand for' them. Thus, 'prejudice' could be measured in a number of ways, for example, by responses to particular items on a questionnaire, attitude scales, voting choice, avoidance behaviour, etc., which depend upon the practical exigencies of the research and the tools of investigation. Most concepts will, likely as not, prove to be complex combinations of indicators rather than measures of a single indicator variable. As most social research will be interested in more than one construct, it is by finding patterns among indicators in terms of their covariation and interrelationships that empirical descriptions are built up, and out of which empirically grounded theories can be devised to explain the patterns found. Quantification, according to Lazarsfeld, is possible through using the idea of variables if only at the relatively crude level of frequency counts of the presence or absence of some property, since even this modest level allows for the identification of covariations between variables.

As hinted at earlier, it is perhaps better to regard Lazarsfeld's endeavours as methodological rather than philosophical; that is, as seeking for a way of making social research an empirically based science. Nevertheless, there is a metaphysics of ontological realism there to the extent that it only makes sense to talk of indices if it can be claimed that they 'stand for' something. However, although Lazarsfeld talked of an abstracted connection between scientific concepts and the world, in practice his strategy is effected by means of correlations among indices and the strength and stability they display, if they do, across studies. Theoretical validity is owed to the sovereign position given to the empirical in that the adequacy of a construct is determined by patterns found among measured variables. Special importance is given to operationalising concepts into observable measured indicators. For Lazarsfeld, indicators are what social science research works with, and they indicate something, to varying degrees, if they show detectable patterns of association with each other.

For empirical social science, then, the language of variables offered a way of expressing relationships in data and, as such, a way of describing phenomena objectively and quantitatively. All phenomena that are of interest to social research, including subjective states, could be conceptualised, measured at some level at least, correlated and variously manipulated by the formal techniques of variable analysis. Hypotheses could be formulated and tested. Although few, if any, of the social sciences could emulate psychology in being able to carry out laboratory experiments, fair approximations in non-experimental settings of social research to the logic of experimental design could be achieved using statistical partitioning methods.

However, despite the fact that the Lazarsfeldian conception has virtually become the orthodox style of social research, in some quarters regarded as **the** method of empirical social research, it has not been without its critics. Some objected to the way in which the reality of social phenomena and processes, in all their fullness, richness, complexity and flux, were concealed behind what was, in effect, a descriptive apparatus whose character owed more to the requirements of quantification and measurement than it did to reflecting the underlying phenomena it was supposed to describe. Some of these matters will be taken up in a subsequent chapter.

A further difficulty was that variable analysis was intendedly atheoretical; a ubiquitous method for pattern searching in data as a route towards theory formulation. Theories explained the patterns, but the patterns were needed first in order to obtain better theories. That is, although 'vague' theoretical ideas will inform the kinds of variables that will be investigated, or will be regarded as independent, as dependent, as mediating variables, and so on, their significance is to be determined by empirically confirmed patterns and correlations shown in the data.[12] The method is, in short, an empirical strategy for theory construction.[13] However, theoretical conceptions could not be ignored altogether in the business of constructing indices. Let us take one example for extended discussion.

SOCIAL WHOLES VERSUS METHODOLOGICAL INDIVIDUALISM

As Durkheim had taken great pains to argue, the social sciences were not concerned with individual phenomena as such but with collective phenomena including, of course, those individual states of consciousness that were due to the operation of social processes. The social sciences dealt with groups of various kinds, institutions, cultures, whole systems of interaction and processes which are, so to speak, more than just the sum of individual phenomena but have, again as Durkheim would put it, a reality in their own right. Economics deals with institutions concerned with the production and distribution of goods; sociology with classes, groups, institutions, even whole societies; political science with governments, political parties, voting patterns, and so on. Yet, as we saw earlier in reference to mental states, such are not observable in any direct fashion. One cannot, for example, observe social classes, the economic system, capitalism, and the like, so what ontological status could such concepts possess? Again, as Durkheim asserted most forcibly about the reality of collective phenomena: 'Society is not a mere sum of individuals. Rather, the system formed by their association represents a specific reality which has its own characteristics.'[14] Social reality, in short, transcends that of individuals. As in nature, there occur in the social world, and definitive of it, wholes which are not simply aggregates of the individual elements composing them but are organic unities, more than the sum of their parts. Such emergent wholes cannot be reduced to the parts composing them.

A successful substantiation of this kind of claim, it could be argued, is necessary to the viability of the social sciences, and Durkheim did so argue for example, for without it the proper study of human behaviour, whether deemed to be social or otherwise, would be psychology or one of its branches. Philosophically, and as Lukes points out, the issue is an ontological one concerning the reality of social entities.[15] As we have seen, Durkheim claimed that social entities were real 'things' even though they were not material 'things'. However, operationally matters were not so easily resolved. The empirical evidence adduced for social facts was, primarily, derived from individuals. Only individual behaviour could be observed in any direct way, whether this be in the form of responses to questionnaires, attitude tests, participant observations, recorded rates of the frequency of criminal activity, rates of suicide, voting preferences, share buying, or whatever. In short, 'nothing about social facts is *observable* except their individual manifestations'.[16]

The paradox here seems firm enough: on the one hand, the claim that social wholes were real depended on it not being possible to reduce completely statements about them to statements about individuals; on the other hand, the evidence for the reality of social wholes seemed to depend almost entirely on evidence derived from observable individual manifestations of behaviour. Even though Durkheim, among others, had claimed to show that individual characteristics and behaviour varied with, or were determined or caused by, social contextual factors such as religion, social class, social status, and so on, the data on which such conclusions were based were always traceable back to their origins with individuals. Nor is the problem one of research technique since, after all, multivariate analysis, contextual analysis, correlation, etc., are all powerful enough *given* the assumptions that the chosen indicators do reflect, to put it crudely, the reality of collectivities in the first place; the problem is to license this interpretation.

It is undoubtedly the case that properties can be predicated of social wholes which cannot be predicted of an individual. A society or a group can be said to be stratified, hierarchical, democratic, class ridden, and so on, while the same characteristics cannot be said of an individual, at least not the same way. Groups, for example, can be said to maintain their identity in spite of the replacement of members. The character of the groups, too, can be shown to influence the behaviour of its members. In many legal systems some associations are treated as if they were persons having rights and obligations distinct from their members. Economists speak of, and even have theories about, the firm. However, these observations are, to a degree, beside the point. Though in legal and in ordinary language we can and do speak in this way, the issue is whether this is legitimate *scientifically*, and, if so, what ontological and epistemological justifications can be offered for so speaking? Answers to this affect the interpretations that can be plausibly offered for research operations supposedly measuring or indicating collective phenomena. There is one additional restraint for the positivist: an acceptable answer must eschew any implication of a 'group mind' or other metaphysical entities – the trap of reification into which Durkheim nearly fell.

Of course, the problem as set out does not require that a choice be made between the reality of social wholes or the reality of individuals; it is not, or need not, be a question of one or the other. To maintain the view that there are both individuals and social wholes, while accepting at the same time that the latter are not observable in any direct way, we need also to claim that, if anything is to be truly predicated of a social whole, this must imply the truth of at least several descriptions of individuals. Without this condition it would be impossible to test statements about social wholes by observation since these are not observable, though individuals are.[17] But, equally, the

description of social wholes, though implying several descriptions
of individuals, must involve more than this; that is, it must mean
that the set of relevant individual descriptions does not exhaust
what may be predicated of the social whole. Thus, for example,
'British society' may be offered as the name of a social collective
and a number of properties predicated of it, such as 'is governed
by the Conservative Party', 'is a monarchy', 'has a low crime
rate compared with X, Y, Z societies', 'has a rate of inflation
of X%', and so on. The question is, however, whether each of
these statements, while implying the truth of a host of statements
about individuals – their behaviour in elections, in the market
place, their obedience to the law, their attitudes and beliefs, and
many more – is reducible simply to a listing of such individual
statements however large in number? If not, then what is left that
is not so reducible?

According to the doctrine of 'methodological individualism'
nothing is left since all so-called collective facts are, in principle,
explicable in terms of facts about individuals. References to social
wholes or collectivities are, in this view, essentially summary
references to the characteristics and properties of individuals,
and the latter could replace the former without residue. The
'real', in other words, is restricted to what can be observed and
these are the characteristics and properties of individuals. The
most that can ontologically be claimed of social wholes, since they
are never concretely given in observation, is a status as theoretical
entities having explanatory convenience only.[18] Ontological reality
is attributable only to individuals while social wholes are regarded
as abstract or theoretical entities not observable but having an
explanatory usefulness rather like similar kinds of theoretical
concepts in physics and the other natural sciences.

For some this interpretation was tremendously important, since
it seemed to bring the social sciences even closer to the practice
of natural science in which a principle of reduction seemed to
operate through a hierarchy of explanation from fundamental
physical processes up to larger more global ones. Moreover, it
appeared, too, to avoid the metaphysical lapses to which the social
sciences seemed heir, such as reifying collectivities and attributing
to them qualities which, properly speaking, could only belong to
individuals and their relationships with each other. In so far as
recourse was made in ordinary language to things like the 'spirit
of the people', 'the racial memory', 'the mind of an age', 'class
consciousness', 'the people', and so on, then either this was a
careless way of speaking done for effect, or, at best, a conveniently
summary way of referring to large numbers of individuals in some
capacity, or at worst, unscientific and ignorant.

For others, however, 'methodological individualism' was too
timorous and, furthermore, seemed to lead to a psychological

reductionism in which all so-called social facts, including those social properties and attributes of individuals, were ultimately reducible to explanations in terms of psychological dispositions. Durkheim would certainly have made this objection. Social wholes needed to be given a less ephemeral character than that of mere theoretical entities and given, instead, a conception more consistent with a view of them as real causal factors.

Of course, as hinted at earlier, methodological reductionism does not necessarily imply a psychological reductionism: that the only valid explanations of social life are those couched in terms of human psychological dispositions. Homans, for example, argued that sociology can be 'reduced' to psychology in the sense that its laws can be logically derived from those of psychology, just as the laws of chemistry can be deduced from the more general ones of physics.[19] For one thing, it can and often does claim that human action is, at least in important and irreducible respects, the outcome of interaction with others. That is, it acknowledges that there are 'emergent properties' arising out of individuals *interacting* with other individuals, properties that are not present in the individual alone. Interaction itself is one such emergent property, and all that flows from this, such as the possibility of power between two or more people, exchange, social status, cooperation, conflict, and many more. Indeed, in describing the actions of individuals we often have to make reference to their institutional status in order to understand the actions they are performing. The actions of a person towards his children cannot be understood without the relational description 'father', arrest by a person unless we understand the institutional identity 'policeman'. In short, the whole relational context that is social life is not reducible to psychological dispositions.[20] This does not, of course, dispose of psychological explanations as relevant to the explanation of human social behaviour; but nor is it meant to do so, it is merely to reserve places for the respective disposition of social and psychological explanations.

What does all this amount to methodologically? What are the implications of these views for social research? The problem occurs for the social sciences in the following way: 'individuals' and 'social wholes' are not discrete, separate phenomena, the latter being defined and conceptualised in large part in terms of the former, because only individuals, their attributes and behaviour are observable. If this is correct, then it is extremely difficult to establish, theoretically and empirically, the reality of social wholes independently of the reality already accepted for individuals. But, for the positivist, if an observational basis cannot be provided for social wholes then they are little more than metaphysical entities, and data presumably about such entities are masquerading as scientific data.

From the point of view of variable analysis, such debates seem beside the point. All that is needed are ways of indicating the properties of 'objects', be they individuals, collectivities, aggregates or even whole societies. Then it is an empirical matter of determining which of these indications, in any particular case, are the important determinative ones. After all, we can calculate rates for regions, for example, develop indices for group properties, and so on.[21] Unfortunately, the ontological claim is prior to choices of indicators since, presumably, the indicator has to reflect the properties of the phenomenon it is designed to 'stand for'. It is not that indicators cannot be produced but, having done so, what inferences does this entitle one to make about the character of the underlying phenomenon? If we lean towards methodological individualism, then the interpretation of the patterns produced will lead to one kind of theoretical interpretation than if we are persuaded of other types of conceptions. The empirical patterns of variable analysis will not resolve matters such as these. This is a problem to which we shall return.

THE STATUS OF THEORY AND THE NATURE OF GENERALISATIONS

It is fair to say that in the empiricist tradition of positivism the philosophical treatment of theory lagged behind the formulation and development of methods of empirical research. This is perhaps not surprising given the emphasis placed on empirical observation as the prime ingredient of science. Both Bacon and Mill, for example, and years apart, eager to exploit and advocate the method of experiment, regarded nature and its laws as there waiting to be discovered by the correct empirical methods.

It was widely regarded that the aim of science was to produce generalisations or laws stating the causal relationships which held between phenomena in the universe. Natural science had progressed by discovering invariant and necessary connections between phenomena in an orderly and lawful universe. Galileo, Newton, Darwin, later Einstein, and others, had each contributed a precise and universal statement as to how certain phenomena operated and, using these statements, scientists had an ability to predict events in the natural world with astounding accuracy. Such statements, it seemed, were universal in the sense that they specified that all events of a particular kind were invariably connected with other events and having the basic logical form of 'all A is B'. The problem was how to regard these statements. However, the idea that laws involved both invariance and necessity began to look less than straightforward. Invariance or regularity were less of a problem since departures from laws could be explained by special circumstances. The real problem was necessity. As Outhwaite points out, the most obvious way was to see the source of necessity as inherent in the nature of things; yet others saw this as anthropomorphic or trivial.[22] Molière expressed the latter criticism in his mockery of the claim that opium makes people sleep because of its 'dormative power'. The positivist tradition, with its presupposition that empirical knowledge was the most fundamental knowledge in the foundation of science, was to give laws an empirical interpretation. In this it owed much to Hume and other philosophers of the British empirical tradition.

Hume argued that the idea of cause is no more than the outcome of repeated observations of one object following another, or one event following another event. For Hume ideas were impressions gained from the senses and his interpretation of cause was consistent with this point of view. Knowledge of causes was the result of sensation and habit. Reason alone, for example, could not arrive at the idea of heat causing water to boil, or of gravity causing bodies to fall, without experience to work on. To say that A causes B is to say that A and B are 'constantly conjoined' in our sensations; the causal connection being attributed to, but not observed in, nature. Through repeated observations of similar conjunctions one comes, by habit, to expect that they will always be related.

The idea of cause and effect is deriv'd from experience, which informs us, that such particular objects, in all past instances, have been constantly conjoin'd with each other: And as an object similar to one of these is suppos'd to be immediately present in its impression, we thence presume on the existence of one similar to its usual attendant.[23]

In some respect, however, this did not seem to go far enough. Universal laws were regarded as exactly that: universal both in time and place applying to the past, the present *and* the future wherever. Hume's reasonings though, by making causal generalisations the result of sensory experience, could provide no guarantee that the generalisations would hold in the future since they were based on evidence which could only be gathered in the past and the present. By definition, constant conjunction could not be observed in the future, and water might, in the future, boil at 80° rather than 100° centigrade. Hume's reply to this would be that, indeed, there could be no guarantee that such generalisations, even the well-established ones of science, would hold in the future as past experience would itself show. Nevertheless, we only have past experience on which to base future expectations, so this is all we can use. Accordingly, knowledge of empirical connections, of causes and their effects, is never certain but only probable; that is, we can never have absolute confidence in their repeated connection in the future.

A general causal statement, on this view, was a summary of our sensations of two sets of phenomena and constituted what is normally called an empirical generalisation. To determine causes we formulate categories of objects or events on the basis of their respective similarities. The relationship between them is observed, naturally or experimentally, and the sequence noted. If we find that in a large enough number of cases there is a constant conjunction of the putative cause followed by its corresponding effect, then we expect that this association will hold for the future, though there is no guarantee that it will. Thus we have our causal generalisation.

Later, J. S. Mill was to provide further arguments for the empiricist interpretation of laws. He defined concepts as referring to classes of objects which demonstrate a likeness with respect to some property. Man, woman, cow, girl, temperature, energy, catholic, etc., would all be concepts in Mill's terms because each word stands for a group of objects having similar characteristics. The method of relating concepts within synthetic propositions, (that is, propositions which are empirical as opposed to *a priori*) – and the only one relevant to science as far as Mill was concerned – he called 'induction'; that is,

that operation of the mind by which we infer that what we know to be true in a particular case or cases, will be true in all cases which resemble the former in certain assignable respects.[24]

Whereas Hume justified generalising from particular instances on the pragmatic grounds that the future will not, likely as not, be unlike the past, Mill argued that the inductive inference could be made that the knowledge we have of some cases will be true of all cases at all times, past, present *and* future. This he justified by an appeal to the uniformity of nature, itself arrived at through an inductive process of reasoning in which the accumulations of inductions of individual uniformities in nature are the basis of the all-encompassing induction that nature is uniform. Induction was justified by induction.

Mill did, however, recognise that life was not quite so simple. In nature things did not appear related to each other in simple fashion. Small empirical regularities would overlap and give the appearance of irregularity, some would appear regular only because they were commonly produced by another not-so-visible causal agent, and so on. The various absolute causal regularities could only be found by systematically sorting out one uniformity from another using experimental methods of manipulation. These methods were his famous 'canons of proof', reasoning procedures that could be used to identify causal relationships from the mess in which the world often appeared. Briefly, the canons were the 'method of agreement', the 'method of difference', the 'joint method of agreement and difference', the 'method of residues' and the 'method of concomitant variation'. The end result of the application of these methods should be absolute causal generalisations, according to Mill.

However, even to the thoroughgoing empiricist this interpretation of the nature of laws had its weaknesses. Mill's methods were firmly based on the supposition that nature is uniform, lawful and causally interrelated and, therefore, the language to describe it had to be a causal one. There was little need to speak of theories. Although there are hierarchies of laws, at the pinnacle standing those of Newton, the ultimate ones are discovered, like any other generalisation, by application of empirical methods of inquiry. The source of all scientific law is empirical generalisation, a conclusion built upon the presupposition that nature is lawful and uniform. Lawfulness being, in other words, a characteristic of nature itself.

Modern positivistic and empirical thinking, however, has been critical of the naive interpretation of causal laws as typified by Mill's philosophy of science. Knowledge in science is certain, not probable. Accordingly, while admitting of the essentially empirical nature of laws, it was argued that certainty arose from the employment of the rigorous connections of deductive inference in mathematics and logic, rather than from induction. Thus, 'all swans are white', if interpreted as an empirical generalisation, has to be tested again and again on each new observation of swans. Such an inference cannot license inferences to the future, just as the statement, 'All British prime ministers are male' merely reports on past experience up and until Mrs Thatcher became prime minister, and could not have said anything about the future as a scientific law would. Pure empiricism cannot generate the universal laws of science. These, it was argued, can only be provided by logic where the determinativeness, the necessity, is a consequence of formal structure. The conclusion of a logical argument must follow from the general premises if the deductive rules are followed. This interpretation of scientific explanation, as a marriage between empirical conception and the certainties of deductive logic, became known as the 'hypothetico-deductive model' of scientific explanation.

On this view a scientific theory consisted of a set of statements connected by logical rules. The law was expressed as a universal statement of the form 'all A's are B's'. From this and other statements of 'initial conditions' a hypothesis was deduced which could be tested against empirical observation. An event was considered to be explained if it could be shown to be a logical consequence of the theoretical statements. This interpretation seemed to solve a number of problems, not least those involved in induction as the basis for the universality of scientific laws.

While statements of the form 'all A's are B's' cannot logically be conclusively proved or verified, they can be falsified by one counter instance of an A not being a B. Popper, for example, denied the possibility of using induction to arrive at a general law. The universality of the law cannot be a matter of probability either, since this would, in effect, say that the law was sometimes true, sometimes not. Nonetheless, scientific laws are empirical laws and subject to empirical confirmation, and involved in the method of testing is deduction. Scientific explanation is causal explanation in which 'the explanation of an event means to deduce a statement which describes it, using as premises of the deduction one or more universal laws; together with certain singular statements, the initial conditions'.[25] Scientific laws are causal statements describing events in nature and are capable of being true or false, their truth or falsity being determined by observation.

Another issue the combination of empiricism and logic seemed to resolve was one discussed earlier in connection with the observability, or lack of it, of social wholes. A theory, interpreted in the way just discussed, was clearly more complex than 'all A's are B's' would seem to imply. The theory may contain postulates and concepts which are themselves not subject to observational testing. Such concepts served a heuristic purpose within the theoretical language. So, although theories were still given an empirical interpretation, more room was allowed for non-observables, concepts not directly depending for their truth on a correspondence with the world. The formal structure of a theory was so complex and detailed that 'theoretical concepts' were often necessary for the convenience of logical and mathematical manipulation. It was no longer considered necessary for all concepts in a theory to have empirical meaning. One way of expressing this was to speak of a theoretical language and an observational language linked together by correspondence rules which interpreted some of the theoretical concepts empirically.[26] In this way the theory was still subject to empirical test through hypotheses deductively arrived at.

These moves away from the rather naive empirical interpretation of theoretical explanation as propounded by Mill and his followers did not, however, destroy the empiricist spirit: reinterpretation merely amended it to conform more closely with was what seen as natural scientific practice. For the social sciences this was a helpful development in that it licensed what are now orthodox research methods. The distinction between a theoretical and an observational language was important. So, too, was the account of the supposed certainty of science. The empiricist interpretation of scientific laws had claimed that they were only probable in the sense of being tentative and open to revision.

How, then, could the certainty be accounted for? According to the hypothetico-deductive account of scientific explanation it was the combination of mathematics-cum-logic and the essentially empirical interpretation of laws that gave laws their 'certainty'. This 'certainty' was a fiction, a convenient and helpful one to be sure, but a fiction nonetheless in that it could not conceal the tentative nature of scientific discovery. After all, it was a matter of historical record that scientific laws had been found wanting only to be replaced by newer and more effective ones. The history of science was a history of wrong theories. For the social sciences this was all to the good since their lack of success in formulating laws of even moderate probability could be attributed to the far greater complexity of social phenomena compared with those of inanimate nature. Social phenomena were also more difficult to measure with the kind of precision achieved in the natural sciences. All of which was taken as a sign that positivistic social science was at least on the right track by emphasising the development of more and more sophisticated *methods* of research and paying less attention to the questions of the theoretical basis of disciplines.

In this connection it is worth noting that Pearson, one of the founders of modern inductive statistics, argued that the precise, pristine laws of science are idealisations: the products of averaging and not descriptions of the real universe where all kinds of 'contaminations' are present.[27] Even in the most advanced of the natural sciences, all kinds of factors are present which affect the causal relationship of interest. The result is that data are prone to variability due to error of all kinds. Accordingly, the distinction between a causal relationship as expressed in a law and a correlation is a spurious one. Causation is simply the conceptual limit of correlation. In which case and on this argument, one distinction between natural and social science – that the former deals with causal relationships, the latter with correlations – falls down since all that this reflects are the conditions in which errors can be estimated.

Problems remained, however. Earlier it was pointed out that the hypothetico-deductive model of explanation required that theory be related to the world through transformation rules translating some of the concepts in the theory into observational concepts. The theory was dependent for its truth or falsity, irrespective of a verificationist or a Popperian falsificationist position, on the facts of the world. The world was 'external' to the theory; the theory did not shape the world but could only be responsive to it. The importance of a neutral observation language was precisely in this, despite the fact that the idea of such a language proved troublesome. The transformation rules also proved equally refractory and boiled down to what came to be widely known as the 'measurement problem'.[28]

Among the positivist solutions to this were various measurement models presumed to apply to social research data and the contexts in which they were gathered. One influential doctrine was 'operationalism' which was based on the assumption that the categories used in empirical research were best defined in terms of the operations used to measure them.[29] Thus, on this doctrine, the concept of IQ is defined as that property measured by IQ tests; similarly concepts such as class, status, power, authority, and so on, would be defined by the indicators used to measure them. Such measures could be, and indeed are, used in statistical analyses of data. Once again, operationalism embodied an empiricist conception of the nature of concepts which did not meet the hopes invested in it. One difficulty was that, as strictly conceived, operationalism created acute problems of validity. Though, strictly speaking, one could not ask what a test *really* measured since the measure *was* the concept, questions of validity did arise. For one thing, different measures of phenomena, such as IQ, could be said to be measuring different things since they were different measures. Similarly, different measures of social class or social status would be measuring different things. Clearly this was not a satisfactory situation since often measures had to be different for very good practical reasons and, yet, researchers still wanted to generalise to all instances of the phenomenon, whatever it might be, despite problems of having to use different measures. Also, even a weak operationalism, that is, one which did not claim that concepts were the measurement operations themselves but, instead, took the doctrine as a useful imperative to guide social research, still led to the problem of relating empirical concepts to theoretical ones.[30]

While measurement procedures in a number of the social sciences are extremely sophisticated, as are those methods of quantitative data analysis, there remains relevant the important question about the theoretical relevance of such techniques.[31] Most have been designed to exploit the principle of association or correlation very much in the tradition of Mill's canons of inquiry, the aim being to measure concepts at a sufficiently high level to meet the assumptions of correlational techniques first developed in genetics at the turn of the century. While the use of such techniques have resulted in any number of empirical generalisations, none has been so far offered as a causal law. Social science has produced a catalogue of associations between any number of variables; between, for instance, class and educational attainment, educational attainment and mobility, class and voting choice, class and mental illness, religion and voting choice, the degree of industrialisation and domestic political violence, and so on and so on.[32] All range from weak to strong, none is perfect, a fact attributed to various kinds of measurement error and the difficulty of controlling for all possible factors. But, some questions arise: What do such generalisations amount to? Are they 'proto-laws' from young and immature disciplines which, nonetheless, could serve as a basis for sounder laws?

Let us first take the question of the nature of such generalisations. Such associations are normally derived from a sample of some population, the measures of association summarising the relationships among the variables in that sample. In any sample any number of such associations could be produced between all kinds of 'disparate' phenomena, so they summarise relationships among those variables felt to be important enough to be considered. So, how is the decision reached as to what to include within a study, given that it is impossible to include everything? The hypothetico-deductive model would suggest that the theory dictates what should be included, what variables should be examined, what variables should be controlled, and so on. Mill himself, although as thoroughgoing an empiricist as one is very likely to find, did not dismiss the importance of hypotheses as necessary if one was to apply any of his methods of inquiry and derive verifiable consequences of the laws themselves. But for Mill, all hypotheses were suggested by experience and capable of being true or false. If we accept this it is still not quite clear how associations between variables could be said to be theoretically relevant. What are we to do about a less than perfect association or correlation? Does it prove or disprove a theory? Alternatively, should we want to say something a little weaker: that it 'lends support to' or 'is not entirely consistent with'? In fact, the interpretation of such associations is usually a *post hoc* affair in spite of the obeisance made to the hypothetico-deductive model's espousel of the test of prediction. All kinds of rationalisations, some more plausible than others but still many plausible enough, are entered into to make the associations theoretically interesting. That classic of positivistic social science, Durkheim's study of suicide, contains many generalisations summarising the correlations between marriage and suicide, religion and suicide, urban living and suicide, and more, while the remainder of the analysis consists of interpretations and arguments, many of them shrewd, ingenious and insightful, elaborating *post hoc* rationales to explain what it is about the correlated phenomena that leads to suicide.

Can such associations be regarded as proto-laws? An affirmative answer to this questions looks remote since what has been said so far points to the conclusion that no empirical generalisation can logically ever be a law. Indeed, not all statements of the logical form 'all A's are B's' can be treated as lawlike in the sense required by science. 'Nomological generalisations', for example, support subjunctive and counterfactual conditional statements whereas empirical, or 'accidental generalisations' to use a phrase of Brown's, do not.[33] For example, the law concerning the effects of dissolved solids on the boiling point of a liquid entitles a subjunctive conditional such as, 'If this solid salt were dissolved in this pan of boiling water, then the boiling point would be raised.' The law, along with statements about the initial conditions stating that the law is applicable in this particular case, entitles us to make such a statement. Similarly, it lends support to counterfactuals such as, 'If this piece of solid salt had been dissolved in water – though in fact it had not been – the boiling point of the water would have been raised.' In short, 'nomological generalisations' or laws allow us to make inferences about cases that do not now occur, have not occurred in the past and may not occur in the future. They state hypothetical relationships of invariable connection irrespective of whether or not the relationships is actually exemplified.

None of these characteristics applies to 'accidental generalisations'. The generalisation that all the people in this room are under 6 feet tall does not entitle the inference that any future incomer to the room will be under 6 feet tall. Although a number of 'accidental generalisations' may have always held in fact, at all times and places, this will still be, as Brown puts it, 'a happy accident and not a consequence of there being a law-like connection between the properties in question or, more basically, of there being a scientific theory from which the generalisation can be derived'.[34] That is, in the absence of any scientific theory to preclude the appearance of anyone over 6 feet tall entering this room, we have no basis for the kind of inferences we can make using nomological generalisations.

The question is, however, whether 'accidental generalisations' – and the word 'accidental' is perhaps unfortunate here since they are certainly not trivial or unimportant – or nomological ones are the kind of generalisations produced by the Lazarsfeldian-type methods of social science. Brown claims that no clear line can be drawn between 'accidental generalisations' and empirical–universal generalisations since both are based on observational processes rather than theoretical ones. They are generalisations based on observed regularities, unlike theoretical laws, and, as a consequence, their explanatory scope is limited.

Suppose, for example, after intensive studies of samples of individuals we find a high positive correlation between the number of siblings in a family and poor educational performance. What kind of generalisation would this be? An 'accidental' one or an empirical one, or what? It is hard to say since the case could be made for both. This, however, is not really the issue. If we wanted to use the generalisation to *explain* why little Johnny down the road with twelve brothers and sisters is not doing very well at school, it might indeed be offered as an explanation. But is this good enough? What about other factors which may play a part? How do we know that it is the number of siblings that causes the poor performance rather than, say, the poor school, little Johnny's passion for fishing, his dyslexia, or whatever else might characterise little Johnny's life and circumstance? Could, to be brief, little Johnny's poor educational performance be deduced from the generalisation? The answer is no, and for two major reasons. First, unlike the laws offered in natural science, the *ceteris paribus* conditions under which the applicability of the law is judged, in this example and in most real-life social science examples, are indeterminate – to say the least. Second, the lack of a theory from which to derive the generalisation, along with some statement of the conditions under which the theory will apply, means that any application will have to be determined *post hoc*. Though the mechanisms involved here have intuitive plausibility – for example, large families means less time for study, less parental attention for any one child, sibling rivalry, and so on – this *ad hocing* process is not quite what is to be expected from a scientific theory and observations that might be deduced from it. Moreover, there are, in fact, any number of theories that could explain little Johnny's poor educational performance, some consistent with the generalisation but many not so, and for which the empirical connection between number of siblings and educational performance is an irrelevance. Third, since the generalisation is drawn from samples, all we have is a statistical generalisation stating that a property (number of siblings) is associated with another property (educational performance) in a particular direction and size. From this, nothing follows about any *particular* instance.[35] A deductive conclusion cannot be found, only an inductive one. Premises made up of such generalisations cannot logically imply a conclusion, only lend support.

In this respect Lieberson offers an illuminating example.[36] He asks: how might social researchers go about studying the question of why objects fall? He visualises a study, based on an analogy with the typical type of social research study, in which a variety of objects is dropped from a height without benefit of strong controls such as a vacuum: a condition, to repeat, which parallels most circumstances in social research where controls, such as they are, enter *post hoc* at the data analysis stage. If the objects differ in the time they take to reach the ground, the question becomes What characteristics of the objects determines this difference? Air resistance in the absence of a vacuum, the size and density of the objects will, on the face of it, affect the speed of the fall. Assume that these factors, even including others, taken together account for all the differences in velocities of fall between the objects.[37] In a social research context, likely as not, it would be concluded that a complete understanding of the phenomenon had been achieved since all the differences had been accounted for. But, of course, the point of the example is that we would not have come up with the idea of gravity. What is wrong here? As Lieberson puts it, data on the *phenomenon* of interest are not necessarily relevant to the *question* of interest. So, an analysis of the rate of fall of various objects might tell us why they differ in the rate of their fall, not why they fall. What we would not have available is the power of the theory of gravity and its statement of the constancy of the rate of acceleration of falling objects to deal with many of the applications for which it is employed.

An important consideration here, and one fully acknowledged by Lazarsfeld in pursuing the ideas of variable analysis, is the non-experimental character of social research. Without the ability to effectively make *ceteris paribus* assumptions about the effects of unwanted factors, identifying causal relationships where 'contamination' by multifarious influences is ever present, is likely to present fundamental difficulties to researchers. As said earlier, in variable analysis controls are normally employed at the data analysis stage, the aim being to see how much of the variability of the values of the dependent variable is accounted for by one or more of the independent variables. Again, as indicated earlier, for such as Pearson this is entirely what the problem is, namely, finding those variables which account for *most* but not *all* of the variance. For him there is simply no point in trying to add causes together until all the variation has been explained. The complete elimination of variability in real world observation is a chimera. It is only highly correlated variables that matter.

Unfortunately for this kind of conception there are serious technical flaws, quite apart from the ones suggested by Lieberson's example. Turner points out, for example, that both the metaphysics underlying this conception of social research and the statistical techniques used to implement it, fail to realise that theories remain underdetermined.[38] Not only is there no attainable goal of the complete elimination of variability, there is usually more than one way of adding or combining variables to the point of redundancy, assuming that this is capable of plausible definition, irrespective of the fact that there is more than one choice about the way in which the variables can be measured. Turner points out that no logical relationship can hold between theoretical claims and generalisations based on statistical data largely because of the assumptions about the order of variables, their completeness, their linearity, or otherwise, and their independence; all essential to the mathematics of statistical modelling, and which always make the generalisations assumption-relative.[39] It is this feature which directs us back to theoretical considerations.

POSITIVISM AND SCIENTIFIC THEORY

The positivist conception of scientific knowledge with its emphasis on observation and empirical method to the relative neglect of theory turns out to be a less than adequate reflection of the natural science logic which it extolled. Certainly in social science the generalisations produced by most current empirical methods do not begin to look like the laws offered by natural science: a fact more often than not attributed to the relative immaturity of the social sciences and the relatively greater complexity of social phenomena compared with the subject matters of the natural sciences. However, what is also clear is that there was much wrong with the positivist conception of science itself.

One persuasive view on this matter takes issue with the predominantly empirical interpretation of scientific laws and theories to be found in positivism. As a system of knowledge empiricism, of which positivism is an important part, is to be found in many diverse activities of widely varying content, from primitive magic to modern technology. Its main and distinguishing feature is that it relates observable to observable.[40] Effectively it is a system of trial and error and no less important in science for this since it can, and does, lead to effective results which, in their turn, lead to routine procedures in investigative work. By contrast, rational thought deals solely with the theoretical, connecting idea to idea, and is characteristic of logic, mathematics and also of some metaphysical systems of thought. Science shares characteristics of both but in a very different way to that presupposed in positivism. Science is concerned with empirical connection and, like logic and mathematics, with the rational connection of idea to idea, but it is through the 'abstractive connection' of theoretical concepts with observations that these concepts are given empirical import. A scientific explanation uses determinative laws and not laws interpreted as general causal statements as positivist thought had it. The determinativeness of its rational connections is what gives greater precision to scientific knowledge.

To illustrate.[41] A relationship between cold weather and cracked car radiators can easily be established using empirical methods. In such a case the connection is made as a result of repeated observations and, Hume would add, habit. Such an explanation, making use of the empirical connection between cracked radiators and freezing weather, can be adequate for its purpose, especially if the aim is to avoid cracked car radiators. A scientific explanation, on the other hand, might begin with the idea that under perfect elasticity, stress is equal to strain. Then an attempt would be made to determine a value for the limit of elasticity for radiators by measuring the amount of force applied before the radiator cracks. By measuring air temperature and that of the water at night the point at which the water freezes to produce enough ice to apply the stress that would bring the radiator to its strain limit can be determined. A stress greater than the strain limit would break the radiator. In this case a law is being used in which stress is equal to strain under conditions of perfect elasticity. The purpose of the law is to derive a measure for the strain limit by applying stress, and to compare the calculated stress at the time of breakage with that limit. In so far as the value of the strain limit was determined from a calculation of stress, it is difficult to see how the laws could be proved false in such an application. The exact calculation of a limit could not have been arrived at empirically. Even though temperature could have been measured as precisely as possible using empirical methods, and the generalisation offered that the colder it gets the more likely the radiator is to break, this could not result in the calculation of a limit. It may result in a probability distribution, but this will not tell us whether or not the radiator will crack. The scientific laws can point to a measurable condition under which breaking will occur; an empirical generalisation only that it will break with a certain probability.

Science and empiricism differ, too, in the way in which they transcend particular instances. The latter does so by generalisation, that is, applying a name to a set of similar objects so forming a particular category through the observational process; car, tree, society, male, female, and so on. These are then related to other empirical categories by means of such methods as correlations. Science, on the other hand, transcends the particular case by abstraction, by a process of selection and not by the summation of similar characteristics. Indeed, observational phenomena abstracted in this way may bear little obvious similarity to each other. Billiard balls are not like rockets, to use another example from Willer and Willer, but both may be abstractively connected to the concepts of the same laws of motion.

The meaning of abstracted concepts is derived not from the similar appearance of objects but from their relationship to other concepts within the theory. The process of abstraction is, in effect, one of conceptualising observations so that they may be deterministically related to other concepts. At once an infinite universe is provided as a conceptual framework for the theory. The rational connection between the concepts in the theory is not like a causal connection at all. We may well use the relationship $d = vt$, and use it often to build speedometers, measure distance travelled, and so on, but we do not observe distance to discover if it is, in fact, velocity multiplied by time. vt *tells* us what distance is in terms of time and velocity.

Abstraction in science moves back and forth between the empirical and the theoretical expounding and sharpening the scope of application of the theory and its explanatory power: a matter of establishing an isomorphism between theoretical terms and empirical observables. This may be aided by manipulation under laboratory conditions, constructing models to fit particular cases, changing empirical conditions and varying models, and so on. As far as the abstraction process is concerned, and unlike in the case of generalisations, there is no problem about how similar is similar since the theory and its model(s) are deliberate constructions, even inventions, to fit and translate the theory to apply to particular cases. Indeed, theories may be applied to a large number of cases, as the law of falling bodies applies to anything that falls or flies. This is not the case with empirical generalisations. Lack of success in the case of a theory does not mean that the theory was false: it may instead indicate a limit to its scope, or mean that an abstractive error has been made.

A very different conception of measurement is embodied in this view of scientific explanation. For the positivist, measurement is effectively a matter divorced from theory. Accordingly, the so-called 'measurement problem' in social science has largely been seen as an effort to scale all kinds of variables, from the macro structural variables to the affective, trying to give them the kind of precision and exactness felt to be characteristic of measurement in science.[42] Energy was devoted to constructing 'indices' for theoretical concepts, the aim being to connect the theory to the empirical world of observables by the use of essentially empirical techniques. However, on the abstractive view of the connection of theory to empirical observables, it is measurement which gives a theoretical concept empirical interpretation. Measurement orders data, not the other way around, and is very much a consequence of theory. 'Length', for example, in a scientific theory has a purely theoretical meaning determined by the postulates and laws of the theory. The concepts that are measured are chosen as a consequence of these postulates and laws and can be empirically interpreted in many different ways according to circumstances. The application of a theory to a broad range of phenomena gives rise to very different empirical interpretations. As Pawson points out, in science the

objective of measurement is to incorporate and embody within an instrument, principles derived from theoretical science. Instrumentation is thus seen as a branch of engineering and engineering is nothing other than the application of the laws, theories, hypotheses and principles of theoretical physics . . . the incorporation of theory into the observational domain is seen not as the problem, but as the true justification of measurement.[43]

Temperature can be measured, for example, using an ordinary mercury thermometer or, with very cold objects, by means of the resistance to an electric current. In both cases, the measurement is the direct result of the laws of thermodynamics applied to different domains, the expansion of liquids in the one case and electrical conductivity in the other. Measurement of a rigorous scientific character is impossible without a strict theory specifying the strict numerical relationship between concepts.

If the views just summarised are correct then the positivist conception of scientific knowledge must go by the board. It emphasised some aspects of science, particularly its empirical character, at the expense of failing to see the significance of others, especially that of theory. Science is empirical but it is also profoundly theoretical; indeed, perhaps a more convincing case could be made that science is more interested in theory than it is in the empirical. Laws, the aim both of positivism and science, are not causal empirical generalisations but rationally connected statements. True enough, in their infancy, some sciences may well proceed in a more empirical manner by correlating observables with other observables, but matters do not end there if it is to progress. Positivism did suspect that rational connection might be more important than some of its adherents would allow and the hypothetico-deductive model of explanation, for example, was an attempt to rationalise the importance of logic and mathematics, but firmly within the empiricist framework.

However, although it may well be accepted that the positivist view of science was misconceived, this is not to say that the methods it authorised as the methods of social science are also entirely useless. It may be that they are not scientific, either in the way that positivism understood or, indeed, in terms of the view just outlined, but does this imply that they are useless as a form of knowledge? Further, it has also been argued that the hypothetico-deductive, or covering law, model of explanation is not a useful one for social science to follow given that, very often, they are more concerned with discovery than with explanation.[44] Genetic explanations, typical of history for example, are concerned to show how certain events came about and, here, there is no explicit reference to laws as such but the deployment of an explanatory narrative.[45] Nor, of course, need it be the case that the hypothetico-deductive model is an accurate rendering of the scientific method. It may be, too, that there is no one method for science in the way in which positivist philosophy understands this. These are, obviously, large questions, some of which I want to take up more directly in the final chapter. For now, one or two remarks are in order. One implication that could be drawn is that the intellectual authority for such methods can no longer be in terms of a positivistic conception of science, or that by using such methods the social sciences are aping the natural sciences. In so far as such methods deal with the production of empirical generalisations, they will be subject to the kind of logical constraints pointed out earlier, but, to reiterate, this is not to say that such generalisations are of no interest.

There are also implications for interpretations of the nature of social scientific theory, most of which become less than scientific. Even within a positivistic framework the relationship of theory to data was a troublesome one. Theory was supposed to be dependent for its truth on the 'facts' of the world which were external to the theory itself. The theory did not shape the world, but was responsive to it. The importance placed on developing a theory-neutral observation language lay precisely in this. However, many of the candidates for theory in social science were, and still are, rejected on extra-empirical grounds. In the 1960s, for example, the great theoretical debate in sociology was between conflict theories and functionalism.[46] Functionalism was attacked because it seemed to ignore the fact of conflict in social life, whereas one of its major aims was to examine the causes and consequences of conflict within a set of concepts stressing the systemic nature of society. Each side of the debate, however, effectively talked past each other. Something other than the scientific status of the respective theoretical positions was at issue, having much to do with what the connotations of concepts like 'conflict', 'stability', etc., carried with them about familiar events and processes in historical societies. Such debates might better be seen as quarrels about how the social world ought to be looked at and less to do with the scientific value of such theories.[47] This brings us to another general point about social scientific theory and one which will be discussed more fully in the next chapter.

Positivism, with its stress on the idea of a neutral observation language, empirical generalisation, and so forth, was disinclined to concern itself with the origin and source of theories. This is illustrated by the relative lack of interest shown in the matter of scientific discovery which was relegated to a sideshow beyond serious philosophical concern. Of much greater importance was the matter of verifying theories once formulated. The discovery of theories was a matter of conjecture on the part of scientists and their imagination, fancy, even induction and speculation, but certainly beyond formal logical description. What could be described as a logical process, it was argued, was the confirmation and testing of theories. To this extent theories had to conform to certain formal criteria in order to be capable of test against the 'facts' of the world. However, although this emphasis might have seemed excusable or justifiable in connection with natural science theories, it is less so with reference to the social sciences. The very notion of a domain of inquiry, whether it be sociology, economics, physics, chemistry, history or whatever, presupposes some conceptual schema ordering the world as a prelude to the observation of the relevant facts. This is what Durkheim, for example, was insistent on establishing, namely, the conceptual distinctiveness of sociology as an autonomous discipline with its own domain of facts, facts which gain their importance and significance because they are distinctively social. In other words, the conceptual ordering necessary to identifying a species of facts begins to challenge the idea that observation is entirely a theoretically neutral affair. It suggests that the knower is an active constituent in the construction of knowledge. On this view scientific theories become like inventions actively engaged in creating a reality, not passively waiting for their substantiation by the facts of the external world. Indeed, much of social scientific theory is underdetermined by the facts of the social world in the sense that no 'strategic experiment' is conceivable that could decide between them. Rather, such theories are better seen as conceptual schemes stipulating, even legislating, what the domain of fact might be.

One final point. Although the positivist conception of science has been shown to be seriously flawed, this is not the same as saying that the social sciences cannot be scientific within another interpretation of science. This issue will have to be dealt with, but before doing so it is necessary to bring some of the debates about the nature of science up to date.

REFERENCES

1. Kuhn, T. S., *The Structure of Scientific Revolutions*. 2nd edn, Chicago, University of Chicago Press, 1970. Kuhn was referring to natural science and it is a moot point as to whether the social sciences are, or could ever be, 'normal' in the sense offered. Nevertheless, positivistically inspired social science is, perhaps, as near as could be got to 'normal science' in the last few decades. See next chapter for fuller discussion of some of Kuhn's ideas.

2. See, for example, Ryan, A., *The Philosophy of the Social Sciences,* London, Macmillan, 1979; Lessnoff, M., *The Structure of Social Science,* London, Allen and Unwin, 1974; Popineau, D., *For Science in the Social Sciences,* London, Macmillan, 1978; Doyal, L. and Harris, R., *Empiricism, Explanation and Rationality,* London, Routledge and Kegan Paul, 1986. See also Bernstein, R. J., *The Restructuring of Social and Political Theory,* Oxford, Blackwell, 1976, for an excellent review of some of the philosophical influences on major social theories. See Anderson, R. J. *et al., Philosophy and*

the Human Sciences, London, Croom Helm, 1986, for a review of most of the major philosophical schools of importance in the social sciences.

3. See Anscombe, G. E., 'On brute facts', *Analysis,* 18, 1957–8, pp. 69–72; Taylor, C., 'Interpretation and the sciences of man' in Beehler, R. and Drengson, A. R. (eds), *The Philosophy of Society,* London, Methuen, 1978, p. 160.

4. Carnap, R., *The Logical Structure of the World,* London, Routledge and Kegan Paul, 1967 (first appeared in German, 1928), for example, gives an account of the whole apparatus of empirical discourse in terms of remembered similarity between sense impressions. These are the basic elements out of which are constructed, with the help of logic, the concepts of material things, other minds, social institutions. Topics of thought stand in various levels each reducible to the one preceding it. Higher level statements are justified by induction from statements of levels below; basic lowest level statements need and can have no inferential justification. At this point the system of beliefs makes contact, through observation, with the world of empirical fact.

5. Many members of the Vienna Circle, as it was known, went to the United States prior to the Second World War and had a major impact on the philosophy of science there, as well as philosophy generally.

6. See the selections in Ayer, A. J. (ed), *Logical Positivism,* New York, Free Press, 1959.

7. Toulmin, S. and Goodfield, J., *The Discovery of Time,* London, Hutchinson, 1963, gives a good discussion of Darwin's contribution to geology and biology.

8. Neurath, M., 'Empirical sociology; the scientific content of history and political economy' in Neurath, M. and Cohen, R. S. (eds), *Empiricism and Sociology,* Dordrecht, Reidel, 1973, pp. 319–412.

9. As Smelser wrote of the language of science: '. . . the language of the ingredients of science; independent variables, dependent variables, theoretical frameworks, and research methods' (*Essays in Sociological Explanation,* Englewood Cliffs, Prentice Hall, 1968, p. 43). It is important to note that he is, in fact, referring to the language of social science not physical science where talk of variables is rare. One textbook gives the following instruction: 'it is necessary to translate your ideas . . . into the language of variables . . . The experienced sociologist develops the habit of routinely translating the English he reads and hears into variables, just as a bilingual person can read one language while thinking in another' (Davis, J. A., *Elementary Survey Analysis,* Englewood Cliffs, Prentice Hall, 1971, p. 16).

10. Lazarsfeld, P. F. and Rosenberg, M. (eds), *The Language of Social Research,* New York, Free Press, 1955, p. 15. This whole collection, despite its age, is a testament to the vigour of variable analysis in its early days.
11. *Ibid.,* p. 13.
12. There is no doubt that Lazarsfeld's thinking owes much to his commitment to survey research as a method.
13. This is evident in the work of Blalock, one of the foremost exponents of causal modelling in sociology. See, for example, his *Theory Construction,* Englewood Cliffs, Prentice Hall, 1969.
14. Durkheim, E., *The Rules of Sociological Method,* New York, Free Press, 1966, p. 103.
15. Lukes, S., 'Methodological individualism reconsidered' in Emmet, D. and MacIntyre, A. (eds), *Sociological Theory and Philosophical Analysis,* London, Macmillan, 1970, pp. 76–88; O'Neill, J. (ed.), *Modes of Individualism and Collectivism,* London, Heinemann, 1973; Sharrock, W. W., 'Individual and society' in Anderson, R. J. (ed.), *Classic Disputes in Sociology,* London, George Allen and Unwin, 1987, pp. 126–56. It is also possible to treat methodological individualism as just what it says, namely, a methodological rather than a philosophical position. See Anderson, R. J. *et al., The Sociology Game,* London, Longman, 1984, pp. 40–3.
16. Lessnoff, *op. cit.,* p. 77. Italics in original.
17. Mandelbaum, M., 'Social facts', *British Journal of Sociology,* 6, 1955, p. 312; Lessnoff, *ibid.,* pp. 80–1.
18. See, for example, Hayek, F. A., *The Counter-Revolution of Science,* New York, Free Press, 1964, pp. 54–5.
19. Homans, G. C., *The Nature of Social Science,* New York, Harcourt, Brace and World, 1967.
20. Structuralist sociologies, mostly deriving from interpretations of Marx's work combined with that of Saussure, see the individual as the 'bearer' of larger relational structures and, since much of the current inspiration of this view arises from the work of Althusser, a French sociologist, it has some Durkheimian tonality. See his, *For Marx,* Harmondsworth, Penguin, 1969.
21. Lazarsfeld P. and Menzel H., 'On the relation between individual and collective properties' in Eztioni. A. (ed.), *Complex Organizations: A Sociological Reader,* New York, Holt, Rinehart and Winston, 1969.
22. It is by the seventeenth century that the idea of 'laws of nature' began to lose its theological overtones. See Outhwaite, W., 'Laws and explanations' in Anderson *et al.* (eds), *op. cit.*
23. Hume, D., *A Treatise of Human Nature,* 2nd edn, Oxford, Oxford University Press, 1978, pp. 89–90.
24. Mill, J. S., *A System of Logic,* p. 188.

25. Popper, K., *The Logic of Scientific Discovery,* London, Hutchinson, 1959, p. 59.
26. Nagel, E., *The Structure of Science,* London, Routledge and Kegan Paul, 1961, for a discussion of 'theoretical' and 'observational' languages of science.
27. Pearson, K., *The Grammar of Science,* 2nd edn., London, Adam and Charles, 1911.
28. This is how, for example, it appears in the work of Blalock. See his *Conceptualization and Measurement in Social Science,* London, Sage, 1982, for example.
29. See Bridgeman, P., *The Logic of Modern Physics,* New York, Macmillan, 1927; Campbell, N. F., *Foundations of Science,* New York, Dover, 1957.
30. For useful review, see Pawson, R., *A Measure for Measures: A Manifesto for Empirical Sociology,* London, Routledge and Kegan Paul, 1989.
31. Such questions are not only raised by philosophers, but also by practitioners. See Blalock, *op. cit.*; Lieberson, S., *Making It Count: The Improvement of Social Research and Theory,* Berkeley, University of California Press, 1985.
32. See, for example, the compendium of 'findings' offered in Berelson, B. and Steiner, G. A., *Human Behaviour,* New York, Harcourt, Brace and World, 1967, shorter edn.
33. Brown, R., *Rules and Laws in Sociology,* London, Routledge and Kegan Paul, 1973, pp. 91–2.
34. *Ibid.,* p. 93.
35. Robinson, W. S., 'Ecological correlations and the behaviour of individuals', *American Sociological Review,* 15, 1950, pp. 351–7, is a classic paper which identifies a number of 'ecological fallacies' involved in inferring about the characteristics of individuals from aggregated data. See also, Sacks, H., 'Sociological description', *Berkeley Journal of Sociology,* 1963, for an examination of some wider implications.
36. Lieberson, *op. cit.,* pp. 99–101.
37. This assumes that one could account for all of what is known as the variance, statistically defined, in a social research context. Such a state of affairs would be unprecedented. Lieberson draws some devastating conclusions about the techniques of non-experimental social research, especially in so far as they fail to match up to the aspirations of producing adequate theoretical accounts.
38. Turner, S. P., 'Underdetermination and the promise of statistical sociology', *Sociological Theory,* 5, 1987, pp. 172–84.
39. Assumption-relative is not the same as stating the conditions of a law. Newton's laws, for example, apply in a vacuum at low speed, without significant light pressure, and so on, but these

are known and measurable factors not assumptions necessary
to deploy statistical models.

40. Willer, D. and Willer, J., *Systematic Empiricism,* Englewood
    Cliffs, Prentice Hall, 1973, p. 16.
41. *Ibid.*
42. Duncan, O. D., *Notes on Social Measurement: Historical and
    Critical,* New York, Sage, 1984, has much to say on the
    so-called exactness of measurement in the physical sciences
    and, at even greater length, on the efforts of the human
    sciences to emulate this. However, the point being made is
    not affected by a modest scepticism about exactness.
43. Pawson, *op. cit.,* pp. 106–7.
44. Brown, *op. cit.*; also Outhwaite, *op. cit.*
45. But see Nagel, *op. cit.,* on the nature of historical explanation
    for an alternative view.
46. See, for example, Rex, J., *Key Problems of Sociological
    Theory,* London, Routledge and Kegan Paul, 1961.
47. Anderson *et al., The Sociology Game, op. cit.,* for a criticism
    of perspectivalism in sociology.

CHAPTER 4

Positivism, theory and science

In this chapter I want to take a rather wider perspective on issues in the philosophy of science, but one which will return to some of the themes raised in the previous chapter. Once again, the beginning is that ambition bequeathed by nineteenth-century positivism to the social sciences, namely, to become scientific in the same fashion as the natural sciences. As said previously, the vision of science was very much a philosophically inspired one generating no little philosophical argument.

I shall begin from a summary recapitulation of the hypothetico-deductive model of explanation.

THE HYPOTHETICO–DEDUCTIVE MODEL OF SCIENTIFIC EXPLANATION AGAIN

On this view a scientific theory consisted of a set of statements connected by logical rules. The law was expressed as a universal statement of the form 'all A's are B's'. From this and other statements of 'initial conditions' a hypothesis was deduced which could be tested against empirical observation. An event was considered to be explained if it could be shown to be a logical consequence of the theoretical statements. In other words, the truth of the explanandum is, in crucial part, guaranteed by logic, – as long as the explanadum is logically deducible from empirically true statements about the initial conditions and the general laws. If the scheme is used retrospectively it gives explanations; used prospectively it provides predictions. If the universal law is true then the prediction will be confirmed; if not, then the prediction will fail. This interpretation seemed to solve a number of problems, not least those involved in proposing induction as the basis for the universality of scientific laws. Scientific laws are empirical laws subject to empirical confirmation, and involved in the method of testing is deduction. Scientific explanation is causal explanation in which 'the explanation of an event means to deduce a statement which describes it, using as premises of the deduction one or more universal laws; together with certain singular statements, the initial conditions'.[1] Scientific laws are causal statements describing events in nature and are capable of being true or false, their truth or falsity being determined by observation. There was no need for any inductive process or, indeed, for any metaphysical refuge in appeals to the uniformity of nature.

The hypothetico-deductive model seemed to offer a characterisation of scientific reasoning that social science could live with and emulate. Further, the adoption of such a mode of reasoning, even at the modest levels the social sciences could realistically achieve, would place the social sciences firmly within the science camp. In other words, the schema served as a criterion definitive of scientific forms of knowledge. However, in the hands of Karl Popper, matters did not turn out quite so straightforwardly.

POPPER'S FALSIFICATIONISM AND THE ROAD TO THE SOCIOLOGY OF SCIENCE

Earlier I drew attention to arguments showing that inductivism failed as a justification for the truth of scientific theories and generalisations. Popper agreed. The classical model of induction could not logically escape the uncertainty of succeeding observations. Scientific knowledge cannot proceed by the verification of theories by means of empirical testing but, instead, has to rely on a critical method of 'bold conjectures' and attempts at refutation. His philosophy of science, however, is more than just a criticism of inductivism; he was also vitally interested in looking for what was distinctive about the scientific method. Not all forms of knowledge are scientific and, like Logical Positivism, he was interested in developing a demarcation criterion that could distinguish 'science' from 'pseudo-science'. Inductivism failed to do this since many activities laying claim to scientific status – such as astrology, which Popper did not want to count as science – relied upon induction. Not only had it failed to provide an adequate justification for the truth of scientific generalisations, but it had run the risk of allowing into the collection of scientific disciplines such activities as astrology, psycho-analysis and Marxism, to mention but three which earned Popper's disapproval. Unlike the Logical Positivists, however, the issue for Popper was not one between verifiable science and nonsensical metaphysics, but between science and pseudo-science.[2]

The 'demarcation criterion' Popper offered was that of falsification. Though no amount of observations could ever confirm a generalisation of the form 'all A's are B's', one counter instance of an A not being a B would disconfirm the generalisation and this, Popper argued, is in fact the characteristic method of science; that is, to seek the disconfirmation of a theory's predictions. Scientific theories state the conditions for their failure as theories, whereas the theories of pseudo-sciences do not. Astrological theories, for example, are unfalsifiable and, therefore, not scientific.

In this way Popper revised the orthodox positivist conception of science. The object of science is not to infer from specific instances to generalisations but to search for ways of rejecting what he calls 'conjectural hypotheses'. Science is not a body of accumulated and accumulating true theories but a collection of conjectures which have yet to be refuted: science is a 'system of guesses or anticipations which in principle cannot be justified, but which work as long as they stand up to tests . . .'[3] Further, it is those theories which make very precise predictions, and accordingly are more likely to fail with one crucial experiment or test, which are the best.[4] The ability of theories to withstand tests, their 'corroboration', is related to the improbability of their predictions. The best theories, like Einstein's General Theory of Relativity, provide for very precise predictions across a range of tests and, therefore, have a high empirical content. It is those theories, which are unfalsifiable-in-principle, which are virtually devoid of empirical content. Science is, as a consequence, ruthlessly competitive forever seeking to destroy or refute its conjectures, even its best ones. It is by critical trial and error that science proceeds, discarding those theories that fail to match up to the tests and hanging on to those, at least for the time being, that have passed the best tests that can be currently devised for them. As long as 'we admit that there is no authority beyond the reach of criticism to be found within the whole province of our knowledge . . . then we can retain . . . the idea that truth is beyond human authority'.[5] This 'evolutionary epistemology' is no different, for Popper, to the way that all forms of life adapt, or fail to adapt. Of course, there is always the risk of holding on to an unsound theory or, for that matter, abandoning prematurely a good one. But these risks science has to live with since, as Popper admits, there are non-logical criteria involved in the selection and promotion of scientific theories. As studies in the sociology and the history of science have shown, there are many reasons why theories are often held on to or thrown over, other than for strictly scientific criteria, including such prosaic matters as personal preference, career advancement, religious conviction, etc.;[6] but, for Popper, although such things are an ineradicable feature of the social history of science, they are not part of its logic, and it is this with which Popper sees himself as primarily concerned. The only defensible concern of epistemology as the theory of scientific knowledge is with regard to the actual procedures and products of science. Science aims at truth in the sense of correspondence with reality, yet we can never conclusively demonstrate that our conjectures are true. Rather truth is tested by eliminating falsehood; 'we are seekers of truth but we are not its possessors'.[7]

Nonetheless, though Popper's criterion of falsifiability is intended as a logical one, reservations have to be expressed as whether its point is descriptive or prescriptive. If the former, then as an account of how science works it is clearly deficient. If the latter, then falsificationism does not only rule out well-known and well-respected theories in the human sciences, it has the same effect on a number of natural scientific theories including, for example, Darwin's theory of evolution. As far as Popper is concerned, theories must be predictivist: it is the predictions that lend theories to falsification. Heuristic theories are not allowable. Further, no notice is taken of the immense amount of taxonomic work fundamental in many sciences. These issues apart, even as an account of the logic of science, Popper's is idealised paying little attention to the other than strictly logical reasons scientists might have for accepting and rejecting hypotheses. This matters if Popper's criterion is invoked prescriptively since it no longer just describes the difference between 'proper' science and pseudo-science, but begins to stipulate how science ought to be done.

As far as the social sciences were concerned, the first impact of Popper's work was devastating. The requirements of falsification effectively ruled out of the court of science many tried and trusted social science theories because they could not state the grounds on which they could stand refuted. As far as Popper was concerned, all they offered was ways of looking at, or perspectives on, social life; they were not *scientific* theories. This aspect of his work was developed in his vehement arguments against collectivist views of society, such as those of Marxism, as inviting not more freedom for the individual but less. Any attempt to impose equality as a major social organising principle would, likely as not, produce tyranny.[8] The arguments are connected, and strongly so, to Popper's sense of the limitations of human knowledge and, in this respect, his suspicions of those inspirations of social science, of which Comte was a precursor, which see it as a way of enhancing the rational intervention in human society to ameliorate its evils. For Popper such an ambition, if conceived holistically, is to invite tyranny. Scientific knowledge is a matter or trial and error and this can only be institutionally realised in an 'open' society where a plurality of points of view can compete with each other. Such a process requires that criticism flower, argument thrive, dissent flourish, and these cannot do so in 'closed' societies.

The hypothetico-deductive schema, whether interpreted in verificationist or falsificationist terms, has been a powerful idea in the philosophy of science, though not without its critics. It was intended to avoid the philosophical difficulties of inductivism but also, sometimes inadvertently, while concerned to maintain the rationality of the *method* of science did, at the same time, highlight the importance of the history and sociology of science if only, to put it in Popperian terms, to understand which theories entered the evolutionary race.

Popper's intervention, however, raised a number of issues which transformed the debate on the nature of science and the scientific method. Though Popper himself rejected the charge of relativism, the claim that science could only, at best, obtain 'successive approximations' to truth along with the view that observations are invariably theory impregnated, do invite relativist conclusions. Popper made two important claims. First, that the logical method of science is falsification. Second, that science progresses through trial and error, by an evolutionary epistemology incorporating a logic of criticism. Kuhn, however, claimed that neither of these assertions is supported by the history of science.[9] Far from the history of science displaying a steady continuity in which theories, subjected to steady but unrelenting criticism, are weeded out leaving only the best conjectures holding the field, conformity and conservatism seem to rule. For most of the time scientists exhibit a strong attachment to general frameworks, or 'paradigms', within which 'normal science' proceeds its uneventful and cautious way. Such prolonged periods are punctuated by upheavals in which 'revolutionary science' overthrows the orthodoxy only to establish itself as a new orthodoxy. Upheavals such as this are relatively rare, however.

Here Kuhn is drawing upon sociological ideas and using them against philosophical conceptions of science, including those of positivism. In brief, science is a social institution into which scientists are socialised: learning how to work and think within the idioms of particular scientific communities. In doing so they become committed to a paradigm which, though it is not always clear just what Kuhn means by this, contains, first, a constellation of values and beliefs, cognitions, rules of order and techniques of procedure shared by a given scientific community, and, second, a collection of exemplary work within a discipline that serve as recipes for problem-solving activity. Paradigms involve a shared set of symbols, metaphysical commitments and values, as well as criteria of judgement and the worth of work done. So, becoming a member of a scientific community involves enculturation into the paradigm. 'Normal science' characterises the kind of attitudes and practices that go on within a discipline for most of the time, in which scientists patiently and undramatically work to elaborate the theories and accumulate findings shaped by the orthodox paradigm. However, such a process always creates puzzles and problems which, though for a time can be put on one side, eventually accumulate until they become so serious that the orthodox paradigm is increasingly seen as inadequate. The search for a new paradigm starts; a search best done by younger scientists with reputations and careers to establish. Out of this turmoil a new paradigm emerges.

For some, Kuhn's version of the development of science overemphasises the irrational and non-rational factors. The change in paradigms amounts to a *gestalt* switch in which things can never be the same as before. A new paradigm is a new way of seeing the 'same' things differently, and the kind of phenomena with which a discipline deals change fundamentally. Paradigms are incommensurable. When the phlogiston theory of combustion was refuted and Lavoisier discovered oxygen, the universe was different for science.[10] In which case, if Kuhn is right there can be no theory-independent view of the world, and if a change from one paradigm to another is a movement between incommensurables, then it is hard to see the development of science as progress towards truth. The history of science is simply a history of changes and science unequivocally a social process and the selection of competing theories dependent on this context. Moreover, such a view seemed to reject a correspondence theory of scientific truth. Theories are radically underdetermined by the facts of the world; the world, to put it slightly differently, is capable of bearing a very wide variety of theories, none of which could be said to be absolutely superior to another. Kuhn himself claimed that he was not a relativist and expressed unease at the apparent abandonment of the idea that sensory experience was fixed and neutral, but did also despair of securing this through the pursuit of a neutral observation language.[11]

The dispute between the Popperian and Kuhnian views is one over the character of scientific logic and its place in the development of science itself, in particular as to whether it is possible, or sensible, to describe science's development as a progress towards truth.[12] Popper wants to say that despite local vagaries and perturbations, the choice between theories, between paradigms even, is, or can be, made on rational scientific criteria. It is the effort to deploy these criteria in a process of criticism, trial and error, that results in the slow progress towards truth as weaker offerings are discarded. Kuhn, on the other hand, seems to suggest that such choices are not rational in this sense, but the outcome of non-rational, extra-scientific considerations and factors, such as the distribution of power and reputation within disciplines, within society itself, personal commitments, wider cultural and political circumstances, and so on. The 'facts' cannot decide the matter because what the 'facts' are is dependent upon the particular paradigm they belong to, as do the standards in force for judging which theories are better than others. Facts, methods and standards are internal to paradigms and there is no independent position from which to judge them – least of all by an appeal of a world independent of any theoretical position whatsoever. Such a thing is a chimera.

Although Kuhn's views provoked no little excitement in social science, it is not clear just what their implications might be, except as a way of writing the history of social science in terms of paradigm changes.[13] In other words, it is not clear just what philosophical or methodological consequences would flow from Kuhn's conception. Are the social sciences at a pre-paradigmatic phase, or do they exhibit a plurality of paradigms which, though incommensurable, can be ignored until a better paradigm emerges? But what follows from any answer to these and other questions of this order? As far as the sociology of science was concerned, however, Kuhn's work proved to be a liberation. Hitherto a relatively minor branch of sociology concerned with studies on, for example, the background of scientists, the social history of science, the rise of science as an institution, and so on, began to see itself as able to make inquiries into the cognitive aspects of science, scientific knowledge itself, and so encroach, it was claimed, upon territory hitherto reserved for philosophy. For some, it meant that philosophical questions about knowledge were at least open to empirical solution. The Strong Programme in the Sociology of Knowledge, for example, saw itself as banishing forever the philosophy of science and all the epistemological and ontological questions that went with it. Science was through and through a social construction and, therefore, a concern of sociology rather than philosophy.[14] It is social, political as well as wider moral attitudes that determine the theories which are held and sustained and those which are rejected. Boyle's atomic theory of matter, for example, crucial to the origins of modern chemistry, had a strong affinity with the corpuscular philosophy that shaped the political opinions of the 'establishment' groups to which Boyle belonged in post-Civil War England. Corpuscular philosophy was the ideology of an establishment class and corresponded with the requirements of their social, political and economic interests.

The claim is that all knowledge, including scientific knowledge, is social. Although knowledge can be analysed and studied as if it were asocial, that is, independent of the social circumstances which produced it, this is a very limited conception and one which will not be able to explain why some theories, some beliefs, are held and others not. If one looks at the history of science one can find many theories, including some that were just as plausible in terms of the evidence available, but which were not accepted while others were. This cannot be explained purely in terms of rational criteria. A proper footing for the examination of knowledge is the sociology of knowledge rather than philosophy. According to the Strong Programme, what such an examination should seek to do is specify the causal connections between social conditions and knowledge, irrespective of whether or not these bodies of knowledge are true or false. In other words, it should not simply seek to explain why false beliefs are held – for example – why some people still believe that the Earth is flat – but also try to explain why true beliefs are accepted. Nor is the sociology of knowledge to be exempted from its own strictures; it, too, is capable of explanation in terms of its causal social conditions. One implication of such a view is to render meaningless the quest for intellectual authority, as positivism did, for example, through a philosophically secure conception of the foundations of human knowledge. For philosophy, too, as a body of knowledge is socially caused and, hence, dependent on the social conditions which produced it. There are no secure foundations for human knowledge; it is relative.

However, what this represents is a mistake traceable back to Kuhn, or at least to some interpretations of Kuhn, of confusing the history and the sociology of science with the philosophy of science. For, even accepting that the boundaries between disciplines are not always clear, it can be argued that history, sociology and philosophy represent different ways of being interested in the world and, as such, are incommensurable in respect of their problems and procedures. In which case, the claims of the Strong Programme, for example, to answer philosophical questions empirically is simply mistaken, for not only is philosophy not an empirical discipline, its problems and interests are not of the kind to be resolved empirically. Its interest in the world is independent of whatever empirical conclusions history or sociology might provide. This is an issue that will surface again; but as far as Kuhn's work is concerned, if he was doing no more, as suggested earlier, than describe the development of natural science in a particular period of European history, then it is debatable as to whether his analysis has any methodological consequences for the social sciences as to how they might meet the requirements of scientificity.[15] Rightly or wrongly, however, one of the implications that has been drawn is that Kuhn's arguments deny the possibility of scientific progress. Science does not grow, it simply changes. As Laudan points out with respect to Kuhn's conception, 'scientific revolutions are regarded as progressive because the "victors" write the history . . .'.[16] This, as said earlier, is, for many, an absurd conclusion. Whatever scientific discipline we choose to take, be it physics, chemistry, biology, mathematics, history, even any of the social sciences, our knowledge has not merely changed but grown, though not always in a straight linear fashion. However, this is not quite the problem. We could still accept that scientific knowledge has grown and still deny that this is solely the result of the rational accumulation of knowledge. Lakatos turned to this in an effort to reconcile some of Kuhn's insights into the historical development of science with the view that science is a rational activity.[17] Falsificationism, as far as Lakatos was concerned, failed as a demarcation criterion between science and non-science because it underestimated, even ignored, the tenacity with which theories were clung to despite disconfirmation; a point which Kuhn dwells upon. However, Kuhn's own conclusions about the incommensurability of theories was far too relativistic for Lakatos' taste. Science, for him, is a rationally accumulating body of knowledge; but it does not progress, as Popper claimed, through trial and error. The key notion for Lakatos is not, as it is for both Popper and Kuhn, the theory but the 'research programme'.

Newton's theory of gravitation, Einstein's relativity theory, Marxism, Freudianism, among many more, would qualify as 'research programmes' in Lakatos' sense. They are characterised by a 'hard core' of definitive propositions protected by a belt of auxiliary theories and hypotheses which connect the 'core' to the domain of facts to which they pertain. Thus, for Marxism, the theory of value formation and the creation of surplus value would be the core, and the theories of alienation, diminishing return to capital and of revolution, would be the auxiliary theories. However, a 'research programme', as its name implies, is not some dead, fixed collection of ideas but a living thing directed by scholars working within it at the problems it poses, suggesting ways in which they can be tackled, exploring its ideas, indicating problems that are best avoided, and so on. It is the last kind of problems wherein lie the dynamics of 'research programmes' since, by eventually confronting them, progress can be achieved. Of course, the problem is knowing which problems are likely to prove promising and which not. For Lakatos, as for Popper, the important criterion is the ability of a research programme to predict novel facts or facts ruled out to be impossible by other research programmes. So, if a theory is running ahead of the facts, or is predicting new facts, then it is a progressive one. If, on the other hand, the theory constantly needs repair and patching up to stay in business, then it is degenerating or, at best, static.

Lakatos' 'rationalist history' of science tries to merge the philosophy of science's traditional concerns for the logic of the scientific method with those of the history of science. The tendency of science to persist with disconfirmed theories is rational in that it delays judgement until a research programme has matured. However, whatever the merits of the views just discussed, there is no doubt that bringing historical and social considerations to bear upon discussions on the logic of science has cast serious doubts on the traditional view that science is a paragon of rational-cum-empirical knowledge.

This is most pronounced in the work of Feyerabend who argues that scientific change and progress is really a conversion from one myth to another. Rejecting the distinction between observation and theory, as well as philosophical rumination as having any relevance for the operation of science, he regards science as a social institution located within a specific set of cultural, political and social concerns, just like any other institution in society. Thus, scientific changes do not simply arise from the application of a scientific method, but from the influences of 'interests, forces, propaganda brainwashing techniques' of 'professional socialization'.[18] In this respect, science is not different to any other form of knowledge; it is part and parcel of 'forms of life'. The conclusion that Feyerabend draws from this familiar relativist argument is that 'anything goes' in science. There is no scientific method. There is certainly no superiority attaching to scientific knowledge. For Western society, science has become an idol, a dogma, and its conception as a progressive rational activity little more than an obsession without foundation. In this he is not claiming the need to 'correct' the actual practices of science, but to bring its ideology more into accord with these practices.

His own examination of the Copernican revolution in astronomy during the sixteenth and seventeenth centuries suggests that Copernicus' theory did not succeed because it was 'obviously' more rational and more progressive than Ptolemaic astronomy. Indeed, Copernicus' theory did not fit many of the widely accepted astronomical 'facts' and made use of some of Aristotle's theories about the harmony of the universe. It was not until the use of the telescope that the majority were eventually persuaded to accept Copernicus' heliocentric theory of the solar system. Other aspects of the theory depended upon Galileo's new theory of motion. But Feyerabend's point is that conversions such as these are not the products of reason, evidence or method, but have much to do with self-interest, ideology and wider cultural beliefs. Although Feyerabend's anarchism is well known and fits well with his rejection of the notion that there is any superiority to the method of science, he is not against science, only against its pretensions and idolisation.

Popper, Kuhn, Lakatos and Feyerabend represent, although in different ways, a response to the epistemological problems posed by induction as the basis of scientific knowledge. Popper revised the scope of the problem by proposing that it was the scientific method that was rational, not necessarily any particular scientific theory. Science is a human activity and, consequently, prone to mistakes, confusion and error. Nonetheless, the rationality of science and the cut and thrust of scientific debate ensures that, in the end, true theories will prevail. This apart, Popper's reflections on science had the further consequence of making science's history and its social context highly visible, eventually leading to the prominence of views which gave science little credence as the epitome of reason. Science did not progress rationally. As Feyerabend would put it, change in science is simply the replacement of one myth by another. Relativism is loosed.

However, although the social and historical nature of science, indeed of any form of knowledge, is well accepted by most, what are less palatable are precisely the kind of relativist conclusions that seem to follow. For one thing, although it might be accepted that observation is theory-laden and there is no theory independent way of observing the external world, and that theories might well be incommensurable, surely nature must play some role in determining which particular theories, categories, methods, etc., are the right ones? Surely we just cannot determine what the world is like in whatever way we choose? If we cannot then a fundamental requirement is the independent existence of an external world which has a character independent of human conceptions of it.

REDEFINING EMPIRICISM

However, positing this requirement for an adequate philosophical empiricism is one thing; demonstrating, as we have seen in the discussion of positivism, is quite another, especially after the forceful attacks made by arguments concerning the social construction of knowledge and, importantly as a consequence, varying standards of truth and validity. If science is a social construct, then any claims it might have to a unique accessibility to the nature of the external world has to go. Our conception of science, its methods, and its findings, are a consequence of our history, our society, and not the result of some privileged method for describing and explaining the nature of reality. Science becomes, at best, simply another way in which the world may be described. As Quine argues, our experience of the world, of facts, does not impose any single theory on us. Theories are underdetermined by facts, and the factuality of the external world, to call it that, is capable of sustaining many different interpretations of it.

This Quine accepts with equanimity, but does not conclude that we should abandon science. While we can have no firmer knowledge than science can give us, this knowledge is always revisable and contingent. What has to be abandoned is the epistemological goal of trying to discover those principles which would guarantee certain knowledge. Such an endeavour is futile. Epistemology is really an inquiry into how we come to know the world in the way in which we do, and not an inquiry into whether we can acquire certain knowledge. Indeed, Quine is prepared to consign epistemology to psychology; that is, as part of an empirical rather than a philosophical discipline.[19] For his own part, his interests are ontological rather than epistemological and begin from the position that there is nothing that can be more certain than science and no philosophy that can be foundational to it. This is not, as said earlier, to claim that science is certain. Philosophy depends upon the foundations of science for this is the best guide as to what kinds of things there are in the world. So what Quine is offering is a limited scepticism about science unlike, say, that offered on some interpretations of Feyerabend's remarks. We do not have to accept or reject science *in toto*, but we should recognise that some of the theories and the findings of science will be wrong, as they have been in the past. This is the best we can have even though they may be the products of *our* culture.[20] For Quine, science and philosophy, though not the same, are joint endeavours distinguished by the generality of their respective concerns. Nevertheless, philosophy must take its lead from science. What Quine seeks to provide is an economical, not to say austere, account of what there is; an ontology that postulates as few entities as possible. There is one important difference between science and philosophy, however. Philosophy does not investigate the world directly, but through language invoking what Quine calls the principle of 'semantic ascent'. Instead of examining 'things' like science, philosophy investigates how things are talked about and, through this, investigates the nature of the world.[21] Quine is a relativist to the extent that, although the aim of both philosophy and science is to discover what there is, neither can claim to do this in any theory independent way.

However, instead of regarding this as the conclusive result of philosophical rumination, Quine, in effect, comes at the issue from another direction. The answer to the question, what exists? can only receive the answer, what exists is what theories posit. Since there are different theories, these will posit different things. Accordingly, Quine is happy to accept some of the implications of the Kuhnian type of view, which argues that different theories postulate different existents and that there is an incommensurability involved in this. But, for Quine, this is to take an 'externalist' view of theories. However, we look at the world *through* theories and though we can accept, from an external point of view, that there can be alternative accounts of the world and what exists, we judge their adequacy from the point of view of our 'home' theory and that is, for us, science.

Quine is claiming that certainty cannot be sought from the places philosophy has traditionally looked for it; that is, what we can know independently of all experience, the a priori, or that which is certain because it arises directly from experience, the *a posteriori*. These are, for Quine, the two 'dogmas' of empiricism.[22] What he intends is nothing less than eroding the distinction that has long been central to philosophy between analytic and synthetic statements. Philosophers have tended to regard the truth of sentences as a matter to be settled for each sentence separately when, in actuality, sentences are part of whole languages. The same is true of sentences within theories. It is language, or the theory, which is the unit of meaning and, accordingly, the truth and the meaning of any one sentence in that language, or in that theory, has to be answered in terms of its relationship within the whole. The sentences that make up theories, for example, are like a spider's web, anchored at some points, but connected by filaments of thread such that perturbations at one point will affect others. Thus, at some points there will be sentences that are directly related to our experience, others will be more remote. Others we may be prepared to readily abandon, others less so. Still, all sentences are linked together and it is this organisation which has much to do with our conception of the world rather than those points anchored to a more direct experience of the world.

The structure can be revised, of course, though there will be some statements we might be more reluctant to give up than others. Some will have more consequence than others and their abandonment involving major revisions to the structure, while others might have only minor effects. The reason, therefore, why the analytic–synthetic distinction cannot be sustained is that questions of meaning and those of fact are thoroughly intertwined within the structure. The discovery of black swans does not suddenly render the statement 'all swans are white' synthetic, for we could choose not to regard black 'swans' as swans at all.[23] In other words, the facts do not necessarily impose either solution on us. The configured web of our beliefs, theories, sentences can be altered to cope in various ways with any changes we might be forced to make: 'a statement about the world does not always or usually have a separable fund of empirical consequences that it can call its own'.[24] Thus, and this is the important point, our experience of the world does not impose any single theory on us, nor any particular response we need to make in adjusting theories to meet new facts. It is this which sets limits to the certainty of our knowledge: theories are radically underdetermined by evidence.

Accordingly, the hope of positivist empiricism that certain knowledge of the world could be provided by sensory experience is rejected by Quine. Even the sentences which report on our direct sensory experiences are also part of the web of sentences and, as a result, revisable as necessary. Quine is not here rejecting the idea that the evidence of our senses is the evidence for the theories we have: indeed, this is the only evidence we have. But theories go beyond that evidence and cannot be limited by it. There will always be more than one logically equivalent theory (note, not *any* theory) consistent with the evidence we have. This is not because that evidence may be insufficient, but because the same facts can be accommodated in different ways by alterations in the configuration of the theory. Of course, there may be lots of good reasons why we should prefer one theory or another logically and evidentially equivalent theory, but these cannot be on the grounds of evidence alone.

Similar problems emerge in translating one language, or a theory, into another. As Kuhn seems to have suggested, theories are incommensurable and that, as a result, changes in scientific theories represent fundamental changes in our conception of the world and, indeed, in the ontology of the world. For Quine, translation between two theories is a matter of aligning two systems, not simply trying to match up the meaning of separate words, concepts or sentences. So, attempts to match, say, separate sentences between two systems will involve making assumptions about how the bits fit into separate but respective wholes; and, as before, we can provide different solutions for particular sentences depending upon the adjustments and compensations we wish to make. Translating involves guesswork, assumptions about the ontologies referred to by the respective theories and, for Quine, there is no right way of deciding which translation might be the correct one. There is even logical room for doubt that even the speakers of a common language hold the same ontology. This, however, makes no practical difference to social relationships. It is the pattern of behavioural dispositions that is crucial and there is no way of telling from these, with absolute certainty, whether a person has the same ontology as we do. In logic there is no compelling reason why our ontology should be chosen over another.[25]

The sort of revisions Quine, and others, envisage for empiricism are major revisions against positivism. In trying to obtain an ontology for science, what we cannot do, as positivism did, is to look to the nature of the world independently of our theories, our language. As one contemporary philosopher of science expresses it, it is 'generally agreed . . . that the idea of a descriptive vocabulary which is applicable to observations, but which is entirely innocent of theoretical influences, is unrealizable'.[26] But looking towards theories simply brings us up against their incompatibility and incommensurability, and their indeterminacy, and the spectre of relativism. Once again, we seem to lose any possibility of justifying scientific knowledge over other forms.

Others, however, such as Putnam, while agreeing with Quine that we can have no knowledge stronger than science, nevertheless want to reintroduce the notion of 'essence' through a theory of 'direct reference'. Thus, although an object might manifest all kinds of appearances, what is essential to this is the nature of the stuff. Gold, for example, can vary in appearance in relation to light, heat, etc., but its physio-chemical constitution cannot vary, cannot become, say, like that of water and still remain gold.[27] What links a word and an object is an act of 'dubbing', and what the name is linked to is whatever it is that makes it the kind of stuff that it is. So, when scientists discover 'essences', what kind of stuff a thing is, then they discover necessary relations; that is, discover what it is that makes something what it is. Such a theory is intended to avoid the Kuhnian and Feyerabend claims that there is no continuity between theories. Even though, before and after a scientific revolution, beliefs about the things theorised may have changed, this is irrelevant since these do not 'fix the reference' of the terms.

One further consequence of these efforts to revise empiricism is embodied in Hacking's recommendation that philosophy turn its attention to the ways in which scientists intervene in the world to produce their theories in order to see what ontologies their methods of experimentation, observation and measurement are committed to.[28] In other words, philosophical interests in science should have less concern with the question of how scientific theories *represent* the world, and more in how they *intervene* in the world in order to investigate it. Such a conception does not require that science has a single unified ontology. Realism for theories only causes us problems when we try to imagine that we can effect a match between the theory and the world independent of the theory. Without theories we have no idea what the external world is like. Realism belongs *within* our theories; what Putnam refers to as 'internal realism'.[29] Propositions are true within a theory, or within a given language, but we can cope with the diversity of the conceptions of the world implied if we regard ontologies as allowing us to make experiments, observations, and so on, to give organised and systematic descriptions of what is found, rather than requiring us to match theories with how the external world *really is* organised. In this there is no need for a unified theory, a unified method, or a unified ontology. The theories of the various scientific disciplines are descriptions of what is observed, measured, experimented on, counted, and so on. The 'phenomenological laws', as Cartwright calls them, are the outcome of many different premises, assumptions, interests, exigencies, and problems that are peculiar to particular disciplines.[30] These laws are correct within their respective domains but do not add up to a theoretical or ontological unity. Any attempt at unification by connecting them to more 'fundamental laws' is bound to distort them since they can only be approximations to the concepts deployed in the original theories. Various orders of observations, measurements and the phenomena displayed in the investigations of different disciplines cannot be reduced to each other without 'lying'. In which case, science has to be committed to multiple ontologies, multiple realities, rather than the myth propounded by the likes of positivism of a single, unified description of the ontology of the external world.

The implications of the new philosophy of science for the social sciences are radical in some ways, inconsequential in others. What is rejected is positivism's effort to build a view of science stressing the unity of its method, its search for laws, and so on, which the social sciences, if they were to become scientific, would have to emulate. However, the views reviewed here cast doubt, in various ways, on the idea that there could be a unified science united by its commitment to a single ontology of the external world. The work of Kuhn, and the sociologists of science, as well as the arguments of Feyerabend, showed that scientific change has little to do with the shape science obtains through the application of a rational method, and has more to do with the fact that it is a social institution. Arguments about the incommensurability of theories raised questions about the truth of theories and provoked damaging doubts about the correspondence theory of truth espoused by positivism. Nevertheless, rather than abandon science to anarchy, as Feyerabend is alleged to want, contemporary realists and empiricists, such as Quine, Putnam and Hacking, have revised the conception of science and knowledge in light of the arguments raised against positivist conceptions of science. What was rejected was not science, or indeed its eminence as a form of knowledge, but the view of science requiring epistemological and ontological unity. What is emphasised is the diversity and the disunity of science. After all, scientists do not worry about epistemology and ontology but about the particular problems they confront from their theories and investigations. And, indeed, as Pawson reminds us, the theory-laden nature of observation is a feature of scientific work that natural scientists find unremarkable and obvious.[31]

A further implication of this kind of view is that the intellectual authority of philosophy is eroded. If all that matters is that scientists go about their business in the ways that they are taught, learn and acquire, using methods appropriate to the problems they have to deal with, then philosophical worries about ontology and epistemology are an irrelevance. Quine, for example, argued for the 'naturalisation' of epistemology by reducing it to one of the sciences of knowledge, such as behavioural psychology or brain physiology, to discover those laws of cognition which determine why we accept and hold the theories and the beliefs that we do. Ontology, too, becomes the business of the respective sciences and their investigations. In which case, as far as the social sciences are concerned, if they want to emulate the natural sciences what they should do, like them, is disregard philosophical versions of science and get on with tackling their problems as they see fit. There is certainly no reason to feel bound by stipulations about a unified method or a unified ontology for science, for on these arguments no such creature exists.

For some realists, especially those concerned with the social sciences, this kind of conclusion is unsatisfactory. While recognising that positivism has been found wanting, they still want to assert that science is concerned to describe real structures, entities and processes which constitute the external world. In this, the regularity that is required by the orthodox notion of laws is less important than identifying and describing the real, operative causal mechanisms which have real effects. It is not required that these operating mechanisms and their entities be observable, *contra* empiricism, but by isolating their causal effects in suitably designed studies, their existence can be plausibly postulated. Many of the more powerful mechanisms postulated by natural science theories, as said before, are not directly observable, though their effects can be. Laws need not be universal in the sense required by positivism but should represent recognisable tendencies.[32] As Bhaskar says,

The citation of a law presupposes a claim about the activity of some mechanism but not about the conditions under which the mechanism operates and hence not about the results of its activity, i.e. the actual outcome on any particular occasion.[33]

The consequences stated by laws happen only in special circumstances, that is, when its operation is not 'impeded' by complicating tendencies and the *ceteris paribus* conditions are in place. All heavier than air objects fall, for a simple example, unless 'impeded' by things that do not allow them to 'realise' the law of falling bodies, so to speak. In the natural sciences, the ability to set up 'closed systems' often, but not always, experimentally, allows for the more detailed specification of the *ceteris paribus* conditions for a law. This is the major difference between the natural and the social sciences. Accordingly, it should not be expected that the degrees of precision attainable in most of the natural sciences should be found in the causal statements of the social sciences. In addition, the view also stresses realism for theories in that entities have their meaning and significance from the theories of which they are a part.

This realist conception of the nature of social science – although in many ways in accord with much of the new philosophy of science and, in this sense at least, tries to avoid many of the problems of earlier positivist and empiricist philosophies of science – contains little of direct guidance to social research itself. It is still a language of causation and in this respect attractive to materialists. But, in addition, it represents a serious relaxation of the criteria for determining causal relationships as exhibited in natural science. Others, however, recognise that any realist social science would have to take into account the fact that social actors themselves have their own theories about the way in which the world operates, and taking this seriously raises the question of whether any causalist conception of the business of social science can be sustained. This is one of the issues to be taken up in the next chapter.

REFERENCES

1. Popper, K., *The Logic of Scientific Discovery,* London, Hutchinson, 1959, p. 59.
2. Halfpenny, P., *Positivism and Sociology,* London, Allen and Unwin, 1982, p. 101.
3. Popper, *op. cit.,* p. 317.
4. For a fuller treatment see Anderson, R. J. *et al., Philosophy and the Human Sciences,* London, Croom Helm, 1986, pp. 236–43.
5. Popper, K., *Conjectures and Refutations,* 2nd edn, New York, Harper & Row, xxxx pp. 29–30.
6. See, for example, the selections in Barnes, B. and Edge, D. (eds), *Science in Context,* Milton Keynes, Open University Press, 1982. Also, Barnes, B., *Interests and the Growth of Knowledge,* London, Routledge and Kegan Paul, 1977.
7. Popper, K., *Objective Knowledge: An Evolutionary Approach,* London, Oxford University Press, 1972, p. 59.
8. See his *Open Society and Its Enemies,* 2 vols, London, Routledge and Kegan Paul, 1945. Also Sharrock, W. W., 'Individual and society' in Anderson, R. J. *et al.* (eds), *Classic Disputes in Sociology,* London, George Allen and Unwin, 1987, pp. 126–56.
9. Kuhn, T., *The Structure of Scientific Revolutions,* 2nd edn, enl., Chicago, University of Chicago Press, 1970.
10. Anderson *et al., op. cit.,* p. 252.
11. Kuhn, op. cit., p. 126; also his 'Second thoughts on paradigms' in Suppe, F. (ed.), *The Structure of Scientific Theories,* Urbana, University of Illinois Press, 1974.
12. See Lakatos, I. and Musgrave, A. (eds), *Criticism and the Growth of Knowledge,* Cambridge, Cambridge University Press, 1970.
13. See Urry, J., 'Thomas Kuhn as a Sociologist of Knowledge', *British Journal of Sociology,* 24, 1973, pp. 462–73.
14. See, for example, Bloor, D., *Knowledge and Social Imagery,* London, Routledge and Kegan Paul, 1976; Bloor, D., 'The strengths of the strong programme', *Philosophy of the Social*

Sciences, 11, 1981, pp. 199–213; Shapin, S., 'History of science and its sociological reconstructions', *History of Science,* XX, 1982, pp. 157–211; Woolgar, S., 'Interests and explanation in the social study of science', *Social Studies of Science,* 11, 1981, pp. 365–94. See also, Laudan, L., 'The pseudo-science of science', *Philosophy of the Social Sciences,* 11, 1981, pp. 173–98; Anderson, R. J. *et al.,* 'Some initial difficulties with the sociology of knowledge', *Occasional Papers in Social Science,* Manchester Polytechnic, 1986. See also Law, J. and Hodge, P., *Science for Social Scientists,* London, Macmillan, 1984.

15. As history, Kuhn's views have been subjected to some criticism. See also his own *Essential Tension,* Chicago, Chicago University Press, 1977.

16. Laudan, L., *Progress and Its Problems: Toward a Theory of Scientific Growth.* Berkeley, University of California Press, 1977, p. 10.

17. Lakatos, I., *Collected Papers,* Vols I and II, Cambridge, Cambridge University Press, 1978 and 1984. Also Anderson *et al., Philosophy and the Human Sciences, op. cit.*

18. Feyerabend, P., *Against Method: Outline of an Anarchist Theory of Knowledge,* London, New Left Books, 1975.

19. Quine is a materialist and the kind of psychology he has in mind here is a behavioural one.

20. Quine, W. V., *Ontological Relativity and Other Essays,* New York, Columbia University Press, 1969.

21. Quine would reject the view that what such studies investigate is language alone. Language is the route for the philosophical investigation of the world.

22. Quine, W. F. V., *From a Logical Point of View,* Cambridge, Harvard University Press, 1953. See also Anderson *et al., op. cit.,* pp. 153–4.

23. Anderson *et al., ibid.,* p. 156.

24. Quine, *Ontological Relativity, op. cit.,* p. 82.

25. Davidson, D., *Inquiries into Truth and Interpretation,* Oxford, Oxford University Press, 1984, explores further Quine's remarks on translation.

26. Harre, R., *The Philosophies of Science,* Oxford, Oxford University Press, 1972, p. 25.

27. Anderson *et al., op. cit.,* p. 169; Putnam, H., *Mathematics, Matter and Method,* Cambridge, Cambridge University Press, 1975, and *Realism and Reason,* Cambridge, Cambridge University Press, 1978.

28. Hacking, I., *Representing and Intervening,* Cambridge, Cambridge University Press, 1983; also selection in his collection *Scientific Revolutions,* Oxford, Oxford University Press, 1981.

29. Putnam, *Realism and Reason, op. cit.*

30. Cartwright, N., *How the Laws of Physics Lie,* Oxford, Oxford University Press, 1983.
31. Pawson, R., *A Measure for Measures: A Manifesto for Empirical Sociology,* London, Routledge and Kegan Paul, 1989, p. 32.
32. Outhwaite, W., 'Laws and explanations' in Anderson, R. J., *et al.* (eds), *Classic Disputes in Sociology,* London, George Allen and Unwin, 1987, pp. 174–82. See also Keat, R. and Urry J., *Social Theory as Science,* London, Routledge and Kegan Paul, 1975; Bhaskar, R., *A Realist Theory of Science,* 2nd edn, Sussex, Harvester Press, 1978.
33. Bhaskar, *op. cit.,* p. 95.

The interpretative alternative

In the previous chapter I mentioned a distinction which, historically speaking, is of fundamental importance in Western intellectual development, namely but rather grossly, that between mind and matter. While admitting of the distinction in some sense or another, different philosophical schools have, as we have seen, interpreted it in different ways. For materialists the aim is to reduce mental phenomena to epiphenomena of the material. Extreme idealists, on the other hand, argue that the so-called material world is simply the resultant of ideas. Both positions, of course, are more detailed and more plausible than this summary statement might indicate. For our immediate purposes in this chapter, what is important is the acceptance of the dualism as representing different orders of phenomena and, accordingly, to be known in different ways.

SOME INTELLECTUAL FORERUNNERS

As with the origins of positivistic thought, the tremendous debates of the seventeenth century form the more immediate intellectual background for the view that the proper study of human society could not be scientific in the manner of the natural sciences. Where the social sciences are concerned, the important figures are Vico and, much later, Dilthey and the development of hermeneutic philosophy. More contemporaneously, the Phenomenologists, among others, have expanded this tradition. The earliest mentioned, Giovanni Batista Vico (1668–1744), saw human history as a process reflecting the maturation of the human mind in its understanding of God's nature. He also stressed that the study of man and society in history was very different from the study of inanimate nature in the sense that the former involved subjective understanding, a theme that was to be developed more fully later, especially by German scholars of the nineteenth century. Important to this particular phase of the debate were considerations arising from Biblical philology. Translating texts which had themselves gone through a number of different translations and modifications from their original language did not simply involve linguistic considerations, but also required them to be related, in order to discover their original meaning, to the wider social context in which they were originally produced. So, making sense of textual materials required a union of philology and history and, one might add, sociology and anthropology. It was this which provided what has become known as hermeneutics with its abiding question: how is an understanding of the past to be gained through its texts and other remains? Schleiermacher, who was responsible for drawing hermeneutics away from its original home in philology and applying it to the problems of historical knowledge, took this as *the* problem of history. To understand the past one has to identify with it. By complementing grammatical interpretation with psychological identification, hermeneutics was introduced into the study of human activities more generally and the possibility of interpretative understanding more particularly.[1] Dilthey (1833–1911), building on Schleiermacher and as part of a widespread romantic reaction against positivism, held that the positivist methodology of the natural sciences was inadequate to the understanding of human phenomena except as natural objects. It left no room for the idea that history and society were human creations and that this constituted the essence of all social forms. The study of human history has to be based on the fact that humans were purposive creators whose lives were bounded by a reality which has meaning for them. The duality of the subjective and the objective was irreducible. History was not simply the succession of events one after another, but expressed the spirituality of social life as expressed in social institutions, law, literature, government, morality, values, and more.

This required a wholly different but still well-grounded method of inquiry to that of natural science. The method had to recognise the actions, events and artifacts from *within* human life not as the observation of some external reality. Knowledge of persons could only be gained through an interpretative procedure grounded in the imaginative recreation of the experiences of others. History, society, art, indeed all human products, were the objectifications of the human mind and not at all like material things. Accordingly, understanding such phenomena required that the lived experiences of others be grasped through the apprehension of their inner meaning; the meaning that led to their production. The socio-historical world is a symbolic world created by the human mind and cannot be understood as simply a relationship of material things.

So for Dilthey and others of like mind, nature and culture were inherently different and required different methods of study. Natural science, conceived mainly in positivistic terms, studied the objective, inanimate, non-human world. Society, a product of the human mind, was subjective, emotive as well as intellectual. What we would refer to as causal, mechanistic and measurement oriented models of explanation were inappropriate, since human consciousness was not determined by natural forces. Human social behaviour was always imbued with values, and reliable knowledge of a culture could only be gained by isolating the common ideas, the feelings, or the goals of a particular historical society. It was these that made each social act subjectively meaningful. The observer, as a human being studying other human beings, has access to the cultural world of others through some form of 'imaginative reconstruction' or 'empathy'.

Others, notably Rickert, did not accept Dilthey's dichotomous view of reality as split, in effect, between nature and culture, but, instead, argued that reality was indivisible. However, unlike the positivists who held a similar view, this did not imply that the methods of natural science were thereby applicable to the world of society, culture and history. Differences between the natural and the social, or cultural, sciences were based on logic rather than a metaphysical ontology. For Rickert, human beings could have no knowledge of the world independently of what was in their minds. They had no way of finding out whether their knowledge faithfully reproduced a reality existing outside the mind and independent of it. They could only know things as they appear as phenomena, never as things as they are as such.[2] Facts, so to speak, are constituted out of the phenomena and given both form and content by the mind. This is a volitional act and its performance an intentional activity. All human knowledge, therefore, is selective, involving abstraction according to particular interests. Objectivity, therefore, is achieved not by matching ideas to some external reality, as the positivists would have it, but by the intersubjective establishment of those facts by those who have an interest in knowing them. Accordingly, if the knowledge of laws of nature is the only knowledge that anyone wants, then the legitimate method leading to their discovery is the method of natural science. If, on the other hand, the interest is in knowing different things, then the basis of knowledge, too, is different.

Empirically, according to Rickert, there are two basic principles of selection at work, each making it possible to arrive at one of two different kinds of representations of reality, namely, the nomothetic and the ideographic. The former, characteristic of natural science, is an interest in discovering general laws, while the latter, more characteristic of history, is concerned to understand the concrete and unique case. This dichotomy represents no fundamental difference in the ontology of the world but in the kind of knowledge required by different interests. Human products embody values and it is these which need to be understood by the social scientist in order to make sense of the unique constellations that make up human history. So, while natural science is interested in forming general concepts by abstracting from the concrete case those features which are in common with other phenomena, historical inquiry is concerned to form individual concepts by focusing on the unique combination of elements that represent a culturally significant phenomenon. Both forms of inquiry use their own principles of selection for the purpose of isolating the elements of empirical reality which are essential to their respective cognitive purposes. The ideal of objective knowledge requires both methods, as any one of them gives only a one-sided picture of reality. The same reality, however, can be presented either as history or as natural science.

Although Dilthey and Rickert differed as to the reasons for the employment of different methodologies with respect to the natural and social worlds, they did concur that positivistic natural science method could not be used to gain adequate knowledge of the social. Weber, much influenced in a selective way by Rickert, accepted the distinctive character of the social sciences but not the implication that they were unscientific in being unable to meet the rigorous standards of objectivity. In Diltheyian fashion Weber accepted the importance of 'interpretative understanding' as the distinctive form of knowledge for the socio-historical sciences but only as a means towards objective knowledge. In Rickertian fashion he supported the view that the essential distinction between the natural and the social sciences was methodological rather than ontological. Indeed, the possibility of 'interpretative understanding' in the social sciences was, for Weber, a tremendous opportunity and not something to be apologised for. By its means human action could be studied in greater depth than a natural scientist could ever penetrate into the nature of the inanimate world.[3] There was, however, a price to be paid in objectivity, precision and conclusiveness. For his own part Weber tried to reconcile the advantages of 'interpretative understanding' with the demands of scientific criteria.

However, to understand quite what this meant it is important to understand something of the road that led Weber to this conclusion. At the time, two general positions dominated the debate over the social scientific method: one we have already reviewed at some length, positivism, and the other, intuitionism. Weber rejected both of these. Any socio-cultural science must use a method distinct from that deployed in natural science, but this is not characterised, as the intuitionists wanted, by any allegedly unique stance. Both forms of knowledge, the natural scientific and the socio-cultural, are 'invariably tied to the instrument of concept formation'.[4] In other words, the problems of the logic of concept formation are the same for both despite the fact of practical differences in the manner in which intellectual inquiry is pursued. The crucial difference lies in the 'theoretic interest' or 'purpose' of understanding which, for the socio-cultural sciences, is understanding subjectively meaningful phenomena. Thus, we understand and expect the historical, the socio-cultural, sciences to be distinctive in their objective of interpreting meaning because of our own historically shaped, exiological interests. It is the values in our own culture which determine the kinds of interests that we take in history and in the social world as subjectively meaningful. By the same token, we take the 'theoretic interest' of the natural sciences to be in the production of universal-general concepts and propositions, or laws. But each of these different kinds of 'theoretic interests' cannot be reduced to the other. This is not for ontological reasons, as the intuitionists argued, but because of differences in the axiological or 'theoretical purpose' of the enquiry, and this does have methodological consequences for the socio-cultural sciences. A different method of inquiry is called for, given the theoretic interest of understanding or interpreting meaningfulness, and this is the method of *verstehen*; that is, attempting to reconstruct the subjective experience of social actors.

To this end Weber advanced two major methodological principles, both of which are still part of the contemporary language of social science, namely, value neutrality and the method of ideal types. So far as the the first is concerned, Weber held that social scientists should never abuse their scientific authority by passing off value judgements as scientific truths. About conflicting values scientists can have nothing to say as to which is to be preferred, but can only review the likely outcome of the various value alternatives. Science deals only with the rational, and is a technically oriented, instrumental activity.[5] The second methodological device, the ideal type, was offered as a means of grasping subjectively held meanings more objectively. All irrational and emotive aspects of human behaviour are to be seen as deviations from a conceptually pure type of rational action. This ideal type is both clear and free from ambiguity. Understanding, then, was transformed into the construction of rational models. Weber felt that the natural science method, transplanted to the study of social behaviour, would produce valid knowledge but of largely irrelevant and unimportant activities, at least as far as the subjective perspective was concerned. The contrast between the natural and the social sciences occurs because, in the latter, human beings are both the subject and the object of inquiry, which means that knowledge of society is a form of self-knowledge. *Verstehen* or interpretative understanding, gives social observers a method of investigating social phenomena in a way that does not distort the social world of those being studied. Since the essence of social interaction lies in the meanings agents give to their actions and environment, all valid social analysis must refer back to these. However, the insights gleaned in this manner must be supported by data of a scientific and statistical kind. All phenomena, no matter how unique and particular, are the products of antecedent, causally related conditions. By this Weber does not mean that social acts are to be reduced to single all-embracing laws, but rather that, from the complex whole of social reality, limited and unique antecedents and consequences are abstracted and related to observed phenomena. Such 'adequate causation' provides probabilistic explanations.

This tradition of thought reacting against positivist conceptions of science and their importation into social science had a powerful impact especially in Europe but, while not ignored, less so in the United Kingdom and the United States. For our purposes one feature above all stands out, namely, the view that the social sciences involve radically different methods from those of the natural sciences. Admittedly, the arguments for this did not always take on an ontological form but pointed instead to the different kinds of knowledge required by the respective disciplines. Either way, different methodologies were involved. It is to an examination of some of the issues here that I now turn.

SOCIAL ACTION AND MEANING

In part, the 'interpretavist' or 'humanistic' programme is a reaction against the very strident claims of positivism and its 'scientised' conception of the social actor which they see as embodied in orthodox social science of a positivist persuasion. The accusation is that those features which make social life a distinctively *human* product are analysed out and reduced to the interaction of variables.[6]

At times such accusations are little more than understandable frustration at the apparent trivialisation of the problems of social science and the betrayal this represents of the moral concerns that motivated the founding fathers. Exactly what positivistic social science had left out was a matter of some debate; was it freewill and choice, moral and political concerns, a regard for human fate, values, the self, the subjective dimension, or what?[7] On a less elevated plane the argument is about the character of the objects of social scientific inquiry. Even though it is more than possible to describe empirically patterns of social action by using all the elegant correlational apparatus of positivist social science, this would fail to get at the proper subject-matter of social science. It would fail, in short, to give an adequate account or interpretation of why the pattern of interaction occurred as it did, when it did and where, in terms faithful to its status as a human product. It would give no account of the fact that human beings of flesh and blood produced the interactions and, accordingly, would at best be only a partial analysis. The argument could go much further than this and claim that positivist methods not only give a partial account of social life but that they distort its nature in profound ways.

The manifold issues here are encapsulated in Weber's famous definition of 'social action': an action is social when a social actor assigns a certain meaning to his or her conduct and, by this meaning, is related to the behaviour of other persons.[8] Social interaction occurs when actions are reciprocally oriented towards the actions of others. Actions are reciprocally oriented not in any mechanistic fashion of stimulus and response, but because actors *interpret* and give meaning both to their own and to others' behaviour. Weber himself devoted considerable efforts to elucidating the implications of this formulation of the central tenet or, as for Weber the objective, of sociology. The important point here has to do with the idea of meaning and its relationship to the kind of knowledge we require in order to understand and explain social phenomena. To speak of meaning is to begin to point to that most important fact, that human beings have a rich and highly varied mental life reflected in all the artifacts by which, and institutions in which, they live. In sociological and anthropological terms this is referred to as 'culture' and includes all that social actors can talk about, explain, describe to others, excuse or justify, believe in, assert, theorise about, agree and disagree over, pray to, create, build, and so on.

One way of regarding meaning is to see it as a subjective or internal component of behaviour. This would be to draw a contrast between the objective features of social action and its subjective elements. The regularities we discover by studying society are only the external appearances of what the members of a society understand and, thereby, act upon. This point can be illustrated using Hart's famous example of traffic behaviour.[9] A stream of traffic controlled by traffic lights displays regularity. If it were to be regarded purely as the product of causal factors, then to explain the patterns we would have to specify the necessary and sufficient conditions which produce a given pattern, and go on to formulate a theory linking the traffic signals to the movement of the traffic stream. We would have to postulate the causal mechanism involved in effecting the connection between the different coloured lights and the movement of the vehicular units. However, as it happens, we do know that there are regulations governing traffic lights which order the drivers of the cars and other vehicles to behave in particular ways in accordance with the pattern of the lights. Thus, the connection between the lights and the movement of traffic is one which can be explained in terms of the *meaning* the lights have within the culture.

An important issue arising from this example is whether an explanation in terms of meaning is compatible with a causal explanation. If the answer is negative then this would seem to indicate a fundamental difference between the social and the physical sciences. The claim would be that the relationships between the traffic lights and the behaviour of the road vehicles is not of the same logical order as, say, that between sunlight and plant growth, between thunder and lightning, or between colliding billiard balls. Though classically regarded causal elements are involved in the traffic lights and the behaviours they produce – for example, in the mechanisms which activate the lights and in the control systems of the vehicles – these are irrelevant to understanding the relationship between the lights and the patterns of traffic. The relationship is a meaningful one, and what we have uncovered is a custom- or rule-governed practice rather than a causal law. The drivers could give *reasons* why they stopped when the light shone red, moved on when it changed to green. In short, they themselves could account for what they did: 'because the red light signalled "stop"', 'The green light allowed me to proceed', 'If you don't stop at a red light you can get in trouble with the police', 'You have to obey traffic lights otherwise the roads would be in chaos', and so on. Such reasons would invoke intentions, purposes, justifications, rules, conventions, and the like, rather than impersonal causal mechanisms.

There are a number of problems here to do with the ontological status of reasons and rules, the status of social science theories versus those accounts offered by the members of society, the nature of social action and its description, among others, all intertwined in complex ways. However, let me begin by trying to establish some preliminary positions.

One task of the social scientist is to give some theoretical account of social life. This requires empirical research in order to bring data to bear on the theory. These data must derive in some way from the lives of the social actors being studied, but unlike physical phenomena, social actors give meaning to themselves, to others and to the social environments in which they live. They can describe what they do, explain and justify it, give reasons, declare their motives, decide upon appropriate courses of action, try to fit means to ends, and so on. As Schutz expresses it:

It is up to the natural scientist and him alone to define, in accordance with the procedural rules of his science, his observational field, and to determine the facts, data, and events within it which are relevant for the problems or scientific purposes at hand . . . The world of nature, as explored by the natural scientist, does not 'mean' anything to the molecules, atoms, and electrons therein. The observational field of the social scientist, however, namely the social reality, has a specific meaning and relevance structure for the human beings living, acting, and thinking therein. By a series of commonsense constructs they have preselected and preinterpreted this world they experience as the reality of their daily lives.[10]

The social scientist, then, must come to terms with these meanings for, as we shall see later, in a fundamental sense the origins of the researcher's data lies in these meanings. The starting point for empirical social science research is the observation of what the members of society do or have done. These observations may be in the form of records, statistical rates, tape-recordings, writings, questionnaires or interviews, archeological remains, diaries, and so on. An essential part of observation is the description of the phenomenon. Actions and behaviours must be classified and categorised. Decisions must be made, for example, about whether a man carving a piece of wood is doing something economic, religious, political, artistic, or whatever. What is also certain is that the man himself would have views on what he is doing. What, then, is the relationship between his account and any that the social scientist might offer? What, if any, should the link be? More generally, what difference does the fact that social actors assign meaning to their social reality make for the study of social life?

Since positivistically inspired social science has not exactly ignored what might loosely be termed, the 'meaningful components' of social behaviour, and since the philosophical positions being discussed in this chapter involve a critique of this treatment, it is as well, perhaps, to begin with some statement of the traditional ways in which reasons, motives, intentions, rules and conventions have been regarded in traditional social scientific theorising.

RULES, MOTIVES AND THE DESCRIPTION OF SOCIAL ACTION

In the traffic light example used earlier two sorts of phenomena were identified as important in a 'meaningful' account of behaviour; rules and dispositional concepts such as reasons, intentions, or motives. These, as it were, point to the 'internal' character of the relationship between the lights and driver behaviour; that is, to the subjective meaning which leads to the sequence of actions we would describe as 'obeying the rules of traffic signals'. The idea that social action is rule-governed is not, of course, new or surprising. Some of the basic concepts of social science, such as norms, institutions, deviance, rationality, authority, profit-seeking, exchange, legitimacy, and many more, all pay more than just passing homage to the idea that social behaviour, whatever else it consists in, involves rules. In its various forms, the notion of rules is used to explain social conduct and is able to do so because rules, even if imposed, are part of the system of meaning actors use to make sense of their reality. Similarly, and in a related fashion, motives, intentions, and so on, point to another aspect of meaning, namely, that social actors pursue goals, have reasons for doing things, explain their conduct in such terms, and so on. Let us look at how these elements are normally treated within positivistic science.

The common mode of explanation is predicated on the notion that interaction is both rule-governed and motivated. Patterns of action are explained by reference to two groups of factors: dispositional ones, such as attitudes, motives, feelings, beliefs, personality; and sanctioned expectations, or norms, to which the actor is subject. These latter are sometimes referred to as 'role expectations' attaching to the incumbent of a particular position within a network of social relationships. The occupants of managerial positions, for example, are expected by others to behave in particular ways as are, though in different ways, mothers, fathers, prime ministers, ministers of religion, bank clerks, and so on. These expectations can be seen as rules guiding or even dictating the appropriate mode of behaviour for someone in one of these positions. A newly employed teacher, for illustration, has to learn the rules, both official and unofficial, that shape what others with whom he or she comes into contact will expect. Moreover, the incumbent of any particular position will be expected to occupy that position authentically by having the right motivations to perform the role properly.

These expectations or rules are, as it were, 'external' to the individual. They exist prior to whomever occupies a position and, moreover, act as coercive elements producing appropriate behaviour. In Durkheim's terms they have a 'thing-like' quality to them. Their 'externality' in this sense produces social patterning because similar rules apply to the same positions; managers are all subject to much the same kinds of expectations, as are mothers, fathers, and all the rest. This is much of what is meant by the idea of a normative order. There is presumed to be a more or less stable linkage between the role performance expected of position occupants and the situations in which they find themselves because of the normative rules governing behaviour in that situation. It is further presumed that actors have been socialised into a common culture so that there is some substantive cognitive consensus among them enabling them to identify situations, actions and rules in more or less the same way.[11] The regularly and routinely occurring patterns enable social scientists to speak of such stable societal elements as 'social structure', 'institutions', 'the political', or the 'economic system'.

For the sake of completeness, it is important to make the point there may be significant subgroup differences within a society in terms of the expectations and normative definitions attaching to particular positions, but these do not modify the general picture. Indeed, such differences pose problems of some interest as the studies of such phenomena as role conflict, marginality, social change, deviance and minorities illustrate.

In a similar vein, motives, reasons, intentions, and so on, are seen as causal antecedents and, therefore, 'external' to action, which impinge upon or coerce persons into certain behaviours. Behaviour, in short, has a motivated character. To ascribe a motive to someone, on this view, is to identify an 'inner' causal mechanism that produces an 'outward' display of behaviour. To say that workers strike because they have anti-management dispositions or attitudes is to say that the 'inner' picture of their working world produces, or causes, their intransigence *vis-à-vis* management. It is to give their striking behaviour a purpose or goal, and offers an explanation in terms of the ends the action is designed to meet. Weber's analysis of the economically innovative behaviour of ascetic Protestants ascribes a particular set of religious motivations which caused the persons holding such beliefs to work harder, be thrifty in their ways, endeavour to succeed in all that they did, and so on.[12] Of course, motives, though regarded as 'internal' and private states, are not considered to be randomly distributed among the population. As with rules, socialisation into a common culture means that motives are patterned, typical to particular socially defined persons and, in this way, produced by the social structure. Thus, occupancy of a particular social position 'leads to' the development of certain socially relevant and consequential dispositions which, in their turn, cause conduct or behaviour of a particular kind. The motivated character of such actions can be said to arise from the interest embodied in the occupancy of particular positions; voting for reasons of class advantage, joining certain associations in order to improve one's career prospects, or striking to improve the earning position of oneself and fellow workers are such examples.

This, then, is the basic model of social scientific accounts using those elements of meaning we have referred to as rules and dispositions. Although I have relied on sociology for the lineaments of this account, it is by no means restricted to that discipline. The assumption of homo economicus in economic theory is to postulate an actor with disposition to act rationally; the sense of history is provided by imputing motives to personages acting within specified historical circumstances, and so on.[13] Nor is it claimed that the accounts are as simple as this; simply that they follow, more or less, this basic mode. What must be added to it are the elements required for a positivist account of social action, though it would perhaps be more accurate to say that the mode of explanation outlined already owes a great deal to the attempt to make the explanation of social life scientific in a positivistic fashion.

The additional elements, stated more explicitly, are, first, that the explanation must be couched in a deductive form showing how the observed behaviour can be deduced from a set of premises containing the theory plus stated empirical conditions. This means, second, that the behaviour to be explained must be defined independently of the so-called predisposing factors or causes; that is, social action must be defined or described independently of the rules or norms supposedly governing that action and independently of whatever motives might be said to cause it. Further, any descriptions entering into the deductive argument – and they enter when specifying the empirical conditions and the facts to be explained as well as in statements of the theory – must have stable meanings independent of the circumstances of their use. They must, in short, be 'literal descriptions'.[14] A deductive argument cannot logically work if the expressions used in it shift their meaning according to circumstance and occasion.

Given that the mode of explanation outlined earlier satisfies these methodological conditions, then the framework is coherent. The job of empirical research is to discover precisely the pattern of the contingent relationships between rules, motives, situations, social relationships and behaviour and formulate them as regularities bringing them under a theory which explains why they have the form that they do. To see just how far this is justified, let us examine the relationship between motives and the description of social action a little more closely.

As pointed out, in the typical form of explanation some internal and private characteristic of persons is offered, often implicitly, as a causal antecedent that predisposes the actor to behave in a particular manner. The motive and the behaviour are regarded as independent, the internal and private state being the mainspring, as it were, for the external behavioural display, the action. However, this formulation of the relationship gives rise to all kinds of methodological problems for social science. Being conceived as internal and private, and therefore not open to direct inspection, the problem is to devise methods of assessing such internal states to which effect a number of techniques, such as attitude scales, questionnaires, interviews, personality inventories, etc., have been devised. The results provided by these are usually correlated with 'objective' indices, such as level of education, social class, ethnic identity, associational participation, voting, spending patterns, etc., to mention but a very few of the kinds of variables employed.

With methods such as these, which rely for attributions as to 'mental states', to use a catch-all term for the moment, on what respondents say, there has always been the problem of relating what people say to what they do.[15] Prior to this problem, considerable effort has been expended improving the validity of such methods so that they can provide more accurate assessments of what is really 'in people's minds'. However, in other cases, motives are inferred less from what people say about themselves and more from what they do or have done. From the fact that a person has tried to commit suicide inferences are drawn as to the state of mind of the person concerned. From the fact that dustbins are increasingly full of empty food packages it could be inferred that people are motivated to create more leisure time by using convenience foods. From the fact that the earliest capitalists were members of ascetic Protestant sects it can be inferred that their religious membership motivated them to engage in behaviour appropriate to capitalist accumulation.

In all the cases the problem has been to formalise the seemingly inevitable inferences that must be made in order to gauge the appropriate mental states of a person or group of persons. For the positivists, such inferences, unless rigorously controlled and measured, could lead to unwarrantable imputations on the part of the researcher. The situation led some to almost despair, seeking salvation in neurophysiology or some other method which would 'permit us to observe what was going on in a person's head in the same way that we can observe stomach contractions or nerve discharges in a hungry organism'.[16] Be this as it may, the contention here is that the conception of the relationship between so-called 'internal states', such as motives, intentions, and reasons, and the behaviour presupposed in the traditional approach outlined earlier is fundamentally misconceived.

Consider the following description of fairly mundane acts: 'I raised my arm', 'I raised the glass', 'I toasted the happy couple', 'I assuaged my thirst', 'I decided that the only thing to do was get drunk'. All these statements describe what could be said to be different actions and yet could also be said to consist of, or involve, much the same bodily movement. This one 'behavioural display' is capable, then, of being part of many different '*actions*' and, generalising from this, we can say that there is no necessary one-to-one matching of an action description with a behavioural display. Pitkin puts the point rather well:

With the same physical movement, the stroke of a pen or the shake of a head, a man can break a promise or make one, renounce his birthright, insult a friend, obey a command, or commit treason. The same movement can, in various circumstances and with various intentions constitute any of these actions: so in itself it constitutes none of them.[17]

So an observer seeing me raise my arm and a glass of beer could describe my action in a number of ways. Any of those offered earlier could be appropriate, though 'I raised my arm' does seem singularly uninformative. The observer cannot, of course, see directly into my mind to inspect my intentions or bodily states. Nonetheless, noting the circumstances – it was a wedding, a hot day, I had just been jilted, etc. – some description could have been supplied without much trouble or anguish about what was really the case. Some of these descriptions might well impute a motive or purpose to my behaviour, such as a desire to get drunk, be sociable, wish luck to the happy couple, assuage a thirst, and so on. In such cases what the motive does is tell us more about the action that is being performed, tells us what the person was doing, 'getting drunk', 'toasting the happy couple', 'assuaging a thirst' or whatever.[18]

In describing many actions we are unavoidably involved in imputing motives of one sort or another. The analytic force of motives, reasons, lies not so much in their being 'internal' and private mainsprings to action or behaviour, but in their being tantamount to rules for formulating a piece of behaviour *as* action of a particular kind. Motives, reasons, and other dispositional concepts can be seen as rules, or embedded instructions, if you will, for seeing behaviour in such-and-such a way, for explicating action further, for giving an account of that action. It follows that any particular behavioural display can be described and explained in a variety of different, and often competing, ways; that is, as several kinds of motivated action. As Austin expresses it:

It is in principle always open to us, along various lines, to describe or refer to 'what I did' in so many different ways . . . should we say, are we saying, that he took her money, or that he sank a putt? That he said 'Done', or that he accepted an offer? How far, that is, are motives, intentions, and conventions, to be part of the description of actions?[19]

The issue here is, perhaps, most apparent where the motivated character of an event is equivocal as in a case reported by Atkinson.[20] An 83-year-old widow was found gassed in her kitchen. She had lived alone since the death of her husband. Rugs and towels had been stuffed under doors and around windows. Neighbours testified at the inquest that she had always seemed a happy and cheerful person. The coroner returned an open verdict on the grounds that there was no evidence to show how the gas taps had been turned on. In this case, the circumstances of the death, which occurred during the winter, were insufficient to lead to a definitive verdict. For example, it was difficult to establish whether the rugs and towels had been used to keep out the cold and the draughts rather than the gas in, and, accordingly, to establish whether the turning on of the gas was intentional or whether unmotivated and due to absentmindedness. If the death had occurred in the summer, the motivated character of the events might have been less ambiguous. The fact that it happened in winter meant that the motivated character of the scene could not be clarified without recourse to circumstantial evidence regarding the widow's state of mind. Different assumptions regarding her state of mind would have instructed those responsible for reaching a verdict to compose an account for the scene in particular ways or, vice versa, assumptions about the scene instruct them to make inferences about the victim's state of mind, and so on.

To argue or presume, as the typical mode of social scientific explanation would have us do, that behaviour can be described as a kind of 'brute fact' independent of motives or reasons, is seriously to misrepresent the relationship these have to the description of action. To describe my action referred to earlier as 'raising a glass to my lips' as if this were somehow more real than other descriptions which involve imputations or inferences about motivations, leaves out those very elements which make it a *social action*, though, it must be said, for some purposes such a description may well be adequate. However, such a description, treated as a description of indisputable 'brute fact' or fundamental 'observational datum', allowing meaning or the imputation of motive, reason or intention, merely as a subjective component, is to misconceive the process of action description.[21] Further, motives can be arguable, indeterminate and doubtful as a matter of course. Conjecture as to motive does not arise out of the absence of evidence we might have but do not – as the despairing positivist spoken of earlier might have it – but is a review of a range of possibilities where behaviour is just ambiguous, though for parties to those activities they may not necessarily be so.

As with motives, so with rules. Any piece of behaviour could be consistent with a vast number of rules, though in practice only some would be deemed relevant on any occasion. We normally think of rules as commandments to do, or not do, something we could engage in whether or not the rule existed. In this sense, rules are seen as independent of and external to the behaviour to which they apply. The Ten Commandments, for example, forbid various kinds of behaviours which, presumably, the framer of the rules regarded as less than wholesome, such as adultery, thieving, envy, worshipping false idols, and so on. There is, however, an aspect of rules which is not entirely separable from behaviour. Many rules can be said to be 'constitutive' of action in the sense that they tell us *how* to do something. It would be hard, for obvious example, to imagine playing chess without the rules of chess. Suspend rules like this and the activity in question ceases to exist. There would, of course, still be the behaviour of pushing pieces of wood or plastic around a chequered board, but this would hardly be playing chess.[22] In the same way it would be hard to conceive of 'obeying traffic lights' without the notion of traffic rules.

A relevant distinction here is that between a process being in accordance with a rule and a process involving a rule; between 'action in accord with a rule' and 'action governed by a rule'.[23] Any observed agent, process or action can be brought under the auspices of many rule-like formulations, none of which is unambiguously *the* rule governing the process or event. As Coulter expresses it, the 'rules which make an action what it *is* are not reducible to any (set of) descriptions of physical or physiological transformations, since virtually any "action" or "activity" can be realized through *different* transformations . . . and the converse is also true . . .'[24] An activity accords with a rule if it exhibits the regularities expresses by the rule. It involves a rule if agents actually *use* the rule to guide or assess their actions. Rules, however, do not determine their own application but have to be used, and one of their more important uses is to bring a set of events, processes, persons or conduct, or all of these together, into some scheme of interpretation. In this sense the notion of rule is tied to that of 'making a mistake' and it is the possibility of this which helps distinguish being 'rule-governed' from mere regularity. That is, it enables us to evaluate what is being done, to attribute fault, to be subject to criticism. Invoking rules is a way of depicting or describing action, of pointing out what it is we are doing, of making our actions accountable. Used in this way, rules are part of our resources for making the world understandable.

The upshot of these remarks strongly suggests a very different sort of relationship between action and its description, and the rules or the motives which could be said to govern the action, from that envisaged in the positivistic approach. For one thing it claims that action and their descriptions are conceptually tied to reasons and motives, neither being describable as if they were separate and independent; on the contrary, they inform each other reflexively.

This discussion of rules, motives and other intentional concepts – let us call them action concepts – presupposes that these are major means through which members of society meaningfully construct their social world. It is making the point, too, that the vocabulary of action displays very different properties to those presupposed in a causal one. Action is predicated on the idea of an agent, specifically a human agent. The vocabulary of action is used by human beings in speaking to each other about what it is they are doing. An agent differs from a causal process because he or she can be said to make a choice, be held responsible for, initiate, do something, and so on. An action can be praised or condemned, commanded or forbidden, because the person performing the action can be praised, condemned, commanded or forbidden.

The use of causal expressions in action contexts should not entice us into thinking of invariant relationships or into thinking that these are somehow more real than non-causal ones. To say something like 'The fact that it was dark caused me to trip over the stool' is to make use of a causal type relationship between the amount of available light and the ability to see, but its import is offering an excuse, suggesting that I was not just clumsy, but could not help myself, and could not be blamed for what happened. Actions do not come along conveniently labelled as 'suicide', 'clumsiness', 'obeying traffic signals', 'walking the dog', 'voting for a party of the working class', 'being motherly', and so on, but have to be described, and doing this is an action. It involves more than just looking at 'concrete behaviour', if this makes any sense at all, but paying attention to circumstances, reasons, motives, rules, and so on.

Of course, it is clearly not the case that intentions, motives, rules or conventions, are necessarily imputations in action descriptions. One can kill inadvertently, deceive without intending to deceive, and so on, while in other cases matters are not so clear; can one murder without the intention to murder, promise without intending to promise, for example? Events can also be described without motive implications: 'The gun happened to be loaded, the trigger knocked, the bullet hit her and she died of wounds received.' Whether or not such a description would be deemed accurate or adequate would depend on the purposes for which the description was formulated. The description of an action is an occasioned event, is itself an action, done for some purpose, informed by some interest, done in some context. The point is, however, that action descriptions are essentially defeasible; that is, it is always possible, in principle, to argue against any particular description by bringing in other particulars about the situation, the person, the event or the object. Let me illustrate with another homespun example.

Some time ago I was walking down a corridor and, as it happened, I stopped to hold open a door for a woman following behind. The woman stopped and made the remark that what I had just done was sexist. I apologised in some confusion and said that holding the door to allow her to precede me was a gesture of simple courtesy which I would have done for anyone, male or female. This did not carry a great deal of weight and the argument went on for some minutes. The point of this anecdote is not the by now familiar one of the same behavioural display – opening the door, standing back, etc. – being open to different interpretations, which it is, but that it is open to different descriptions as an action. The issue is not one of fitting the right description to an event as one might have to fit round pegs into round holes or the right words into the lines of a crossword puzzle. It has to do with justifying an action, describing it in socially consequential ways. To ask whether the right description of the act I performed was 'a courtesy' or 'male chauvinist piggery' is to miss the point. Neither description could be right in any absolute sense. The matter of description is bound up with justifying my action or my point of view with appropriate reasons and arguments, to do with persuading, cajoling, threatening, coercing, etc., someone that what happened was of such and such a character. The woman and I could have argued our case sensibly. I could have pointed to my exemplary record of courtesy in all things, while she could well have taken this as more evidence for her case, arguing that such behaviour merely indicated a patriarchal attitude on my part and that sexism was part and parcel of this. As in the case of motives, various arguments could be invoked, reasons adduced, in order to support the claim that the scene should be looked at in a particular way. We could only have come to some agreement if we held, as it were, a framework in common whereby such disputes could have been resolved.[25]

However, the failure to find 'common methods', so to speak, is not some failure of our knowledge but a characteristic of our vocabulary of action. In pointing to the essential defeasibility of action descriptions it is being claimed that the vocabulary of action is part and parcel of moral discourse and, as such, is concerned with the appraisal of conduct. In this realm of discourse what we have done or are doing has no well-defined description in ways required by positivistic science, though such descriptions work well enough in the context of action. Knowing what it is you are doing, what you are going to do, what you have or have not done, cannot be fully explicated by looking at what in fact you do. To know what you are doing is to be able to elaborate the action, say why you are doing it, excuse or justify it if necessary, and so on.[26] What is at stake, in short, is what in fact was done. Was my opening the door a flagrant piece of chauvinist piggery or the last throw of knightly courtesy? What the dispute is about is precisely this and not the sort of issue that can be resolved by consulting some putative dictionary of social actions.

These arguments suggest that the description of social action is a problemmatic matter both for social actors and observers alike. Descriptions are, it has been pointed out, deeply sensitive to context and defeasible. They are social activities done for particular purposes and are deemed adequate or inadequate, as the case may be, in terms of these purposes. This leads on to another general property of descriptions, namely, that they are always, in principle, incomplete. Whatever is included in a description is always selective and cannot exhaust all that can be said about an object, event or a person. More could always be added: a person could be described, for example, as 'dark haired', 'tall', 'selfish', 'reticent', 'a worker', 'of higher than average intelligence', and so on, but these could not exhaust all that could be said about the person. Descriptions are selections from what could possibly be said and, depending on the occasion, be perfectly adequate for that occasion and that purpose. Although descriptions have a fringe of completeness about them, or, as

Wiseman puts it, an 'open-textured' quality, this does not impair their ability to do the job required since nothing like absolutely definitive completeness is ever attempted by speakers of a natural language.[27] As said before, often a single descriptor will provide an adequate description – 'this friend', 'my colleague', 'the landlord of the Plough', 'that stupid dog' – the remaining particulars being, as it were, bracketed away for present purposes or their sense 'filled in' using the specifics of the contexts in which uttered. It is always possible, however, to produce alternative descriptions of an object, event, action or person. Other properties may be added which modify the original description, or other aspects come along which provide additional elements to qualify, modify or even undercut the original. The relationship between the features of an object, an event, an act or a person and some description is not a determinate one. A speaker's selection of a descriptor from all that could be said or predicated of some phenomenon normally tells the hearer something about the practical purposes of the speaker in offering that particular description. It calls forth a host of possible elaborations, and this means that, on the occasions of its use, a description can only index what it might mean; a quality referred to, by Garfinkel, as 'indexicality'.[28]

The arguments reviewed here would seem to challenge many of the assumptions and claims of positivistic science. The social science tradition from which they derive takes meaning as central to social life and points to important differences between what I have termed the 'vocabulary of action' and that of science. The rather grand, and overworked, term 'meaning' more than hints at the intersubjective character of social life and, in its way, points to the fact that human action is not as predictable, as determined in its course, as the inanimate subject-matter of natural science.[29] Whereas positivism might perhaps attribute this lack of the paucity of good measurement, good theories and the infancy of the social sciences, or to the greater complexity of the social world compared to the natural, what is being claimed here is more fundamental, namely, that human life is essentially different, and that this difference requires another methodology to that required by a positivistic conception. It might also require a different kind of knowledge. (For the moment I shall beg the question of whether the fact that social life is meaningful can be reconciled with the alternative view of science outlined in Chapters 3 and 4.) Of course, matters hang heavily on the banal observation that human beings are capable of giving accounts of their own lives and their relationships to others. However, what is also being claimed is that this ability is essential to there being a social life at all. Giving reasons, justifications, explanations, making descriptions, are themselves profoundly social activities and, consequently, make social life what it is. What we have to examine now is whether or not these considerations do imply that a social science is impossible.

REASONS VERSUS CAUSES

One major methodological consequence of binding reasons, motives and other dispositions to the notion of action is that it raises questions about whether social science can be concerned with causes of action. The conceptual tie between the imputation of reason and motive and the description of action argues that one of the major criteria for identifying a causal relationship is not met; that is, the logical independence of the antecedent factor, the reason, and the effect, the action. Instead a very different relationship is claimed in which the reason (or the motive) and the description of action are mutually informing, though not in any determinate way. A further objection to the causal account arises from issues addressed in connection with the description of action itself, and is an objection to the use of the hypothetico-deductive model of explanation. It is argued that such a method can only be used if literal description is possible; that is, description not dependent for its sense or meaning on the occasion of its use.[30]

As has been pointed out, descriptions enter into the hypothetico-deductive form of explanation in at least two places: in statements about the initial conditions and in the deduced prediction that constitutes the explanandum. The burden of the argument here, however, is that literal description is possible in the social sciences only by ignoring the interpretative nature of social action and forcing categories into a framework to satisfy the requirements of literal description. *Knowing what* people are doing (including oneself) is *knowing how* to identify what they are doing in the categories of a natural language, which requires *knowing how* to use those categories in discursive contexts . . .'[31] Thus, if I want to describe a piece of behaviour, which may be an utterance or a bodily movement, as, say, indicative of 'mental illness', neither the utterance itself nor the movement will indicate this without the use of some interpretative schema which enables me to compose this as an instance, an indicator, of mental illness.[32] It goes without saying that different schemas would prompt different descriptions, though not always inconsistent ones. Similarly, if I make use of someone else's descriptions of the same elements, to understand this I must use the same interpretative procedures in order to appreciate how the instances were gathered into the description used. Garfinkel refers to this as the 'documentary method of interpretation' in which a set of appearances, which may be objects, events, persons, or symbols, is taken as evidence for some underlying pattern, while the postulated pattern serves as a guide for seeing how the appearances themselves should be read. Thus, the classification of the description of any piece of behaviour on a given occasion as an instance of a particular type of action 'is not based on a set of specifiable features of the behaviour and the occasion but, rather, depends on the indefinite context seen as relevant to the observer, a context that gets its meaning partly through the very action it is being used to interpret'.[33] The meaning, hence the action being performed, of a raised arm would depend on the context; similarly, the context itself would be partly made intelligible by the meaning or the description given to the movement. It follows that any interpretation is always both retrospectively and prospectively revisable in 'light of further evidence'.

These arguments, and we shall examine more in the next chapter, seriously question the idea of a social science based on the search for causes. Winch, among other critics, argues that action concepts are logically incompatible with the idea of causal necessity and, thus, with natural scientific causal explanation.[34] There have been attempts to deny the force of this distinction between reasons and causes. MacIntyre, for example, bothered by the fact that agents may offer many reasons for why they do something, wants to argue that an agent's possession of a reason may be a state identifiable independently of an agent's performance of an action and, accordingly, a candidate cause.[35] The difficulty here lies in specifying what is meant by an agent being in a state of possessing a reason. It would seem that this condition could only be based on the avowals of the agent concerned, although others, too, are equally free to impute what reasons they may to an agent without that agent necessarily having formulated that reason to himself or herself prior to the action. Reasons enter as justifications, as further elaborations of actions and are not necessarily formulated as prior antecedents to the action for which the reason is relevant. Nor does the argument destroy the conceptual link between reasons and the description of action: a relationship which is not one of independence or contingent invariance.

There are, nonetheless, other difficulties with the distinction between action concepts and causal ones. The fact is that we sometimes talk about the causes of actions and give causal accounts of actions. Some would want to say that this is merely a careless habit of speech, but this is hardly satisfactory. The whole issue here is bound up with an old philosophical problem to do with free will, a debate which can be briefly summarised as follows. On the one hand are arguments which say that we hold people responsible for what they do, blame them when they behave badly, and so forth. So, since there would be no point in blaming someone for doing something beyond his or her control, then at least some of our actions must be the agent's doing and free. On the other hand, there is the view that what an agent does is the function of upbringing, personality, situation, and the like, and therefore, he or she is merely the helpless victim of all these factors. While we may all feel free to choose and act, this is, in fact, an illusion.

The conflict here, while easily stated, is not so easily resolved. The notion of cause itself is used in a variety of ways, not all of them accommodated within a Humean conception. Sometimes we give a causal account of action. Peters suggests that we are likely to do so when something has gone wrong, 'where there is some kind of deviation from the purposive rule-following model; when people, as it were, get it wrong'.[36] In such cases doubts are raised as to whether an action was fully performed. Also, we tend to give causal explanations of action where the actor's choice or responsibility is minimal or, alternatively, have no interest for us. We might do this, as Pitkin illustrates, in considering how to get a third party to do something.[37] Here causes are not incompatible with reasons, motives and intentions. In historical explanation, for example, we tend to be rather more interested in accounting for why a person did what they did than in holding him, or her, responsible or attributing blame.

One could say that this is all very well. The practices of ordinary language in respect of causal attributions versus the imputations of motives or reasons are well taken in connection with particular actions, but are not exactly relevant to social science which is concerned with the explanation of whole classes of actions. In reply, one could say that in trying to achieve explanation of this kind one runs the risk of stretching language until insoluble conceptual difficulties are created. 'Free', 'determined', 'cause', are concepts connected to many other concepts. If asked the question, 'what is a free action?' we could, with little difficulty, give many illustrations, synonyms, analogies, offer concepts roughly equivalent in meaning, and so on. If we denied that any actions were free then we would be involved in rejecting whole categories, and relationships, denying, in effect, whole regions of our language. This is something that we might wish to do but, in doing so, we would also ban a host of actions in the process. Terms such as 'free', 'cause', 'determined', and concepts associated with them, are used in particular contexts, used for assessing some particular action taken or contemplated. Whether a person has or has not a choice are questions partly dependent on the position adopted by a speaker in the situation at issue. I might say to a close friend, 'I can't come to the cinema with you because my parents are visiting' and intend that the force of the parental obligation means that I am not 'free' to go. If, on the other hand, my friend wanted me to accompany him to the hospital, it is possible that I might override parental obligations. I might not for an acquaintance, though even that might be dependent on the seriousness of the reason for the visit to the hospital. The point is that in each of these situations I am taking a position with respect to others, and it is by this I will be judged. What is difficult is to generalise from these particular cases to distinguish criteria by which *all* actions are to be seen as causally determined.

In any event, it is difficult to see how one might *discover* whether all our actions are really causally determined or whether they are really all free. In fact, it looks as if the issue is hardly a matter about the facts of the world at all. If, as was suggested above, we seriously entertained the idea that all action was caused (or free) this would involve vast changes in the conceptual system in which and through which our lives are constituted. It would be difficult to speak of responsibility, blame, punishment, honour, achievement, generosity, valour, skill, quality, failure, conduct, and so on. We may, it is true, retain the use of these and like terms, but their point would be lost. One might still 'punish' but this would be the application of another causal mechanism designed to modify behaviour. One might still 'praise' but this would not be giving credit for some personal achievement and would only add another factor to induce a particular behaviour, one that we as 'blamer' or 'praiser' could ourselves taken no credit for since, we, too, could not help ourselves. The point is that though our language and our understandings do change and are conventional they are not arbitrary. They are shaped by our conduct as human beings. The determinist might argue that the distinction between actions and causes arises because we are ignorant of the causes of some actions, but this is to miss the point.

It begins to look as if what we are dealing with here are two different perspectives, Pitkin calls them 'that of the actor engaged in action, and that of the observer'. both deeply embedded in our language and form of life.[38] We cannot take either one alone without losing, in some way, crucial aspects of social reality. A purely observational science of society using a causal vocabulary independent of our action vocabulary might be possible but the question is: What would we then be observing? We would not be able to see promises, power, interests, war, worship, organisations, exploitation, deprivation, and the like, since these, definitionally, could not strike the action-concept free observer. In short, such a science 'could not answer the questions we can now formulate, for they are formulated in the concepts we have'.[39] In this connection, structuralist and post-structuralist theories seek to evade the dilemmas reviewed here by 'decentring the subject'; that is, to overcome subjectivity and individualism by rejecting any form of empiricist epistemology in favour of an analysis of the structural relations and realities underlying the surface appearances of social and cultural phenomena.[40]

It appears, then, that the old dichotomy of reasons versus causes is not as simple as either of the protagonists would have it. What is perhaps clearer is that it is inappropriate to use a purely causal vocabulary as the only one suitable for a social science. The arguments of this chapter, while not resolving many of the issues, do strongly suggest that the traditional manner in which this causal vocabulary has been used in much of social science is seriously flawed. In the next chapter I shall examine further arguments relevant to this matter.

REFERENCES

1. See Anderson, R. J. *et al., Philosophy and the Human Sciences,* London, Croom Helm, 1986, ch. 3; Bauman, Z., *Hermeneutics and Social Science,* London, Hutchinson, 1978; Mueller-Vollmer, H. (ed.), *The Hermeneutics Reader,* Oxford, Oxford University Press, 1985.
2. Burger, T., *Max Weber's Theory of Concept Formation: History, Law and Ideal Types,* Durham, Duke University Press, 1976, ch. 1, for a discussion of the influence of Rikert.
3. Weber, M., *The Theory of Social and Economic Organisation,* New York, Free Press, 1969, ed. Parsons, T., p. 101; also Bauman, *op. cit.,* esp. ch. 3.
4. Weber, M., 'Knies and the problem of irrationality' in *Roscher and Knies: The Logical Problem of Historical Economics,* trans. Oakes, G., New York, Free Press, 1975, pp. 184–5.
5. Hazelrigg, L., *Social Science and the Challenge of Relativism,* Vol. 1: A Wilderness of Mirrors: On Practices of Theory in a Gray Age, Gainsville, Florida State University Press, 1989, pp. 257–70: and Weber, M., *The Methodology of the Social Sciences,* New York, Free Press, 1949.
6. See, for example, Blumer, H., 'Sociological analysis and the variable', *American Sociological Review,* 21, 1956, pp. 683–90.
7. See Hazelrigg, *op. cit.,* for an extensive discussion of such issues.
8. Weber, *The Theory of Social and Economic Organisation, op. cit.,* p. 88.
9. Hart, H. L. A., *The Concept of Law,* Oxford, Oxford University Press, 1961, and discussed at some length in Ryan, A., *The Philosophy of the Social Sciences.* London, Macmillan, 1970, pp. 140–1.
10. Schutz, A., 'Concept and theory formation in the social sciences' in Natanson, M. (ed.), *Philosophy of the Social*

Sciences, New York, Random House, 1963, pp. 231–49.
11. See, on this, Wilson, T. P., 'Normative and interpretative paradigms in sociology' in Douglas, J. D. (ed.), *Understanding Everyday Life,* London, Routledge and Kegan Paul, 1974, pp. 59–61; also Weider, L., *Language and Social Reality,* The Hague, Mouton, 1974.
12. Weber, M., *The Protestant Ethic and the Spirit of Capitalism,* trans. Parsons, T., London, Allen and Unwin, 1960.
13. See Anderson, R. J. *et al.,* 'Some thoughts on the nature of economic theorising', *Journal of Interdisciplinary Economics,* 2, 1988, pp. 307–20.
14. Wilson, *op. cit.,* p. 71; also Quine, W. V. O., *Word and Object,* Cambridge, Mass., MIT Press, 1960.
15. See, for example, Deutscher, I., *What We Say, What We Do,* Glenview, Scott, Foresman and Company, 1973.
16. McClelland, D., *The Achieving Society,* New York, Van Nostrand, 1961, p. 39. I am indebted to Jeff Coulter for drawing attention to this.
17. Pitkin, H., *Wittgenstein and Justice,* Berkeley, University of California Press, 1972, p. 167. This chapter owes a great deal to this remarkable book which, though nearly 20 years old, is still worth reading.
18. See, for example, Melden, A., *Free Action,* London, Routledge and Kegan Paul, 1961.
19. Austin, J., *Philosophical Papers,* Oxford, Oxford University Press, 1961, ed, Urmson, J. and Warnock, G. See also Anderson, R. J. *et al., Philosophy and the Human Sciences,* London, Croom Helm, 1986, ch. 9.
20. Atkinson, J. F. M., 'Societal reactions to suicide: the role of coroner's definitions' in Cohen, S. (ed.), *Images of Deviance,* Harmondsworth, Penguin, 1971, pp. 165–91; also Heritage, J., 'Aspects of the flexibility of language use', *Sociology,* 12, 1978, pp. 79–103.
21. See Weider, *op. cit.* Also, Blum, A. and McHugh, P., 'The social ascription of motive', *American Sociological Review,* 36, 1971, pp. 98–109, Coulter, J., *The Social Construction of Mind,* London, Macmillan, develops this theme at some length.
22. On 'constitutive rules' see Searle, J., *Speech Acts,* Cambridge, Cambridge University Press, 1969, pp. 33–42; and Taylor, C., 'Interpretation and the sciences of man' in Beehler, R. and Drengson, A. R. (eds), *The Philosophy of Society,* London, Methuen, 1978, pp. 159–200.
23. See Coulter, J., *Approaches to Insanity,* London, Martin Robertson, 1973, p. 141; Rawls, J., 'The two concepts of rules', *Philosophical Review,* 64, 1955, pp. 9–11. The distinction is owed to Wittgenstein, L., *Philosophical Investigations,*

Oxford, Blackwell, 1952, paras 199–202, trans. Anscombe, G.

24. Coutler, J., *Mind in Action*, New Jersey, Humanities Press, 1989, p. 14.
25. Ryle, G., 'The world of science and the everyday world', *Dilemmas*, Cambridge, Cambridge University Press, 1966, pp. 68–81.
26. Pitkin, *op. cit.*, ch. VII.
27. Wiseman, F., 'Verifiability' in Flew, A. (ed.), *Logic and Language*, Oxford, Blackwell, 1951, pp. 117–44; also Pitkin, *op. cit.*, pp. 61–2.
28. See Garfinkel, H., *Studies in Ethnomethodology*, Englewood Cliffs, Prentice Hall, 1967, esp. ch. 1; Sacks, H., 'Sociological description', *Berkeley Journal of Sociology*, 8, 1963, pp. 1–9; Heritage, *op. cit.*
29. To social actors, of course, social life is immensely and routinely predictable most of the time.
30. Wilson, *op. cit.*, p. 75.
31. Coulter, *Mind in Action*, *op. cit.*, pp. 15–16. Italics in original.
32. See, for example, Smith, D., 'K is mentally ill', *Sociology*, 12, 1978, pp. 25–53.
33. Wilson, *op. cit.*, p. 75; also Garfinkel, *op. cit.*, pp. 76–103.
34. Winch, P., *The Idea of a Social Science*, London, Routledge and Kegan Paul, 1963.
35. MacIntyre, A., 'The idea of a social science' in Wilson, B. (ed.), *Rationality*, Oxford, Blackwell, 1977, p. 117.
36. Peters, R. S., *The Concept of Motivation*, London, Routledge and Kegan Paul, 1960, p. 10.
37. Pitkin, *op. cit.*, p. 269.
38. *Ibid.*, p. 272.
39. *Ibid.*
40. See Anderson *et al.*, *op. cit.*

CHAPTER 6

Meanings and social research

In the previous chapter a number of points were made about the nature of the vocabulary we use to talk about action. Many of these arose from the fact that human beings themselves describe and explain their social conduct using concepts belonging to this 'vocabulary of action'. This has not, of course, been ignored by social scientists since the actors' talk, reasons, the rules they invoke, their beliefs and such like, are used as a source of data through methods such as questionnaires, interviews, documents, reports, and so on. Some critical differences between causal and action vocabularies were also discussed in an effort to throw some light on the question of whether a social science dealing with causes was possible in the way presumed or postulated by positivism. While it has not been suggested that social science, whether or not it deals in causes, is impossible, the preceding considerations do have crucial implications for the nature of social scientific accounts. Moreover, the arguments presuppose a rather different ontological conception of social reality from that presumed by positivism with consequent epistemological implications. In this chapter I want to bring some of the foregoing arguments to bear more directly on research methods traditionally associated with positivistic social science, and then move on to discuss the relationship between actors' concepts and those of social science in an attempt to approach a somewhat clearer formulation of what a social science dealing with meaning might involve.

THE CRITIQUE OF POSITIVIST METHODS

To begin, let me review in a general fashion some of the main features of the positivist method as used to construct its version of social reality. The principal manner in which positivist social science constructs its version of social reality is by drawing a distinction between identifiable acts, structures, institutions, such as 'brute facts' or 'brute data' on the one hand, and beliefs, values, attitudes, reasons, etc., on the other. These two orders of reality are correlated in order to provide the generalisations or regularities which are the aim of a science of social life. What is real is the 'brute data' considered as objective social reality, and the values, beliefs, ideologies, and so on, of merely subjective status. This subjective status of meanings is evidenced by the disputes which occur over the 'brute facts' of life. Are lorry drivers striking for higher wages, protesting against government policy, or manipulated by agitators, just angry and frustrated, or what? Such beliefs are given a subjective reality in that they are seen as having some effect on the prime social reality itself; and, of course, the fact that persons hold such beliefs, attribute such meanings to their social world, is itself a fact about that world. However, the social reality that is the object of these beliefs, versions, meanings, or whatever we choose to call them, can only be made up of objective 'brute fact'. In short, meanings are only allowed into scientific discourse if placed 'in quotes and attributed to individuals as their opinion, belief, attitude'.[1] What are being referred to as subjectivities are allowable providing they conform to the canons of positivist description.

This conception, if we accept the arguments of the preceding chapter, seriously misconstrues the nature of social action, and hence social reality. It does this by relegating the elements of meaning to a 'subjective' role as merely versions of social reality and in so doing confuses 'objectivity' and 'subjectivity' as, briefly, 'inner' and 'outer' features of human action with standards to do with the appraisal of some claim as being partial or impartial. When, for example, we describe someone's opinion as 'subjective' we are not commenting on its ontological status, but asserting that it is partial, formed without weighing up the alternatives, unreasonably blind to facts, and so on. Confusions such as these rampage through the objective–subjective dichotomy. But, this apart, what is also implied is 'that there is a social reality which can be discovered in each society independently of the vocabulary of that society, or indeed any vocabulary, as the heavens could exist whether men theorised about them or not'.[2] This is far from being the case. As discussed in Chapter 4 in connection with the correspondence theory of truth proposed for scientific theory presupposed by positivism, there is no theory independent way of looking at the world. On the view being discussed here, an additional twist is added to this, namely, that as far as social reality is concerned, it cannot be studied independently of the theories, conceptions, subjectivities if you will, of the members of that society; and, as an arguable implication, there is no reality apart from the subjectivities for our theories to correspond to. As far as social reality is concerned it is constituted subjectively. An alternative formulation is to postulate social realities as being constructed in and through meanings and to say that social realities cannot be identified in abstraction from the language in which they are embedded. Meaning is profoundly to do with language considered not as a system of grammatical or syntactical rules but as social interaction. To adapt a statement from Austin: language does not merely report on the world but is itself performative of action in that world.[3] The language and the practices, things and events in the world are inseparable, and the distinction between social reality and the description of that reality an artificial one, to say the least. Generalising from what was said earlier about 'constitutive rules', we can say that the 'language is constitutive of reality, is essential to being the kind of reality it is'.[4]

We must be as clear as we can on what this view involves. At this stage I shall assert some of its main features and elaborate on some of them later. First, it claims that reality, whether natural or social, cannot be conceived of or known independently of the concepts in language. Second, it asserts that as far as social reality is concerned, this is constructed through the use of language. The relationships we have with others are not independent of the language used to describe and invoke them. Moreover, the relationships thus invoked and described through language and its meanings are occasioned (that is, constructed as instances of relationships of a certain type by the use of reasons, rules, conventions and other action concepts) on *that* occasion in the course of the day-to-day lives of individuals.

Third, language and meaning are not private subjective things but, rather, public and intersubjective. This is not a matter of converging beliefs or, as it is sometimes put, value or normative consensus. A high level of intersubjective meaning is consistent with sharp division and conflict, the protagonists having no doubt as to what divides them. Common meanings are embedded in the language of a community and in all the ways in which the members of that community are able to talk about, agree upon, disagree upon, make sense of, pray to, describe, revolt against, or investigate the social reality constructed through that language, and without which no society would exist.

Fourth, and referring back to what was said about descriptions, meanings are not finitely specifiable but receive their sense from a background of context and interpretation employed by speakers of the language on the occasions upon which elements of the language are used.

Fifth, the disputes which occur about actions, about social reality, are not deficiencies arising from the inadequacy of natural language in saying what we mean, but are a feature of that language as a social activity and part of society's nature as a moral order.

According to the ontological presuppositions just outlined, in studying social realities we are not dealing with a reality made up of 'brute fact' or a reality of external 'thing-like' forces and objects, but one that is intersubjectively constituted by persons relating to each other through practices identified and given meaning by the language used to describe them, invoke them, and carry them out. Proponents of this view argue that social reality conceived of in this way cannot be studied by the methods associated with positivist social science. The argument, in brief, is that such methods are predicted on a false ontology and presuppositions which cannot be supported. Some of the arguments relevant to this have already been discussed. The argument can, however, go further by pointing out the paradox that positivist methods 'work' only to the extent to which they are themselves embedded in the alternative ontology just outlined. If this argument were found to be substantial, then it would clearly have serious consequences for the authority of social scientific accounts to the extent that they depend for that authority on positivistic epistemology. Accordingly, let us examine the issues here and bring out some of the remarks made earlier in this and the preceding chapter to bear more directly upon positivist methods of social research.

The starting point, though not always in an obvious way, for social science data are what were termed the 'first order' constructs used by the members of a given society. However, for precisely the qualities discussed earlier in relation to the description of social action, these 'first order' constructs were deemed inadequate for a science of social life. Often vague by the standards required of scientific discourse, often imbued with emotion, often opinionated, often value laden, ambiguous in meaning, they were held to be hopelessly inappropriate as precise 'scientific' concepts. The spirit of this objection can be captured from Durkheim's remarks on the official statistical categories he used in his study of suicide. He dismisses the official statistics on the motives of suicides, arguing that the 'statistics of the motives of suicides are actually the statistics of the opinions concerning such motives of officials, often of lower officials, in charge of this information service'.[5] He goes on: 'These are known to be defective even when applied to obvious material facts comprehensible to any conscientious observer.' Whether or not higher officials would have done any better in the recording is not addressed. Nonetheless, the objection to 'first order' constructs, in this case those of 'lower officials', is clear enough. They must be repaired in some way, made more objective, or scientific ones substituted. The issue is precisely the nature of such a transformation.

Take an example of a scaling procedure. These are used in the measurement of attitudes and in personality assessment mainly, though they are sometimes used to measure phenomena other than psychological dispositions. Such scales are normally constructed by selecting items from a series presumed to tap the relevant attitude or trait. The items are cast in the form of questions or statements which the respondent has to affirm or deny. The affirmation or denial is scored appropriately depending on whether the response can be said to represent more or less of the attitude or trait. The following example is taken from a Faith in People scale[6]:

1. Some people say that most people can be trusted. Others say you can't be too careful in dealing with people. How do you feel about it?
2. Would you say that most people are more inclined to help others, or more inclined to look after themselves?
3. If you don't watch yourself people will take advantage of you.
4. No one is going to care much what happens to you, when you get right down to it.
5. Human nature is fundamentally cooperative.

On the basis of the pattern of responses to these items respondents were judged to have 'high', 'medium' or 'low faith in people', and each of these subgroups was shown, by correlation with other attitude scales, to have different attitudes towards success in life.

It is important to note that the items themselves are phrased in recognisably ordinary language as is required by the rationale of questionnaire design, and could have been uttered in a variety of familiar situations. On these occasions the answers might have ranged from grunts of assent, or dissent, to more extended justifications; might be uttered ironically, jokingly, and so on. In interviewing or testing situations, however, the respondent is normally limited to making one of a restricted choice of answers already provided: 'yes' or 'no', or choosing one from a set of alternatives expressing the degree of agreement or disagreement with the item. It is this feature which allows the researcher to assign a numerical score to the pattern of responses. If the numbers are to have any meaning as counts of the property of persons, such that person A's score of 3 is equivalent to person B's score of 3, and both of these scores expressing a greater quantity of the property than person C's score of 2, then the meaning of the items as checked must be equivalent.

An important question that arises, however, is whether the meaning of the items intended by the researcher is equivalent to that understood by the respondent. The open-textured quality of ordinary language which the investigator tries to remedy, in part at least, by the provision of forced-choice answers and such like, places a question mark against the assumption that the respondent and researcher do share 'the same community of subjective meaning structures for assigning cultural significance' to the items.[7] If this assumption of meaning equivalence cannot be upheld then it is no longer clear in what sense it can be said that the attitude measure is a quantitative measure at all.

If we take seriously the earlier arguments about the open-textured quality of ordinary language, it is by no means certain that in providing an answer a respondent understands either the item itself or the response to it in quite the same way as another respondent, let alone the investigator, or indeed that any respondent would understand an item on another occasion in the same way that it was understood on a previous occasion. This is not to say that a respondent cannot give an answer: the issue has to do with the meaning of that answer and the implications that can be drawn from it. What do we infer about a respondent who affirms item 3, say, and also affirms item 5? Is the respondent being inconsistent, irrational, or just not thinking? He or she may be all of these things and more, but it is difficult to judge without asking such a respondent to elaborate further. It is possible to give perfectly good and rationally connected reasons for agreeing with both of these apparently 'inconsistent' statements. The circumstances in which the question or statement is offered may make a difference to the kind of answer it elicits. Item 5 would, I suspect, receive a very different response if it appeared on an examination paper. Item 3 might receive a different response if offered by a shady-looking stranger who sidled up to me in some alley during the early hours of the morning! These observations, obvious though they might be, are relevant to understanding why, on occasions, respondents have difficulty answering questions constituting such scales since they are detached from any context where they might have some point. Including items such as these on a questionnaire or interview schedule gives them a disembodied and almost pointless character such that respondents want to ask 'in what circumstances', or qualify by a phrase such as 'it all depends'.[8]

The questions just raised are concerned with the sorts of inferences we might want to draw from the results of such a method. These, as I have shown, are not always clear. What implications, for example, could we draw, to give another example, from the fact that a respondent achieved a high score on such a scale? Do we infer that he/she will always be trusting, will lend money to anyone, will be a sucker for any sales pitch, will join any group? We could infer all of these things and more, but what conclusion would we draw if a high scorer did not lend money to her closest friend? Say that she cheated on the scale, had a momentary lapse, had no money to lend, or what? Without knowledge of the person, the particularities of the occasion and any elaborations or justifications that the person might offer, we would not know what to conclude. Nevertheless, the Faith in People notion does have a commonsense meaning, and we understand the sorts of things it could refer to, stand for, when it could be used, and so on. It is this ability that constitutes knowing the language and gives the scale itself some plausibility as a device relevant to the understanding of human action. If, after all, the researcher had called the property being measured XZ we would still want to know how this related to our concepts for talking about action. In other words, the ordinary usage is a resource essential to our understanding the supposedly scientific concept and the items presumed to measure it: a resource used by both the researcher in designing the scale and the respondent in answering it. However, this ordinary usage, being open-textured and open to further elaboration, can only index all that it might mean on any particular occasion of its use.

These comments are of wider import than personality assessment or attitude measurement. The coding of questionnaires, for example, depends for its validity on some presumed equivalence between what the respondent has replied or checked and the intention of the researcher in asking the question. There are, however, strong grounds for questioning whether such an equivalence is achievable in the way presumed. As Cicourel points out with respect to his own work on fertility, 'having children' does not necessarily have the same meaning for the researcher or the interviewer as it does for the respondents.[9] Meanings shift over every interview. 'Having children' means one thing to virgins, another to a pregnant woman, yet another when giving birth and, more than likely, still another when talking to an interviewer. These do not exhaust the possible varieties and elaborations of meaning, nor is it always possible for a coder to go back to a respondent to ask for an elaboration of an answer that might be unclear or ambiguous. Even if this were possible it would be unlikely to help very much since it would add to the problems of coding as more and more detail was added. Similar problems arise in experimental situations where it is not clear that subjects perceive or understand the experimental situation in the same ways presumed by the researcher.

The criticism of social scientific use of official statistics is particularly well documented, especially as they arise from Durkheim's pioneering use of them in his study of suicide. As has been pointed out, Durkheim himself voiced many doubts about their accuracy, which he tried to resolve by interpreting them as reflections of certain moral currents within society. However, as others have pointed out, those responsible for the compilation of such statistics, such as officials, police, coroners, have themselves to decide upon the appropriate description of the death before them. As studies have demonstrated, such personnel 'rely on background expectancies, commonsense theorising and typifications which enable them to make sense of and objectify the phenomena with which they are faced'.[10] In short, they rely on their own meaning frameworks in order to assemble the particularities before them and so achieve a description of *this* social event and classify it along with other 'similar' social events. The so-called 'objective facts' measured by official statistics are the creation of the practices individuals use to render their world an accountable and meaningful thing. It is their versions, admittedly through many negotiations and processes, which find their way into the figures, a record which cannot stand for an objective reality, or be 'brute data', in the way proposed by social scientists of a positivist persuasion. That such statistics may be taken, by social actors, as referring to objective features of their world is a matter for their procedures, their methods, their meanings; a matter, so to speak, of the practices embedded in their language.

The points just iterated are not solely concerned with the technical validity of methods, but rather to do with general questions arising from such efforts to transform 'first order' constructs into concepts appropriate for a deductive or generalising social science. The structure of the interview, for example, is based on procedures to produce 'clear' and 'unambiguous' responses which can be precisely coded for machine processing and statistical analysis. Unfortunately, these procedures do not necessarily reflect the ways in which respondents meaningfully order their daily interactions. Talk about attitudes, values, beliefs, actions, etc., is presumed to provide an adequate literal description of what they believe and do. Yet the interview is detached from the circumstances in which persons act, which makes the responses artificial, to say the least. The coding and manipulation of such data further removes and abstracts them from the social lives of those they are supposed to reflect. The indexical characteristics of natural language ensure that the things said in that language only have their sense against the background or context of the occasion in which they are said. Words, utterances, indeed any symbolic form, has to be 'filled in' on each occasion of it use, and this is a major stumbling block to efforts to construct a mathematical-type language for social science. Positivist methods, it is claimed, decontextualise 'first order' constructs so distorting the reality they are designed to investigate. They impose, by fiat, a version of reality insensitive to the ways in which the social world is a meaningful one and one constructed by those who live within it. In other words, positivist methods produce or construct the social reality they intend to investigate as a discovery science through the methods themselves; methods which do not so much discover facts about social life as construct a version of that life by its methods.

So far in this critique it has been argued that methods of research associated with positivist social science are based upon assumptions which ignore, or even violate, the presuppositions of the conception of social reality as produced through meanings. Yet the fact remains that researchers have produced 'findings' and analyses of social life which, to put it no stronger, have some plausibility. Although a full answer to the question as to how this is possible is difficult in general, let alone within the compass of this survey, there are one or two points worth making since they incorporate a view of social scientific knowledge which is different to that of positivism. The first of these has already been mentioned briefly. This has to do with the extent to which social scientific concepts, whatever else is done with them by way of research operations, are parasitic for their sense on concepts available within the culture and language – concepts, that is, in everyday use. If, in addition, we take the point made about how the speakers of a natural language achieve descriptive adequacy on particular occasions for practical purposes by the use of their taken-for-granted and commonsense knowledge of the world in which they live, it can be argued that researchers implicitly trade on the same corpus of knowledge in order to do their research in the first place. This would include knowledge of the typical motives, reasons, situations, rules, conventions, etc.; in short, knowledge of the practices embedded in the language. Indeed, without the use of such knowledge it is hard to see how research activity could be done in the first place. Thus, the 'sense', if I can use that word, of the research findings owes a great deal to the implicit and commonsense knowledge the researcher shares with other actors about the social world. Put this way, social science depends for is authenticity on meanings and understandings already available within the culture.[11]

There is another aspect to this and one which harks back to some of the comments made in Chapter 4 in reference to Kuhn and the new sociology of science. Science can be regarded as a cultural practice involving the use of rules of procedure collectively accredited and identifiable as 'doing science'. As Wilson expresses it.

Scientific research is a practical activity, which is embedded, as is any practical activity, in a context of implicit commonsense knowledge and is carried on by members of a particular scientific community for the purpose of developing descriptions that serve as the bases for eventual theoretical understanding.[12]

If we regard research as an activity done in accord with rules then we run into the problem arising with all rules, namely, that no rule dictates its own application but must be *used*. Many, if not all, of the rules used in social science research methods are themselves based on theories, many of them commonsense theories, of social behaviour. The interview, for example, depends for its validity on theories about the relationship between respondent talk and action, beliefs, etc. One of the difficulties here lies in drawing an effective distinction between talk in different contexts, one of which, the interview, becomes talk-as-scientific-data. Positivist methods seem to draw this distinction mainly in terms of the extent to which that talk conforms to certain criteria, such as clarity, consistency, lack of ambiguity, and so forth, which are themselves formulated in logical rather than commonsense terms. Talk becomes indicative of the properties of social actors. As an aid to this, fixed-choice responses may be provided, tests for consistency used, questionnaires rejected if they contain too many 'don't know' responses or inconsistent ones, and so on. But these rules have to be applied to each and every case. Is *this* questionnaire authentic? Does *this* attitude scale score truly reflect this person's attitude or is it a response set? Is *this* answer compatible with the previous answer or was the respondent being careless through tiredness or boredom? Answers to these, and similar questions, cannot be provided by the rules alone but must be 'filled in' so that the rule is seen to apply in a particular case. This will involve invoking typical motives, typical models of the respondent, typical situations, and other imputations in order to accord with some conceptions of acceptable scientific practice. The extent to which the researcher's solutions will be acceptable is, in part, a matter for the other accredited members of the relevant scientific community. Scientific practice, like other practices, is an enforceable matter in which results, conclusions, findings, theories, and so on, are subject to the scrutiny of legitimate others. It is this public scrutiny which gives the rules of scientific research their warrant and their force. 'Objectivity', 'truth', 'relevant description' are, as it were, established through the interpretative procedures of scientific practice. While we may regard the rules of scientific procedure as abstract formulations defining the proper method of obtaining objective knowledge of social reality, like all rules they have to be applied and this is profoundly a matter of judgement and social practice. Scientific descriptions and explanations are the products of research activities carried out by accredited members of a scientific community and consist in the application of rules of procedure provided for and understood by those adjudged to be competent members of that community. Any researcher must rely upon those understandings in order to create, analyse, and communicate findings. These are the bases of the intersubjective agreement which is the resource for seeing research as 'objective', 'consistent with the evidence', 'provisional', or whatever quality it may possess.

These observations on positivist research methods imply a radically different conception of knowledge. The positivist enterprise saw itself as operating according to an epistemology based primarily upon observation. Efforts to formulate a neutral observation language were felt to be crucial to establishing the scientific authority of a discipline since this was the source of objectivity. The external world described in terms of the neutral observation language was regarded as the arbiter of the truth of scientific propositions. An observation language referring to real phenomena and operated in accordance with a strict logical calculus would provide knowledge of the laws of nature, including those of social life. Some of the difficulties arising from these efforts, especially in connection with social science, have already been discussed. One objection argued that positivism misconstrues the nature of science by its espousal of an empiricist version which underrates the importance of the abstractive connection between theory and the empirical world. The view just discussed, however, postulates that knowledge, far from being a passive product of the empirical world, is an active constituent in the construction of the world, whether natural or social. It does so by, first of all, pointing to the interpretative basis of social life and arguing that efforts to construct so-called scientific 'second order' constructs out of 'first order' ones destroy the very reality being investigated and substitute in its place a 'scientised' version. This is to tamper with the concepts used by persons in their lives to make sense and constitute that life in order to make them scientifically usable. The trouble is that the meaning and significance of such supposedly neutral terms such as power, legitimacy, profit, deviance, integration, social system, in large measure derive from the uses, and varied uses at that, they have within action itself and the language used to constitute that action. In the second place, the critique draws attention to the fact that science, natural or social, is a human activity. It is also social and its rules work because there is a strong element of intersubjective agreement about their application. 'Objectivity', 'knowledge', 'truth' and other such concepts, have a conventional quality firmly based on the social practices which can be said to constitute a discipline.

Clearly this kind of argument has important implications for the status of science *vis-à-vis* other claims to knowledge. It raises, too, the spectre of relativism. If scientific practice is conventional in the sense of being rule-governed, like any other activity, what happens to the claim that these rules, and not others, represent a superior form of knowledge? One cannot appeal to the superior ability of science to explain the world since, on this view, the world itself is constructed out of the practices that constitute a discipline and so cannot provide independent witness. One cannot go beyond the circle of interpretations, as the positivists tried to do with the notion of a neutral observation language, to judge the relative merits of different and competing claims to knowledge in terms of how well they describe and explain the nature of the external world. All we are left with are various kinds of activities, science, art, religion, literary criticism, poetry, and so on, each justified internally, as it were, by its own conventions and standards. To judge one in terms of the other would be tantamount to assessing football in terms of the rules of cricket.

There are, of course, many important issue arising from this critique of positivism, some of which I shall look into in more detail. I shall begin by considering the relationship between lay concepts and scientific ones.

LAY VERSUS SCIENTIFIC CONCEPTS

The arguments advanced in the preceding chapter claim that action is unique to human beings – although it does not depend solely on this – involving notions of choice, responsibility, meaning, sense, conventions, rules, intentions, motives and so on. Moreover, such concepts are used and shaped in courses of action; they are, to repeat the point, constitutive of the social world. This has been taken to imply that actions can, therefore, only be identified through the actor's own concepts in accordance with the actor's view of the world. This argument relies heavily upon the distinction between the physical and the human world and the different forms of knowledge this implies. Winch states that, while both the physical and the social scientist bring a system of concepts to their subject-matter, what the physical scientist studies has

an existence independent of these concepts. There existed electrical storms and thunder long before there were human beings to form concepts of them . . . it does not make sense to suppose that human beings might have been issuing commands and obeying them before they came to form the concept of command and obedience.[13]

The subject-matters of social science have their own conceptions of what they are doing and the 'conceptions according to which we normally think of social events . . . enter into social life itself and not merely into the observer's description of it'.[14] Any human activity that involves language, and it is difficult to think of any that do not, will present the observer with a pre-articulated interpretation of what that activity is.

For man does not wait for science to have his life explained to him, and when the theorist approaches social reality he finds the field pre-empted by what may be called the self-interpretation of society. Human society is not merely a fact, or an event, in the external world to be studied by an observer like a natural phenomenon . . . it is a whole little world, a cosmion, illuminated with meaning from within by the human beings who continuously create and bear it as the mode and condition of their self-realisation.[15]

Observations such as these exemplify the thesis that the identification of actions must necessarily be in the actor's terms and, as such, draws upon some of the matters discussed in the previous chapter concerning the identification of actions, describing them, specifying what was done, saying whether two actions are the same, and so on. Again to quote Winch:

Two things may be called the 'same' or 'different' only with reference to a set of criteria which lay down what is to be regarded as a relevant difference. When the 'things' in question are purely physical the criteria appealed to will of course be those of the observer. But when one is dealing with intellectual (or, indeed, any kind of social) 'things', that is not so. For their *being* intellectual or social . . . in character depends entirely upon their belonging in a certain way to a system of ideas or modes of living. It is only by reference to the criteria governing that system of ideas or mode of life that they have any existence as intellectual or social events. It follows that if the sociological investigator wants to regard them *as* social events . . . he has to take seriously the criteria which are applied for distinguishing 'different' kinds of actions and identifying the 'same' actions within the way of life he is studying. It is not open to him to arbitrarily impose his own standards from without. In so far as he does so, the events he is studying lose altogether their character as social events.[16]

What is being argued by Winch, and others, is more than a simple injunction calling on social scientists to investigate the ideas of individuals, but that not only is the identification of actions dependent on concepts employed by actors in the course of their life, so too are the criteria of evidence, proof, rationality, and so on. The rules which make social actions what they are must be the rules of use of the concepts of those actions shared by users of a language and a culture. Thus to be able to see that someone carving a piece of wood is engaged in a religious act requires attribution to that person the concept of 'religion', the possession of which is the ability to use the concept properly and effect other distinctions between this and other activities. Conceptions of reality and how it may be studied, while independent of any one individual's views, are dependent on the human activity concerned which, in its turn, must be defined by its participants. This is as true for science as it is for magic, religion, and any other human activity. In our culture, according to Winch, we have difficulty seeing this because of 'the fascination science has for us' making it 'easy for us to adopt its scientific form as a paradigm against which to measure the intellectual respectability of other modes of discourse'.[17]

These arguments have a specially dramatic force in connection with cultures very different from our own. Anthropologists, although they are not the only social scientists to concern themselves with other cultures, face the problem of categorising the behaviour they witness. What, to use a previous example, is a man doing carving a piece of wood? Is it an economic activity in which he is engaged? Is it an act of worship? A political gesture? Or is it simply a way of passing the time? The problem is, as Schutz points out, that activities may look alike but may have different meanings within their respective cultures. Whether a pattern of activity is 'a war dance, a barter trade, the reception of a friendly ambassador, or something else', only the participants themselves can say.[18] Winch uses Evans-Pritchard's study of magic among the Azande to make much the same point.[19] For the Azande, witchcraft and magic are ordinary enough phenomena, as familiar to them as refrigerators, cars and television sets are to us. There is nothing especially miraculous about it. For them it is a coherent system of thought and though mistakes and errors are possible, as they are within our science, this does not lead to a wholesale questioning of magic as a system of knowledge. For them magic and witchcraft are incorrigible elements in the world and actions which, for them, are evidence of the existence of magic and witchcraft, would present us with problems. From our scientific standpoint we want to say that their system of thought is in error; that it is wrong about the nature of reality since it postulates the existence of forces and beings that cannot, according to our view of things, exist. This issue is one version of the problem of cultural relativism and, among other things, has to do with whether or not we can understand another culture.

The issue of cultural relativism arises in a similar form in connection with the incommensurability of different forms of knowledge. A culture very different from our own can be seen as a distinctive, self-justifying realm of discourse with its own logic and standards of rationality, and so cannot be described or judged except by these, its own criteria and conventions. Be this as it may, what is less clear is whether this logically precludes our being able to understand in any sense at all a society or culture other than our own. Winch himself is not clear on this. At one stage, for example, he seems to be saying that explanation and understanding in the actor's own terms are richer and deeper while, at another, that explanation not framed in these terms is not a genuine social scientific explanation.[20] A more moderate position he argues is that actions can be explained in terms not necessarily intelligible to those concerned if these are translatable in some way into the actor's own concepts. Thus, Winch seems to accept, as many positivists would, that social science need not restrict itself to the 'unreflective kind of understanding' typical of social actors. For example, 'liquidity preference' is not a term commonly used by businessmen in the course of their lives but by economists in the explanation of certain kinds of business behaviour. Nonetheless, it is logically tied to concepts which do enter into business activity and its use in economics presupposes an

understanding of what it is to conduct a business, which in turn involves an understanding of such business concepts as money, profit, cost, risk, etc. It is only the relation between his account and those concepts which makes it an account of economic activity as opposed, say, to a piece of theology.[21]

What is in some ways a more seriously radical relativism arises from the ideas of Sapir and Whorf who have been construed as arguing that differences among languages reflect differences in metaphysics or 'world views'. This thesis is not simply about the differences in vocabulary among languages but about the way vocabularies are organised by grammar and, thus, organise the forms of thought among the speakers of the language. Grammar is a theory of reality. Different ways of viewing the world are expressed in different classificatory systems which are indicated by differences in grammar and, in this way, it is grammar which determines thought and the way the world is seen and constituted. There is no way of moving outside of language to determine the truth value of metaphysics. We cannot rank one metaphysical system, as a complete theory of reality, against another. Though it might be argued that Apache, for example, in turning nouns such as 'sun-set' into verbs, better displays the processual character of the event than does English, this is no licence to judge Apache, *in toto*, as superior to English. Grammatical structures are underdetermined by the way the world is. The world and its words can be formally organised in a variety of ways.[22]

What we have so far, then, are a number of issues turning on the relationship between actors' concepts and those used by social science. Positivist social science, as a consequence of its efforts to be scientific, effectively degraded the status of actors'concepts by seeing them as the subjective counterpart, and therefore less causally efficacious, of an objective social structure. On the other hand, the views represented by Winch and others claim that describing and analysing social life, whether radically different to one's own or not, in positivist terms leads to descriptive asymmetries of a moral nature. Louch, for example, states that to the extent social science borrows its methods from physics it cannot adequately treat the subject-matter of action.[23] The vocabulary of action is concerned with moral appraisal not with scientific prediction. Action concepts deal with rules, reasons, motives, intentions not with causal laws and invariant relations. Also as was suggested in the previous chapter using the episode of opening the door for a lady, the description of action is not only a defeasible matter, it is intimately concerned with evaluation. The language of action, as Louch says, contains values as inextricable elements and to try to remove these by inventing 'operational definitions' supposed to be value-free, means that one can no longer identify actions and the meaning they have for the actors. The processes of identifying, describing and appraising an action are not distinct activities. Moreover, as Winch claims to have shown with the case of Azande magic, systems of knowledge are internally self-justifying containing their own ontologies, epistemologies and standards of rationality which, as it were, reflexively shape and legislate for their respective object of knowledge. Science is not different in this. It is simply another way of looking at the world and, therefore, cannot claim absolute superiority over other forms of knowledge.

Let us look at this position more closely and begin by examining the thesis that actions must be identified in terms of the actors' concepts. As Pitkin points out, this thesis is argued at different levels; that only an actor's own conceptions can define what he or she is doing; that only the concepts and rules of a given human activity can define actions within that activity; and, cross-culturally, that only the norms and concepts of a given culture can define actions.[24]

The argument to the effect that only the individual actor knows what he or she is doing, or has done, is misleading if not false. There are many circumstances in which we could say that the actor did not know what he or she was doing. The actor may not be able to see quite what he or she has done, or that despite good intentions the action turned out otherwise. Similarly, an action might have unintended consequences of which the actor is ignorant or, perhaps, as he or she later comes to see the action in a different light. All of these cases we allow for through our descriptions and our assessments of actions. Though there are cases where it can be said that only the actor knows what he or she is doing, it would be far too strict an implication to claim that this is always the case. As was pointed out earlier with respect to intention, the kind of action itself is relevant to considerations such as these. Some actions are contingent on a relevant intention, others less so. Pitkin refers to the temptation to say that the more an action approximates to physical movements, the sort that can be done by animals for example, the less it would seem to hinge upon relevant intentions, or awareness, on the part of the actor.[25] The more complex, abstract and rule-governed an action is, the less likely it is that we would attribute it to someone lacking the relevant concept of action. For example, one can eat without the intention of eating, kill without the intention of killing, escape without the awareness of escaping, but can one dine, murder or flee without the awareness of such things?

Matters here are complicated indeed. As suggested earlier, the description of action involving motive, intention, or awareness is not a matter of hypothesising an 'inner state' to account for some 'outward' display of behaviour. Nor is it confined solely by the character of the 'outward' behaviour itself. Actions are described against a background of appropriate context or circumstance, and there are always various combinations of elements out of which a description can be assembled. Moreover, with respect to actions there are always possibilities of ambiguities of interpretation because actors are able to voice their reasons and intentions and argue about any particular description. The frequent occurrence of such disputes, arising as they do out of the nature of action description, is one of the reasons for referring to it as a moral activity. The point is, however, that with respect to such disputes the view of both an observer and an actor are relevant. That is, while it is not always the case that the actor, and the actor alone, knows what he or she is doing, neither is it the case that only the observer knows. Sometimes we might conclude in favour of the actor, sometimes in favour of the observer, sometimes in favour of neither. Our conclusions would depend very much on the situation, our interest in it, the action at issue, and a host of other possibly relevant matters. Nevertheless, as far as human action is concerned, intention and the actor's views are always potentially relevant, if never decisive.

A more vexing issue here, and one perhaps more directly associated with describing actions for the purposes of investigations or data, is the claim that actions within any activity can only be defined in terms of the rules and concepts of that activity; that is, within that region of discourse. What is our man doing carving the piece of wood? Is he engaging in a religious ritual, an economic project, passing the time, or making a doll for his child? Winch uses the example of prayer and says that the question of whether an activity is prayer or not is a religious question and must be identified within that realm of discourse. However, if he means by this that disciplines, or other realms of discourse, such as psychology, economics, sociology, or anthropology, cannot address the matter of prayer then this has serious implications. One of these is that forms of knowledge, or realms of discourse, are incommensurate with one another. This thesis, as pointed out earlier, is especially powerful at the cross-cultural level. Without knowing the language, the customs, conventions and institutions of an alien society we are likely to be misled in attempting to describe the actions of the people concerned. Even with some knowledge of the society concerned we can be seduced by 'an overpowering faith in the omnirelevance of one's professional scheme of classification' and see social life only in those terms so editing away, as it were, the actor's own version of that life.[26]

To repeat: matters here are complicated, and the choice of examples important. What we might call complex action concepts, such as prayer, obedience, barter, politics, and so on, are often ambiguous in their use and highly variable and indeterminate in their meaning. Other concepts, such as eating, sleeping, planting, running, jumping, are less so. One would, I suspect, have little difficulty in identifying the latter actions wherever and whenever they occur. However, and this is the real point of the thesis, there still remains the problem of the significance of such actions within the culture concerned. What are they doing by eating, jumping, running, and so on? Few social scientists would be content to describe cultures purely in terms of people running, jumping or eating, amusing as these Monty Pythonesque accounts might prove to be.

Another point to bear in mind is that sometimes anthropologists, or any other social scientist dealing with other cultures, must diverge from actors' own accounts in order to communicate with readers. This is a very real difficulty in anthropological work. Were the researcher to report solely in terms of the actor's system of knowledge this would, as likely as not, involve commitments completely at variance with those of the researcher's own culture; a bias in the other direction would fail to be at least partially faithful to the culture under study. Winch, as we have seen, allows for the possibility that the social scientist must use concepts not known to the actors provided that these are logically tied to those of the actor; exactly what this means is another matter. What Winch wants to avoid is competition between the actors' and the social scientists' accounts in which the latter are regarded as superior to the former. However, there is no reason why the two accounts cannot coexist. As Pitkin puts it, the anthropologist need not say 'although they claim it's A, it's really B they're doing', 'but in doing A, I can see that they are at the same time doing B, though they may deny or ignore it'.[27] Thus, though the tribe may be engaged in a 'rain dance' which, for them, is designed to produce rain, the anthropologist might claim that at the same time they ae 'reaffirming tribal norms'. They may be 'reaffirming tribal norms' without realising it, but they are not doing this instead of what they themselves say they are doing. They are doing both, one by way of the other. Of course, the researcher must show that the actors are doing what is claimed and this may require relating his concepts to some tribal ones but there are no hard and fast rules of logic involved here. The point is that the actors' activity can be spoken of either way, just as a piece of wood can be spoken of as an art object, a weapon, a tool, a marker, or whatever an occasion we take it to be.

For some this conclusion would be less than satisfactory in that it seems to suggest that anything goes. Further, it glosses over the very real problems of translation that can occur when studying cultures radically different to our own. One can admit, perhaps, that there is no necessary conflict between actors' accounts and those of social scientists, but this still leaves open the problem of defining and describing what actors are doing. There are many steps an investigator must take between observing the members of culture and proving some theoretical account of that culture. Though the rain dance may serve to reaffirm tribal norms, the performance still has to be identified as a ritual dance, and tribal norms given some formulation, and those actions have to be counted as an affirmation of those norms. Problems of description proliferate. Nevertheless, this is one of the important implications of Winch's arguments against Evans-Pritchard, namely, that we need to be very careful before identifying another culture's institution, such as witchcraft, as if it were really like one of our own, such as science. It may be that, for the Azande, witchcraft and science can coexist. In which case, regarding witchcraft as a nascent science is to miss the point of witchcraft as a feature of Azande culture.

The anthropological problem here is not unfamiliar. Ascribing or imputing beliefs and other 'cognitive states' to actors in an attempt to clarify what they do is part and parcel of what it is to describe action; but, whereas a social scientist studying his or her own culture has all the advantages of an 'insider', in the anthropologist's case this is less likely. Take an extreme illustration of radical translation, that is translation of a language belonging to a culture completely alien. Here it can be argued that all the anthropologist has available as data are what earlier were called 'concrete behavioural displays' of those being studied. To these can be added the linguistic performances which, it is presumed, derive from and embody the meanings that give sense to the 'behavioural displays'. In this case, however, all we have are the performances from which meaning has to be inferred. To translate African tribal utterances into, say, English, the anthropologist would want to begin by relating some of them to the world. In this way a collection of utterances could be made whose situations of use could be specified. Thus, if a particular set of words were said whenever food was being eaten, this might give some clue as to the meaning of the words. Unfortunately, there is no guarantee that the translator has actually perceived the situation correctly. The words uttered in the presence of food could be recipes, a form of grace, despairing moans, or even the equivalent of a belch; it might be that the presence of food is irrelevant to the words uttered. The only way to solve these problems would be to translate what the Africans said about what they perceive and mean. But this is precisely the problem: the anthropologist would have to translate the language before discovering what the actors perceive, and to know what they perceive before being able to translate.[28] We have, therefore, a vicious circle and there seems no way out. It has been argued, for example, that in the case of radical translation where meaning has to be inferred from purely verbal behaviour there is an inbuilt indeterminacy. As Quine formulates it:

Two men could be just alike in all their dispositions to verbal behaviour under all possible sensory stimulations, and yet the meanings or ideas expressed in their identically triggered and identically sounded utterances could diverge radically, for the two men, in a wide range of cases.[29]

Are there any arguments which would enable us to break the vicious circle in a principled way? Hollis suggests that we assume a charitable and substantive *a priori* principle that all social actors, alien or not, share the same standard of rationality.[30] Winch and others argue that the researcher must participate fully in the life of those under study. Both these suggested solutions, while having pragmatic plausibility, and this may be all that we can have, seem to offer no principled resolution. One might begin to have sympathy with the positivist attempt to discover a neutral observation language referring to, or based upon, the common experience of human kind. Perhaps, after all, there is no resolution of this kind: no way, that is, of effectively routinising the process of identifying actions objectively, determinatively and unambiguously. It has already been suggested that within a single culture the description of action is always defeasible, prone to ambiguity, vagueness and imprecision; bringing in the issue of translation merely highlights by extreme example what is an inescapable feature of action concepts. Where translation is concerned its adequacy will, in part, be judged in terms of its purpose. If we require of any translation that it establishes an exact equivalence between our concepts and those of some culture different from our own, then obviously we shall have tremendous difficulties. It may just be that there are no exact equivalences in our language for some of their concepts, but do we take this to imply that we cannot make sense at all of the other culture? The answer surely has to be no. We can draw parallels, analogies, offer illustrations and so on, in an effort to make sense, for us, of what the other culture is like. It may be that we have to modify or extend our own concepts in some way so that they portray the other culture's concepts more adequately. To presume that what is required is some exact equivalence is to presume also that our own concepts are free of problems. All that has been said so far suggests that this is far from being so.

Pitkin draws attention to parallels between the problems of understanding another culture and understanding action within our own culture.

Action is ultimately dual, consisting *both* of what the outside observer can see *and* of the actors' understanding of what they are doing. The duality . . . is what distinguishes action [and] sets the problems for social science. The problem is not . . . our inability to observe actions objectively or identify them without consulting the actors.[31]

Action concepts developed in the course of action, are themselves performative of actions and, as such, rich in implications which are not always consistent.

They work well in context, in particular cases; but anyone attempting to articulate broad, general, abstract principles about the nature of promises, obedience, voting, and the like, will encounter conceptual puzzlement and paradox. Anyone attempting to study such phenomena scientifically, through empirical observation, will be troubled by just what phenomena count as instances of promises, obedience, voting.[32]

Thus, like a child learning a language, a researcher investigating a different culture will have to learn the language of that culture from the particularities of both action and language, by trial and error.[33] Of course, the researcher may get it wrong, just as an action description in one's own culture may be said to be mistaken, but this is far from saying that it is impossible.

As has been more than just hinted at, the 'other cultures' issue is in many ways a dramatic statement of a problem that arises in the study of one's own culture, namely, the identification of actions. Although Winch, and others who have made much the same point, illustrates the important practical difficulties in understanding other cultures, he has not convincingly demonstrated (assuming that this is his intention, which is doubtful) that it is impossible. His own work, in fact, is a testament to the contrary in that he presents us with an account, an understandable account, of Azande witchcraft. Yet, and this is perhaps the real issue, what criteria are available for deciding whether it is the *right* account?[34] Winch's own views on this matter are not always clear and consistent, but it would seem, almost certainly, that the actors themselves must play some part in that judgement: exactly what this might involve is another matter. Nor, as has been suggested earlier, is there any reason why, in every case, we should take their word for it. That would be to abnegate our responsibilities.

What of the larger question Winch raises concerning the status of social science? The philosophical problems we have been discussing in these two chapters constitute an accumulation of serious objections to positivist social science both as regards its conception of the subject-matter of social science and its relationship, as a corpus of knowledge, to that subject-matter. While these general issues about knowledge, its grounding and its justifications, are of paramount importance, I want to delay their consideration for the final chapter. I shall pause here to look briefly at the positive side of the interpretavist critique in order to see what it suggests about the nature of social research.

MEANINGS AND SOCIAL RESEARCH

Perhaps not surprisingly, the alternatives to the positivist approach are varied and lack the confident clarity that positivism once possessed. Some of them are not new but represent a theme running parallel to positivism in the history of social thought: others are comparatively recent and are a direct response to some of the criticisms of positivism we have discussed. A common idiom is the rejection of a scientific conception of social study, usually seen in positivistic terms, and a sensitivity to the social nature of knowledge itself. Within this general posture, however, are particular, and crucial, slants. The objection to science, for example, can be one against specific versions of science, such as positivism, rather than an espousal of a non-scientific, even anti-scientific, ambition for social science. As we shall see later, Schutz talks about a 'theoretic' interest in the world as opposed to a practical one; the former characterising the distinctive attitude of what we might refer to as science. In other words, for Schutz and other Phenomenologists, science is not especially characterised by a particular method but rather by an attitude. Earlier, Weber also expressed a rather different conception of the human sciences to that propounded by positivism. There are, of course, and Weber debated with many such, schools of thought which do reject the scientific ambition for social science altogether. However, it is the claims about the social construction of knowledge that have proved the most philosophically troublesome. Once doubts are cast on what has been called a 'neutral observation language' in which to describe the world external to whatever subjective experiences we might have of it, scientific detachment and objectivity begin to seem illusory goals. The social sciences, however they may try to ape the natural sciences, have forever to face the difficulties posed by the fact that their subject-matter also has a voice. Moreover, though this voice might be influenced by social position and social processes, it is not alone in this. The social scientist, too, is a member of a society and a culture, has a position within a collectivity of colleagues, and these similarly are likely to affect the way in which he or she sees the world. One conclusion from this is that drawn by Weber:

There is no absolutely 'objective' analysis of culture – or perhaps more narrowly but certainly not essentially different for our purposes – of 'social phenomena' independent of special and 'one-sided' viewpoints according to which – expressly or tacitly, consciously or subconsciously – they are selected, analysed and organised for expository purposes . . . All knowledge of cultural reality, as may be seen, is always knowledge from particular points of view.[35]

There is, in short, no Archimedean, no neutral, point from which to stand back and perceive the social world 'objectively'.

Of course, the notion that knowledge is socially grounded could also be applied to the natural sciences, but in this case few issues of a moral kind would arise since, as far as we know, rocks, molecules and plants do not speak. The difficulty for the social sciences is to come to terms with the fact that their subject-matter and those who would study it live in a world constructed through meanings. The ways, methodologically speaking, of coming to terms with this have been various. Some, such as Mannheim, and to a degree Marx, suggested that objective standpoints could only be attained by those in specially privileged positions of detachment, 'intellectuals' being, more or less, the major candidates for such positions.[36] These were people who could develop a more comprehensive and hence more objective point of view from which to locate the real processes at work within society.

Weber's own response to the problem he did much to identify is important. Accepting the social and historical grounding of knowledge and the partial perspective this implied, he took it that in our own time cultural values had fused with scientific ones, making objectivity universally acceptable. The standards of objectivity embodied in science were socially grounded but in social practices which had themselves changed so that they conformed to those very standards. These changes were brought about by the rise of industrial society. As we have already seen, Weber did offer two ideas, the 'ideal type' and *verstehen*, as techniques towards understanding meaningful social forms. The latter required that the researcher empathise with the point of view of those under investigation so that their world, constructed out of meanings, could be rationally formulated. Using data from a number of sources about the values, aspirations, etc., of ascetic Protestants, Weber developed a meaningful portrait of how such people in their situation at that time, with the motivations deriving from their values, could have been encouraged to engage in the developing forms of capitalist enterprises. The 'ideal type', too, was a device essentially concerned with aiding the construction of rational, simplified and deliberately one-sided representations of social forms rigorously formulated as systems of meaning arising from one or two central values. Of the 'ideal types' Weber himself formulated, those to do with authority are among the better known. He identified three core types of authority in terms of their sources of legitimacy – charismatic, traditional and rational-legal – each type constructed as accentuations of empirically relevant materials. None of them is likely ever to have existed in pure form, but this was not their point. They served both to clarify a 'messy' empirical world and, thereby, isolate some of its salient elements.[37] As has just been suggested, the types can be regarded as rigorous formulations of system of meaning and practices deriving from one or two core values. Thus, the 'ideal type' of bureaucracy can be seen as a model of what organisation would look like if the principle of rational and calculative efficiency, *and only that*, were to be the organising principle. Of course, no concrete organisation is ever likely to be affected in its structure by just this one principle. Nonetheless, by gauging how far actual organisations do conform to the ideal type, researchers can begin to isolate those other factors which determine the character of organisations along with rationality. Finally, and an important point, for Weber 'ideal types' were not the end of inquiries but the beginning.

Much of hermeneutic philosophy, however, sits uncomfortably with Weber's attempt to bridge the gap between interpretative understanding and causal explanation in order to void relativistic conclusions of a nihilistic kind. For Gadamer, on the other hand, this preoccupation of hermeneutics with the constitution and the methodology of the social sciences forgets that understanding and interpretation are essential features of human nature.[38] For Gadamer, much of hermeneutics in the tradition of Dilthey fails to disengage from the Enlightenment idea of the 'pure reasoner' forgetting that 'historicity', as he terms it, is an ontological condition of understanding. It is because of our historical and cultural location that we can engage in interpretative understanding; our present understandings, conceptions of life, open up the past so that we can have knowledge of it. Our historical and social position is the 'given' which shapes our experience and our understanding of that experience. Our own historical position has already been shaped by the past, and it is this which provides the tradition, the ground upon which we, as interpreters, stand. In which case, interpretative understanding is not reconstructing the past in and for the present, but is 'mediating' the past in and for the present. This involves attention to the continuity of heritage and tradition as 'dialogue' and a 'collision of horizons' in which our own deep-seated assumptions and historicity are revealed. The circle of hermeneutic interpretation becomes a process of hypothesis and revision as understanding develops. Hermeneutics, for Gadamer, is not a method or an ideal, but the original form of 'being-in-the-world', a universal principle of human thought. There is no definite meaning to be attained and no standards of objectivity independent of the intersubjective 'fusion of horizons' reached in a dialogue of interpretation.

Underpinning all of this is the fact that we possess language and, through this, possess and experience the world. Language is the precondition for truth and understanding, and since there is no experience of the world independently of language, this sets limits upon the world. This, the way to escape the relativist trap. Language has a 'disclosure power', and just as tradition is the starting point for understanding, so to know a language is to be open to a dialogue with others that can transform and broaden the horizons from which we begin. Also, since there can be no experience of the world independently of language, there is nowhere else to view the world from and so the question of relativity does not arise. The process of transcending our own historicity, our own partial understandings in broader and broader horizons goes on in an endless process. Tradition and language form the context of interpretation and there can be no understanding outside of these and nothing, therefore, for our understanding to be relative to. Our interpretations contribute to history and the further sedimentation of tradition.

Despite Gadamer's claims about the essential character of interpretation within human life, for Habermas this does not go deep enough since it almost celebrates the necessary impossibility of discovering independent and objective standpoints. Instead, he wants to argue that the expression of our subjectivity is determined by forces that we can know objectively; that is, from without the community of life interests. The exemplar of method here is that of Freud which, for Habermas, extends and complements Marx's theory by giving a fuller account of the nature of 'distorted communication'. Psychoanalysis is essentially hermeneutic rather than scientific in character but can admit causal processes into its accounts of psychopathologies. By bringing out the latent significance of the repressed parts of a patient's life history, it reveals the 'underlying' forces which generate the surface meanings. The same 'depth hermeneutics' can be deployed, according to Habermas, to apply the same therapeutic gaze to communication and behaviour in social life; breaking through the constraints and distortions of language and experience to that which determines our experience. Accordingly, reconstituting historical materialism as a 'depth hermeneutics' we would have a realisable critique of ideology and a new philosophy of liberation and emancipation. The argument explicitly appeals to a notion of non-distorted communication in which interests are fully acknowledged and open to critical inspection. Because we would know the preconditions giving rise to it, we could detect false consciousness, and so transform the conditions of human life.[39]

Although that strand of the interpretavist perspective represented by Weber recognised the partiality of social scientific accounts, and hermeneutics their inevitability, the phenomenological tradition did not abandon the quest for the indubitable grounds of knowledge, but sought it in a different place to that of positivism. Phenomenology took very seriously, and still does, the view that knowledge is an act of consciousness.[40] For Husserl, the 'world' means a world experienced and made meaningful in consciousness. It is through acts of consciousness, and through such acts alone, that the world is given and presented to us. This is as true for science as it is for any other mode of knowing. The subject-matter of science, for example, is a system of constructs resulting from conceptualisations, idealisations, mathematisations, etc., based on a 'pre-given' everyday experience. One of the tasks of phenomenological philosophy is to describe this everyday experience of the 'life-world', the world, that is, as given in immediate experience independent of and prior to any scientific interpretation. Admittedly, life-worlds belong to specific socio-historical groups, and from this point of view, there could be no special privilege attached to any particular life-world. For Husserl, however, a 'transcendental phenomenology' could be developed as a universal theory of consciousness. Such an 'ontology of the life-world' would be an *a priori* science of the universal structures of the perceptual world and therefore enable us to derive any particular socio-cultural product, including science and logic. Such a theory, if it were possible, would perform the same role positivism envisages for the neutral observational language.

For our purposes, the important figure in this tradition is Alfred Schutz who elaborated and modified Husserl's work.[41] However, Schutz's starting point was Weber's view that it was possible to provide sociological explanations adequate at both the level of meaning and that of causality. As far as Schutz was concerned, Weber's ambition was admirable but had failed to provide the necessary philosophical premises of an interpretative social science. So, in turning to Husserl's philosophical method and his analysis of the life-world, Schutz aimed to indicate the ontological framework of an interpretative social science. In doing so, he treats the concept of understanding as the problem which Weber, though identifying, failed to examine thoroughly enough.

Borrowing from Husserl, Schutz argues that the life-world of ordinary understandings is carried into the scientific in a manner which leaves it unexamined. The reality the social sciences take as their topic has its origins in the life-world, and it is this which Weber, as well as the positivists, failed to realise. To place interpretative social science on a firmer footing it is necessary to examine the character of daily life as the outcome of the actions of social actors.[42]

Central to Schutz's examination is the 'postulate of subjective interpretation' which requires that social scientific accounts have to treat social actors as conscious beings whose activities, and those of others, have meaning. The social reality in which we act

as interpretative social actors is the outcome of the interpretations
made and the courses of action initiated. The problem is, then,
what 'objects' this postulate makes available for study within this
intersubjective life-world. The social world, claimed Schutz, is
presented to us in the form of an objectified system of share
designations and expressive forms. It is a world of everyday
life as lived and appreciated by 'commonsense' and displaying
a 'natural attitude'. The world, under this attitude, is 'taken for
granted'. The subject does not question the meaningful structure
of this life-world but has purely a practical interest in it. The task
is, in the natural attitude, to live in the world rather than study
it. Moreover, the world has meaning because of the intentionality
of consciousness. For most of the time, what persons are doing is
self-evidently meaningful. Such meanings are shared; the social
world is intersubjective. We make sense of our own actions and
those of others through a 'common stock of knowledge' we inherit
as members of a society. Though such knowledge has its own
personal biographical tonality and is continually changing, its
intersubjective structure is familiar. As Husserl emphasised, we
do not experience a stream of sense data but experience objects
constituted for us in consciousness, such as roads, houses, friends
and acquaintances, bicycles and cars, and so on. The structure of
life-world is displayed through 'typifications' constructed out of
whatever relevances arise from the actor's interests and purposes
at hand. As used by Schutz, such typifications would include the
universal and the stable as well as the specific and the changing.
The primary world in which actors live is an intersubjective one
of everyday life; a world of the natural attitude with its pragmatic
motives and interests. In addition, actors live in other worlds of
'finite provinces of meaning', such as art, religious experience,
dreams, childhood, and so on, each with a particular cognitive
style.[43] What Schutz means by this is not that we can simply
imagine the world to be as we choose, but that each province of
meaning has its own, though not unique in all respects, system of
relevances, and that the available 'stocks of knowledge' enable us
to bestow 'factuality' in different ways. The paramount reality is,
however, that of daily life. Of special concern to us is the world
of scientific theory. This style is that of the disinterested observer
who is only

concerned with problems and solutions valid in their own right for
everyone, at any place, and at any time, wherever and whenever
certain conditions, from the assumptions of which he starts, prevail. The
'leap' into theoretical thought involves the resolution of the individual to
suspend his subjective point of view.[44]

The private and pragmatic concerns of everyday life are bracketed
away. Science, both natural and social, adopt a theoretic attitude

to their subject-matter. They are not primarily concerned with practical consequences except as these are theoretically given. These are bracketed away in the attitude of science. The relevances are determined by the problem at hand and the procedures of the science concerned. These are the things that limit the horizons of the theorist who can, in principle, and contra the requirements of the 'natural attitude', doubt anything.

In this way Schutz tries to face what he sees as the basic epistemological problem of social science, namely, how, as sciences of subjective meanings, are they possible? Like all sciences they make objective meaning claims, or at least aspire to do so, but in the case of the social sciences these have to be within the context of the human activity which has created them and which cannot be understood apart from this scheme of action. Schutz's resolution of the difficulty is to argue that the social scientist must recognise the difference between social actors' experience of daily life and social actors as constituted for social science. This is required in order to make subjectivity available under the theoretic attitude. The social scientist is concerned with 'typical' schemes of action, using models which are 'lifeless fictions', 'constructs', 'ideal types', 'puppets' or 'homunculi' created by the social scientist. These models are distinct from the actual ontological conditions of individual everyday existence and are constructed according to the following postulates: logical consistency, subjective interpretation and adequacy. The first of these says that the construct must conform to the requirements of formal logic, the second that it must be concerned to incorporate a model of the human mind and its typical contents such that the observed facts can be seen as the result of its operation. The third criterion suggests a principle of objectivity, namely, that the construct must be formulated in such a way as to be understandable to the actor using his/her own commonsense.

It is worth noting again the third of the postulates, that of adequacy, since it recognises the problem that has been a major theme of this chapter, namely, the relationship between actors' concepts and those of the social scientist. Positivism's attempt to evade the socially grounded nature of knowledge by trying to formulate, as we have seen repeatedly, a neutral language of observation created tensions between actors' concepts and those of social scientists. The alternative here is to give actors' standards and concepts a much more salient role as a yardstick of successful understanding on the part of the social scientist. The social scientist's interest and purpose is merely to display the meanings that enter into actors' worlds. Various devices, the 'ideal type', 'homunculi', or whatever, are important to this, but Schutz's concerns are with how 'objectivity' or 'truth' are established within a natural life-world and its socially organised settings. There is no question of one form of understanding being absolutely superior to any other.

The shift this represents can be seen in a more recent sociological practice inspired in large part by Schutz's work: ethnomethodology as developed by Garfinkel who achieved what Lazarsfeld achieved for positivism, namely, to transform a philosophical doctrine into a methodology for social science. Although Schutz shared the aspiration of his mentor Husserl, of constructing a 'transcendental analytic' of knowledge by deduction alone, ethnomethodolgy is concerned to elucidate human interaction by empirical examination of those processes through which meanings are produced in social practice. As such it takes a neutral line, being content to describe the procedures of meaning production in any social activity it cares to examine rather than address the meanings themselves. In the tradition of Simmel and Goffman, ethnomethodology is a formal sociology interested in the properties of intersubjectivity as exhibited by social actors in the day-to-day world. Thus, and for example, any stretch of naturally occurring talk about whatever topic might be the subject of investigation for those formal properties of practical reasoning. One consequence of this stance is that nothing is required to be said about 'objectivity' or, for that matter, 'truth' except in so far as these are established through agreement 'work' on the part of the social actors concerned. All knowledge, including ethnomethdology itself, is communally grounded in human practice, and there is no way of reaching beyond this.[45]

This all too brief excursion into social philosophies which try to come to terms with meaning and all that this implies, illustrates once again the tensions arising out of the relation between the social sciences and their subject-matter. Research methods, where philosophical conceptions get their hands dirty as it were, reflect these tensions since their ability to do the job asked of them by researchers depends, in its turn, upon the researcher's own commitments to one or other of the available philosophies of social scientific knowledge. As far as social research is done under the auspices of interpretavist philosophies as I have called them, there is no doubt as to a difference in style and conception. More discursive, less quantitative and more qualitative, more argumentative and philosophical in tone, but no less rigorous (bearing in mind that very good rigorous research using any method is difficult to do), and, obviously, less ready to offer hypotheses or theories. Further, it would also be fair to say that much of the work within the traditions discussed remains philosophical rather than empirical in character in trying to argue for a point of view, though ethnomethodology, for one, is profoundly empirical. But, to the extent that such work is empirical, the emphasis on explanation as the point of empirical research has far less salience than has description of, to use a shorthand phrase, ways of life. Having said this, however, it must be pointed out that the kind of research methods one would associate with interpretavist social research, such as participant observation and ethnography, and the kind of sociological ideas of symbolic interactionism, developed quite independently of the kind of philosophical ideas we have been discussing in this chapter. Perhaps only ethnomethodology as an empirical social science has strong connections with a philosophical tradition. This particular point apart, from what has been said it is clear that an interpretavist social science would require methods that provide access to the world experienced by social actors themselves, and methods appropriate to the phenomena being investigated. The catchword might be, 'fidelity to the phenomenon', namely, the experiences and knowledge social actors exhibit in the course of their daily lives. And, as suggested earlier, the prior requirement of this is the development of a descriptive apparatus rather than an explanatory one. Also important to note is the methodological transformation of philosophical ideas. Again as remarked on before, both Lazarsfeld and Garfinkel, in their different traditions, placed philosophical interests on one side in favour of a more methodological concern to direct such ideas towards developing ways of investigating the social world empirically. The results are very different but, as a small irony, entirely consistent with what the new philosophies of science suggest as the preferred picture of science. Ontologies belong to theories not to some world independently of theories. What this also emphasises is the importance for science not so much method, but of rigour in carrying through the theoretical project.

I shall look at some more general implications of this last comment and arguments in the previous chapters in the next and final chapter. I shall try to briefly summarise the discussion of the previous chapters by considering rather larger questions about the nature of social science, its relation to the empirical world and, equally important, the relationship of the social scientist to the world he or she investigates. Such questions are, I would want to claim, questions about social research and its character as much as they are questions in philosophy.

REFERENCES

1. Taylor, C., 'Interpretation and the sciences of man' in Beehler, R. and Drengson, A. R. (eds), *The Philosophy of Society,* London, Methuen, 1978, pp. 159–200.
2. *Ibid.,* p. 174.
3. Austin, J. L., *Philosophical Papers,* Oxford, Clarendon Press, 1961, ed. Urmson, J. O. and Warnock, G., esp. pp. 66–7.

Also his *How to do Things with Words,* Oxford, Oxford University Press, 1965, ed. Urmson, J. O. A sociological exploitation of some of these ideas is to be found in Turner, R., 'Words, utterances and activities' in Douglas, J. D. (ed.), *Understanding Everyday Life,* London, Routledge and Kegan Paul, 1971, pp. 169–87.

4. Taylor, *op. cit.,* p. 175.
5. Durkheim, E., *Suicide,* trans, Spaulding, J. and Simpson, G., London, Routledge and Kegan Paul, 1952, p. 148.
6. Rosenberg, M., 'Faith in people and success orientation' in Lazarsfeld, P. F. and Rosenberg, M. (eds), *The Language of Social Research,* New York, Free Press, 1955, p. 160.
7. Cicourel, A. V., *Method and Measurement in Sociology,* New York, Free Press, 1964, p. 198. See also Pawson, R., *A Measure for Measures: A Manifesto for Empirical Sociology,* London, Routledge and Kegan Paul, 1989, for a critique of occupational rating scales.
8. Problems such as these are excellently treated in Heritage, J., 'Assessing people' in Armistead, N. (ed.), *Reconstructing Social Psychology,* Harmondsworth, Penguin, 1974, pp. 260–81.
9. Cicourel, A. V., *Theory and Method in a Study of Argentine Fertility,* New York, Wiley, 1973; also Phillips, D., *Knowledge from What?,* Chicago, Rand McNally, 1971.
10. Atkinson, J. M., *Discovering Suicide,* London, Macmillan, 1978. p 45; Cicourel, A. V., *The Social Organisation of Juvenile Justice,* New York, Wiley, 1968; Eglin, P., 'The meaning and use of official statistics in the explanation of suicide' in Anderson, R. J. *et al.* (eds), *Classic Disputes in Sociology,* London, George Allen and Unwin, 1987, pp. 184–212, for an excellent review of the issues.
11. Baccus, H. D., 'Sociological indication and the visibility criterion of real world social theorising' in Garfinkel, H. (ed.), *Ethnomethodological Studies of Work,* London, Routledge and Kegan Paul, 1986.
12. Wilson, T. P., 'Normative and interpretative paradigms in sociology' in Douglas (ed.), *op. cit.,* p. 74. The idea of 'tacit knowledge' is owed to Polanyi and deployed in much of the new sociology of science. See Polanyi, M., *Personal Knowledge,* London, Routledge and Kegan Paul, 1972.
13. Winch, P., *The Idea of a Social Science,* London, Routledge and Kegan Paul, 1963, p. 125.
14. *Ibid.,* p. 95. Also Schutz, A., *The Phenomenology of the Social World,* trans. Walsh, G. and Lehnert, F., Evanston, Northwestern University Press, 1967.
15. Vogelin, E., *The New Science of Politics,* Chicago, University of Chicago Press, p. 27.
16. Winch, *op. cit.,* p. 108.

17. Winch, P., 'Understanding a primitive society' in Wilson, B. (ed.), *Rationality,* Oxford, Blackwell, p. 81.
18. Schutz, A., 'Concept and theory formation in the social sciences' in Natanson, M. (ed.), *Philosophy of the Social Sciences,* New York, Random House, 1963, p. 237.
19. Evans-Pritchard, E. E., *Witchcraft, Oracles and Magic Among the Azande,* Oxford, Clarendon Press, 1965.
20. Winch, *The Idea of a Social Science, op. cit.,* pp. 23, 77, yet cf. pp. 46–7.
21. *Ibid.,* p. 89.
22. See, for example, Whorf, B. L., *Language, Thought and Reality,* ed. Carroll, J. B., Cambridge, Mass., MIT Press, 1956; Horton R. and Finnegan R. (eds), *Modes of Thought: Essays on Thinking in Western and Non-Western Societies,* London, Faber and Faber, 1973; Crick, M., *Explorations in Language and Meaning,* London, Malaby Press, 1976.
23. Louch, A., *Explanation and Human Action,* Oxford, Blackwell, 1966. Also Anderson, R. J. *et al., Working for Profit,* Aldershot, Avebury, 1989, for a discussion of sociology as irony.
24. Pitkin, H., *Wittgenstein and Justice,* Berkeley, University of California Press, 1972, p. 254.
25. *Ibid.,* p. 255.
26. Moerman, M., 'Analysis of Lue conversation: providing accounts, finding breaches, and taking sides' in Sudnow, D. (ed.), *Studies in Social Interaction,* New York, Free Press, 1972, p. 233.
27. Pitkin, *op. cit.,* p. 259.
28. See, for example, Hollis, M., 'The limits of rationality' in Wilson (ed.), *op. cit.,* pp. 214–20. Also Hollis, M. and Lukes, S. (eds), *Rationality and Relativism,* Oxford, Blackwell, 1982.
29. Quine, W. V. O., *Word and Object,* Cambridge, Mass., MIT Press, 1960; also Hookway, C., 'Indeterminacy and translation' in Hookway, C. and Petit, P. (eds), *Action and Interpretation,* Cambridge, Cambridge University Press, 1978, pp. 17–41. See Anderson, R. J. *et al., Philosophy and the Human Sciences,* London, Croom Helm, 1986, ch. 7 for a review of this thesis.
30. Hollis, *op. cit.*
31. Pitkin, *op. cit.,* p. 261.
32. *Ibid.*
33. Of course, the problem can be posed in such a form that it becomes practically insoluble. As Wittgenstein points out: 'If you went to Mars and men were spheres with sticks coming out, you wouldn't know what to look for'. But in dealing with human languages and actions one can learn to understand them in so many different ways. See Wittgenstein, L., *Lectures*

and Conversations, ed. Barret. S., Oxford, Blackwell, 1978, p. 2. Quine's point about the indeterminacy of translation is addressing a philosophical problem not claiming that translation is impossible.

34. Ryle, G., 'The world of science and the everyday world' in *Dilemmas,* Cambridge, Cambridge University Press, 1966, pp. 68–81, makes the point that descriptions are the result of different activities in the way in which 'objects' are made relevant for various interests. This point is also made, from a different philosophical tradition, by Schutz and emphasised in ethnomethodological work.
35. Weber, M., *The Methodology of the Social Sciences,* New York, Free Press, 1949, trans. Shils, E. and Finch, M. A., pp. 72–81.
36. For a selection of articles on the sociology of knowledge, see Curtis, J. E. and Petras, J. (eds), *The Sociology of Knowledge: A Reader,* London, Duckworth, 1970. For more recent work see also Mulkay, M., *Science and the Sociology of Knowledge,* London, Allen and Unwin, 1980.
37. Weber, *op. cit.*
38. Gadamer, H.–D., *Truth and Method,* London, Sheed and Ward, 1975. Also, Dallmyr, F. R. and McCarthy, T. A. (eds), *Understanding and Social Inquiry,* New York, Notre Dame Press, 1977.
39. Habermas, J., *Knowledge and Human Interests,* London, Hutchinson, 1971. Also Held, D., *Introduction to Critical Theory,* London, Hutchinson, 1978, and Taylor, *op. cit.* Anderson *et al., op. cit.,* pp. 76–81, contains an exposition of Habermas' views.
40. On phenomenology see, for example, Natanson, M. (ed.), *Phenomenology and the Social Reality,* The Hague, Nijhoff, 1970; Luckman, T. (ed.), *Phenomenology and Sociology,* Harmondsworth, Penguin, 1978; Anderson *et al., op. cit.*
41. See Schutz, A., *Collected Papers: The Problem of Social Reality,* The Hague, Nijhoff, 1962.
42. This is parallel to the path Husserl recommended for the proper constitution of the natural and the mathematical sciences.
43. Schutz never fully worked out the typology of domains, though he is clear that they shade into one another.
44. Schutz, *op. cit.,* p. 248.
45. On ethnomethodology, see Benson, D. and Hughes, J. A., *The Perspective of Ethnomethodology,* London, Longman, 1983; Anderson, R. J. and Sharrock, W. W., *The Ethnomethodologists,* London, Tavistock, 1986 and Heritage, J., *Garfinkel and Ethnomethodology,* Cambridge, Polity Press, 1984.

CHAPTER 7

Concluding remarks

I began in the first chapter by talking about the philosophy of social research as concerned with the intellectual authority of the claims to knowledge of the social world. The ensuing and inevitably selective discussion was built around two major themes which have characterised the history of social science. The first of these I referred to as the positivist orthodoxy which drew its inspiration from a particular conception of natural science, one which relied heavily upon an epistemology stressing observation as the route towards an objective knowledge of the external and 'real' world: that is, the world independent of the knower. This conception gave rise to, or at least justified if it did not originate, what are today the orthodox research methods of empirical social research. Even though the majority of these views recognised that human phenomena were not identical to those of inanimate nature, this was not regarded as a barrier to the deployment of the method of science in social science. Such differences had consequences for the kind of investigative tools available for research, but not for the logic of scientific knowledge itself.

The alternative theme to that of positivism took a rather different attitude towards the distinction between the human and the inanimate orders. In this case, emphasis was placed on the way in which the social world, and in some versions one could also add the natural world, was created in and through the meanings that human beings used to make sense of the world around them. Although positivist approaches had not ignored this feature of social life, they had not taken it as far as interpretavist conceptions, and instead retained the Durkheimian conception of a 'thing-like' objective, external social world 'outside' meanings and language as the prime determinant of the character of social life. Indeed, in some conceptions, Marxism being perhaps the most well known although it is also in Durkheim's work, the forces which impel societies and their members in their course are not known or understood by those members of society and can, in the end, only be revealed by the deployment of a special method. Just what this special method consisted in was, and is, highly debatable. For positivism, and in brief, the method was to be found in the supposedly empirical methods of science itself. For Habermas, to mention but one contra example, it required a fusion of the interpretavist method of hermeneutics and historical materialism.

As we have seen, each perspective met with a number of philosophical difficulties. For positivism, these included problems to do with the notion of a neutral observation language, the nature of theory itself, the relationship of theory to data and the problem of induction, the nature of social wholes, and the problem of aligning a scientific, especially mathematical, language with that used by persons in the construction of their ordinary conceptions of the world in which they live. As far as the interpretavist conception was concerned, difficulties centred around the nature of understanding and its criteria, social and cultural relativism, and the relationships between actors' conceptions and those of an observer.

It is, of course, impossible to, somehow, weigh and 'add' such criticism in order to see which of the two traditions ends up the superior one. Both are, we might say, in the same boat as far as their respective problems are concerned. There is no doubt that, of late, positivism – largely one suspects because it is the orthodoxy and there to be attacked – has suffered severe damage. Nor is this too surprising given its originally virulent and crusading tone. But its empiricist account of scientific knowledge failed to live up to its aspiration of providing laws of social life equivalent in scope, certainty and predictive capacity to those offered by natural science. Further, as exemplified by its own research methods, it failed to take adequate account of the fact that the social world, its topic of inquiry after all, is constructed through meanings and the practices predicated on them. In fact, some arguments went so far as to claim that such methods distorted the very phenomena they were designed to investigate. The almost inadvertent recognition of science as a social institution, as a social practice, dependent for its warrant on the often tacitly held beliefs that have their life within particular social and political communities, weakened presumptions about the superiority of science and the gates were open to attack by constructivist views. As indicated earlier, the chronically elusive idea of a neutral observation language failed to provide the bedrock upon which positivism's intellectual edifice depended, with the reluctant admission that investigation of the world was inevitably theory-laden. There was no theory independent way of observing the world. Accordingly, far from being a passive reporter, the researcher is an active agent in the construction of accounts of the world through the ideas and themes incorporated in forms of knowledge.[1] All of these difficulties, and more, seemed to make science simply another belief system with no special claims to absolute superiority over others. Nevertheless, as is often the case with philosophy, the empiricist tradition which positivism represents has not died. On the contrary, as we saw in

Chapter 4, it has tried to meet many of the problems identified to incorporate them into the tradition with the result that the notion of science, its objectives and its claims as a body of knowledge have been revised.

The alternatives to positivism had their own difficulties. If forms of knowledge are grounded in social practices, what then becomes of objectivity, the search for the laws of social life, the evaluation of different claims knowledge, and so on? Are we not condemned to an awesome relativity in which no claim to better knowledge can be made against another? Is a science of social life possible at all?

Perhaps this last question is not an appropriate one to ask. Certainly, it is inappropriate if it is assumed that an answer can be provided just like that. One of the lessons of the long and complicated story partially reviewed in this book is that philosophy is, in many ways, an equivocal guide to what is or is not a science. Philosophical arguments go on almost independently of the practices of, in this case, science because, as was indicated in the introductory chapter, philosophy's problems are not seeking for empirical solution but for rational clarification in the way that philosophy understands this. Philosophy is, one might say and not by way of criticism, obsessively concerned with argument and justification and, particularly, with its own nature as an activity. As said at the beginning, philosophical arguments go around and around, not to the point of nether sphincterial entry, but certainly to the point that nothing can ever be settled for philosophy. This is not, I hasten to repeat, a deficiency for philosophy; it is one of its features as an intellectual activity that its arguments, theses, doctrines, are there to be persistently scrutinised, examined, wrenched apart, analysed to destruction, etc., as *the* point of philosophical activity. Philosophical scepticism is, one could say, not an irritant for philosophy but a condition of its being the kind of subject that it is. Accordingly, looking to philosophy to tell us what science is, what the nature of the social sciences is/ought to be, is not unlike seeking guidance from an inveterate gambler on how to save money. One *can* learn, if only that it is wise to stay out of casinos, but one has to be careful. In which case, it is not bad advice to take the view that philosophy is parasitic on science; it cannot alter the practices or the findings of science in any way; a view, incidentally, held by many philosophers. Indeed, to the extent to which it legislates for what science is, or ought to be, as positivism was encouraged to do, philosophy becomes prescriptive not only of what the method of science ought to be, but also of what the world is like independently of any empirical investigation of the world; a view, incidentally, which encapsulates what metaphysics as species of philosophy is about. Accordingly, the question of whether the social sciences can become scientific is not necessarily one that philosophy can answer without engendering more philosophical debate, and quite properly from a philosophical point of view. The consequence is that the question of whether there can be a science of social life is not a question that we need necessarily look to philosophy to answer. We have a choice here. Moreover, it is just as plausible to argue that natural science's development owed more to 400 years of alchemy than it did to philosophical rumination.[2] At least alchemy provided a basic experience of 'trying things out' to see if they worked, to see if the combination of certain compounds produced gold, to see the effects of various manipulations on materials, and so on; a sound experience that provided valuable knowledge, if crude not to say erroneous by our own standards, which could be built upon. The alchemists, one could say, simply got better, grew into scientists, and sought for gold and wealth in more appropriate ways. However, the point is that the question of whether a science of social life is possible is very much a matter for the social sciences themselves.

Having said this, however, there is no doubt, too, that many of the social sciences do, as a matter of fact, take philosophical pronouncements seriously – some, far too seriously. Moreover, a number of the social sciences – especially perhaps sociology, though others are not immune – share with philosophy in being thoroughly debatable. In sociology, for example, there are differences of viewpoint at almost every level, including, and as we have seen, not just the 'technical' but the philosophically fundamental. However, the point is that given this argumentative character, and the range of issues within which debates range, especially those to do with the nature of sociological knowledge, then it is not surprising that there is a turn to philosophy in order to help decide among the perceived alternatives. But, in doing so, it is as well to bear in mind Popper's diagnosis of the 'scandal of philosophy': '. . . while all around us in the world of nature perishes – and not the world of nature alone – philosophers continue to talk, sometimes cleverly and sometimes not, about the question of whether this world exists'.[3] Ally to this Marx's dictum: 'The philosophers have only *interpreted* world, in various ways; the point, however, is to *change* it.'[4] Given the concerns of this book, if we see these remarks as directed toward the *investigation* of the world, then we can begin to see a difference in objectives between philosophy and scientific activity that is crucial to understanding something about the place that philosophy can be accorded within the social sciences. Empirical investigation is the business of social science, as it is of science, and any conception of the relationship between philosophy and disciplines has to take this on board in a way which does not, whether by default or by intention, award philosophy juridical status. In this respect more recent philosophy of science should prove more liberating, if without definite conclusion as to what the right way forward is to be for the social sciences. The recognition that science is a social activity, even though this is a troublesome notion, wedded to an abandonment of the ideal of absolute certainty – as this has been traditionally understood – has placed philosophical conceptions of science on a more plausible if, in some ways, less elevated footing. As far as empirical knowledge of the external world is concerned – the world that exists independently of thought even though it is 'thought', to put it this way, which gives us access to it – science is the best that we can do. But this is not a claim for any particular theory, any particular approach, as epistemologically and absolutely superior to any other. This becomes, in significant part, a matter for disciplines themselves. Given that the search for the indubitable grounds of knowledge, in the way that philosophy has traditionally understood this, looks to be a very long haul indeed to say the least, then we have no good reason to doubt science as a form of knowledge.[5]

For some, of course, this might seem to imply a total relativism of knowledge. For these the claim that all forms of thought, including science, are historical and social constructions would seem to rule out not only any notion of certitude but of knowledge, too, by relegating it to a species of belief. The search for absolute and certain knowledge has to be abandoned and in its place substituted a never-ending series of interpretations of the world. This is, in general terms and for example, the hermeneutic view. A large part of the problem here has to do with the notion of knowledge itself. Implied in the search for the indubitable grounds of knowledge – a search to remind ourselves, in which positivistic and some interpretavistic philosophies were involved – is the idea that a knowledge claim can only qualify as such if it is true in all respects; in short, if it is certain. Unfortunately, as a guiding principle this is particularly unhelpful since it would seem to rule out science itself because it, too, would fail as knowledge by this criterion. But to question this criterion is not to assert the contrary that no such thing as knowledge is possible. One need not to be trapped, as happens so often in philosophy and, one might add, social science argument, by a seeming dualism such that denial of one side is taken, often without further ado, as a subscription to the other. Rather, instead of abandoning the idea that there is certain knowledge, to put it this way, one can ask what qualifies as knowledge within various domains. Such an inquiry might not lead to some overarching conception of knowledge, but is this so necessary? I shall return to aspects of this question later.

Another consideration here, and one which makes the claim to knowledge such an important one, has to do with the status of science and, as far as the social sciences are concerned, their increasing role in the fields of public policy, economic management, social and health care, and so on. The very beginnings of social science were prompted by a desire to reconstruct society on rationally scientific lines, and such a step could only be taken after proper and accredited sciences of social life had been established. Of course, what this meant was seen very much in terms of the organisation and method of natural scientific knowledge current at the time. This legacy is still with us. Social scientists are now experts, though not always happily entertained as such, and play an increasing role in social, economic and public policy. Important in this is their status as scientists and that what they recommend has the force of knowledge and not mere opinion behind it. The accolade of science is important because of its association with the notion of incorrigible knowledge, even when this is offered in a qualified manner.

If this account is on the right lines then we can, I think, begin to see the source of some of the resistance to the interpretavist perspectives that have been reviewed. If all knowledge is socially grounded in human practice and nowhere else, how can we establish the objectivity and impartiality of scientific knowledge? How can it be shown that the social scientist's views are more privileged than those of the layperson, the novelist, the politician, the practitioner, etc. After all, the pronouncements of social scientists have the layperson's world as their referent, a world which is itself the subject of interpretation by those who live within it. Once again we are pushed back towards philosophy and the search for authoritative justification.

It would seem that almost wherever we begin, wherever we turn, given this need on the part of many social scientists to seek authoritative justification for their approaches and ideas, then the road will inevitably lead back to philosophy. This, of course, could be symptomatic of many things, but what it does suggest is that what is at issue is the relationship between the social sciences and philosophy itself, particularly in the manner in which philosophy has been awarded a juridical status in determining what is to qualify as social scientific knowledge.

As should be blindingly obvious from all that has been previously discussed, there are many aspects to this issue, one of the more important being, of course, the tendency to allow philosophical argument to dictate the terms of the relationship. Allied to this is an unfortunate reluctance to think in other than an uncharitably dualistic conception of the nature of philosophical argument and philosophical positions. This book itself is guilty of fostering such a conception by collecting together wide-ranging philosophical arguments and doctrines and organising them as if they were two opposing tendencies: the positivistic and the interpretavistic. There are, naturally enough, many practical heuristic reasons why this method of presentation is not an unreasonable one, especially since this is the way in which the issues, on the whole, enter into social scientific debate. However, there are manifold dangers here, not least, and as suggested earlier, that of reading opposing arguments in terms favourable to one's own position by regarding them as a more or less absurd antitheses without very much further ado. There is, it might be said, an absence of charitable interpretation.[6]

A good illustration of this can be found in one of the major issues arising from the preceding discussion, and one related to that of relativism, namely, the idea that knowledge is a social construction. Positivist doctrines are strongly committed to the notion that it is meaningful to ask what there is in the world independently of our ideas and thoughts about it. Further, they also lean heavily towards the idea that, from a scientific point of view, there can only be one complete description of what there is, of reality. It is this commitment which lent energy to the efforts to discover a neutral observation language, the invocation of the need for 'objective' data about 'objective' phenomena, and so on. The way the world is determines our classifications, our theories, and there is a vital, irreducible difference between how we think things are and how things really are. We can only determine which theory is best, is the correct one, by judging how well theories correspond with reality. Any other conception of the relationship between theories and the world would undermine the very point of science.

The task of any opposing, or even merely demuring, views against such an 'externalist' doctrine is going to be difficult and not only because 'externalism', to call it that, has a commonsensical plausibility. Denying 'externalism' is likely to be heard as denying that there is an external world and, accordingly, asserting that there is no difference between the way things really are and our ideas about them. Such a denial would be an absurdity. It would be to deny science, the credibility of its theories, and make the world a whimsical artifact of whatever ideas we might choose to entertain about it. Huge and vital areas of our lives would be rendered chimerical. To deny science in this way – and this is not a matter of our approval or otherwise of what science has produced – would be a denial of science itself and all that its investigations of the external world have made possible, including radio, television, computers, medical advances, bridges, technologies of all kinds. This is an obvious absurdity whatever attitude one might take to any of these creations. Therefore, arguments opposing 'externalist' views must also be absurd.

Once a response such as this is in place, then the arguments and the issues that depend upon them, in all their essential subtlety, become obscured on what comes to be seen as a clash of two diametrically opposed viewpoints. The stakes become nothing less than the absolute credibility of one or the other. There can be no compromise; only total victory for one or the other.

Of course, the picture I have just drawn is hyperbolical, but does, I think, capture some of the tone and manner in which arguments, particularly philosophical ones, are advanced and countered within many of the social sciences. But, a closer and more patient look at what the opponents of 'externalism' could be arguing does not necessarily, or even very often, result in the absurdity that is alleged. None of the opponents of positivist ideas, for example, denies that there is an external world, or claims that there is no point in investigating it, or that all the theories of physics, chemistry, biology, or what you will, are false. The objection is a logical one directed towards the crucial question of how theories and ideas are to be matched to the world. One of the more important functions of theories is to tell us what the world is like, otherwise there would be no point to theories. If we know what the external world is like independently of our theories, there would be no need for theories at all and, moreover, no need for science. In which case, and *contra* the externalist view, the matching requirement cannot logically be sustained since it needs a conception of the external world independently of theories; a conception which metaphysics sought to provide. We can only match two, or more, things if both can be inspected in their relevant particulars. To say that a photograph of a person is a good likeness of that person, matches them in a word; we need some procedure whereby we can compare the two. The photograph alone will not do. So, it is with the 'internalist' position. On logical grounds, not empirical or theoretical, the externalist position takes the matching procedure as too straightforward. This is not, to repeat, an argument against science or against empirical inquiry of any sort, but a query against the externalist's understanding of the basis of science.

An important lesson here is that it is crucial to get to grips with the issues of difference, and these are not always what they might appear to be at first sight, between viewpoints. Admittedly, this is not easily or cheaply won. Another lesson worth repeating is that the issue just reviewed, a classic philosophical argument, does not have a solution which makes very much difference to the practices of, in this case, science. The epistemological basis of science is a philosophical not a scientific matter.

But, of course, matters cannot be left here, if only for the reason that, as a matter of their history, philosophical arguments about the basis of science, of knowledge itself, are seen as crucial for the social sciences. The Strong Programme in the Sociology of Science, for one example, explicitly espoused relativistic doctrines as a necessary condition of its inquiries into the cognitive nature of science in order to substantiate the claim that all knowledge, including that of science, is a social construction. And it is not difficult to see the kind of reservations, not to say anxieties, externalists might begin to entertain about the direction in which such claims might lead. The argument that theories tell us what the world is like, tell us what observations are relevant to theories, and so on, comes perilously close to saying that theories determine their own truth; and this is but a short step towards the sociological constructionist views represented in the Strong Programme. Such views carry the implication that there are different ways of describing the world, whereas, for externalists, science is about discovering reality and there can only be one description of that. However, these conclusions do not necessarily follow. Ways of describing the 'same' thing are not necessarily at odds. Descriptions, to remind ourselves, are done from points of view, and without reference to that purpose we can easily embrace the idea that, to put it this way, there can be only one correct description of something. Doreen, who cleans my office, would no doubt describe the contents of my office from the point of view of someone whose task is to 'keep it clean', whereas I see it, and would so describe it, as an expeditious arrangement of books, papers, pencils, notes, computers, telephone, student handouts, etc., which reflect the fact that a publisher's deadline is due.[7] Neither of these descriptions is at odds with the other.

This brings me rather neatly to an additional point concerning one of the consequences of positivism, namely, the overemphasis placed on the business of science as predominantly concerned with explanation, hypothesis-testing, the generation of theories, etc. While these are obviously not unimportant in science, they do not exhaust the enterprise. More to the point, it also obscures some of the matters just raised in connection with descriptions and their dependence on points of view. Another important function of theories, classifications, perspectives, and so on, and the descriptions that belong to them, is that they are intended to get us to notice, to bring out, display aspects of things. This is, of course, a routine feature of science. Life-forms can be classified in different ways including their structural similarities. But this may not be expeditious in showing their evolutionary linkages. Bats and wrens have wings, but both are not birds. Whales and fish live in the sea, but whales are not fish.[8] Classifications, theories and descriptions depend not only upon the way the world is but also upon what it is we want them to show or display. It is not reasonable to suppose that there could be one classificatory or descriptive scheme which could serve for all purposes.

If we take these observations on board, then the kind of debates and arguments reviewed in the previous chapters begin to assume a very different patina. For one thing, the kind of social constructionist claims about the incommensurability of theories look far less melodramatic than many externalists, and many constructionists for that matter, make them out to be. Different descriptions might well represent different points of theoretical view. Or, the same description might have different consequences depending upon the difference in theoretical points of view. Once rid of the 'one description' prejudice, such variations become a commonplace feature of scientific, or even commonsense, inquiry.

Much the same points can be made in reference to explanation. What can often look to be incompatible explanations may well turn out to be answers to different questions. When talking about the explanation of some phenomenon, or a theory of some phenomenon, we are talking about the explanation, or the theory, of something about a phenomenon. Forgetting this means that we are likely to overestimate the extent to which different theories and explanations are trying to do the same things and, accordingly, the extent to which they are in competition with one another.[9] Explanations, it might be said though with some trepidation as to how this might be interpreted, are relative to the kind of question asked.[10] Being sensitive to the idea of 'explanatory relativity' means that we might be less likely to view, for example, disciplines as necessarily in competition with one another, sociology, say, with psychology, or that theories are necessarily answers to the same questions, that psychological theories of suicide, for one example, are necessarily in competition with sociological ones. Less likely, too, to imagine that perspectives, theories, approaches can be 'added' together, or synthesised, without serious loss of a clear sight of just what problems each of them is addressing.

Similarly, what can also be rejected is the claim that arguments about the social construction of knowledge necessarily imply a rejection of the idea that theories, descriptions, classifications are unconstrained by the world. They may be underdetermined but they are not thereby unconstrained. What is claimed is that the world, to put it that way, is interrogatable from different and varying points of view, even *within* science, and properly so. We can, indeed, have a great deal of choice about the frames of reference we deploy but not about what can be done within them. Again, what is rejected is the 'one story', the 'one reality–one description' conception as an adequate rendering of the objective of science.

Nevertheless, and even accepting the last point just made, the idea that descriptions, frames of reference, even science itself, are dependent upon socially shaped human points of view, human purposes, would seem to make science far too contingent a matter; a product, so to speak, of our history as a society. Science becomes, in a word, conventional. Once again, we find ourselves in the dilemma of, on the one hand, accepting the conventional elements in science and yet, on the other, struggling hard to see how, in this event, science could tell us anything about the world.

In significant respects the trouble here lies not so much in trying to find a solution to a philosophical problem, but with the way in which philosophical thinking can sometimes prevent us seeing things clearly. As Wittgenstein diagnosed one of the 'diseases' of philosophy: it can 'bewitch' our intelligence by not allowing us to see what is before our eyes.[11] Such is the problem here. In calling science a conventional pursuit one is saying little more than, like games or language, it could have been very different if our history as a society had been very different. But although we are aware of its objectives, its norms, its social organisation, its way of working, and so on, all the conventions of science and the result of agreement, this has nothing to say about the results of science. Soccer is a game and, accordingly, a conventional activity. Soccer could have been different. It could have been played with 13 players, have no offside rules, two goal keepers, and so on, but these would not determine the results of a match. This would depend upon what happens when the game is played. So, science as a social institution, gives scientists their objectives, tells them what will count as legitimate moves, what will count as the fulfilment of their objectives, and so on, but the results of the game will stand as how things are and as the result of inquiries into how things are in the world. To claim that some phenomenon, or its properties, is 'socially constructed' is not to relegate it to being an arbitrary consequence of social agreement or consensus. 'Objectivity', 'findings', 'truth', 'inquiries', and the rest, 'are rendered possible *only* by the acculturated, concept-laden and fundamentally social . . . operations of their producers and consumers'.[12] As Popper stressed, though with different purposes in mind, it is because science is a social and public institution that it can pursue its inquiries at all, test its theories, etc., with the evident success that it has. Scientists can be blind, prejudiced, deluded, partial, misguided by their values, personal idiosyncrasies and the rest, but it is the process of mutual criticism incorporated in the institution of science that, in the end, cancels these out. The social organisation of science makes scientific activity possible, but does not, thereby render its findings false for such reasons.[13]

The point of this lengthy excursus into the 'internalist' and 'externalist' controversy is not necessarily to commend or decry one over the other, though the balance of the arguments probably weighs against certainly the simple 'externalist' conception. Rather it has been to warn against a too dualistic and oppositional argument against viewpoints, especially philosophical ones, and, as a palliative to this tendency, the need for a charity in interpretation.[14]

After all, both the internalist and the externalist positions are not unreasonable. Both have much to say that is both serious and plausible. The discussion is also intended to warn against the tendency of much of social science to take philosophy either too seriously or not seriously enough; the point being to find a place for philosophy which allows social science, like natural science before it, to get on with its business as it sees fit. To allow itself to become embroiled in philosophical disputes will mean making a choice between doing social science or philosophy. Above I mentioned Wittgenstein's remark on the 'bewitching' nature of philosophy. In doing so, but in a very prolonged and detailed engagement with philosophical argument, he draws attention to the fact that the words, the concepts, which give the most trouble in philosophy are words from our ordinary language; words such as 'know', 'mind', 'body', 'true', 'perceive', 'relative', 'real', and so on. As speakers of language in ordinary contexts we know how to use such words without very much trouble. Once incorporated into philosophical debate they can so easily become detached from their 'homely' context; so much so that it becomes difficult to see quite what the problems are. Only by bringing them back to the ways in which words are used, when language is working properly, can we begin to appreciate what it is words will or will not do. For Wittgenstein, the aim of his philosophy was therapeutic in trying to rid philosophy of the urge to engage in theorising and did so by trying to offer reminders of the grammar of our concepts and so obtain a suitably perspicuous perspective on what can sensibly be said.[15] Wittgenstein offers no new theories of language, sociological or otherwise, but tries to get us to see what sort of questions can be asked about such things as meaning, reality, knowledge, etc., and where the differences lie between empirical questions, about which philosophy has nothing to say, and conceptual ones, about which philosophy is in danger of saying nothing that is of any sense.

Nonetheless, Wittgenstein does recognise that the craving for philosophy, the craving for generality, the craving for explanation where none is needed, is endemic. And although he himself did not address social science directly his strictures against philosophy are relevant to many social science theories.[16] Theories, perspective, points of view are often treated as if they were 'metaphysical pictures'; that is, as if they were intended to fulfil metaphysical tasks by nominating what the ultimate constituents of reality are.[17] We have already seen one example of this in the way in which the social constructionist view of scientific knowledge is taken, often by proponents and antagonists alike, as an answer to the philosophical question of whether knowledge is relative or absolute.[18] As I said earlier, the stakes become very high since what becomes the issue is nothing less than the nature of knowledge and reality. Empirical questions suddenly become confused with the epistemological and the ontological. But, as social scientists, we can just as well refuse to take a stand on whether scientific knowledge is relative or absolute as a precondition of our inquiries. Indeed, we can go further, as Wittgenstein did, and argue that neither position makes very much sense. The question of whether knowledge is relative or absolute is not an empirical question and, as a philosophical one, 'reminders' about the grammar of our concept of knowledge, along with the myriad of other concepts with which it is associated, should lead us to say that neither position is intelligible.

The upshot of these concluding remarks is that there is no necessary reason why the solution of philosophical problems should be a precondition for social scientific work. The philosophy of science, after all, did not precede science nor did it affect its practices and procedures overmuch. In which case, one of the ways in which the social sciences could learn from the natural sciences is not by trying to ape its logic or its procedures, but by refusing to accord philosophy any arbiter role. Certainly, and to repeat an earlier point, the philosophical attitude and interest almost precludes its having such a determinative role in empirical inquiry. Moreover, approaching the matter of the relationship between philosophy and social science as if this was a general and unitary one conceals, or glosses, the often complicated, certainly changing, and essentially debatable connection between the two bodies of thought. It is always possible to take any two disciplines and provide a general statement of their connection, and such a statement can be more or less useful depending on the context and the purpose. However, once we begin to pay attention to the details of the disciplines concerned, the general characterisation becomes denuded of informativeness. There are, for example, multifarious relationships, commonalities as well as differences, between sociology and economics, sociology and biology, sociology and philosophy, and so on, but none of them unitary or all-encompassing. Philosophy as a whole does not have a relationship to sociology as a whole in except the most general of terms. Rather, some philosophical arguments have a bearing on some arguments in social science.

Although many of the issues in the social sciences are arguments about philosophical matters, as a general rule it does not follow that all issues in social science depend upon the solution of these before getting down to empirical inquiries. Certainly, if philosophy could produce a method which guaranteed assured knowledge, then it would be foolish to ignore this; but, as I have argued, philosophy has long been arguing about such matters without final resolution and there is no reason to think that it will soon cease to do so. The search for a sound method simply opens up disagreements for philosophy and, to the extent to which it embraces philosophical issues, so too for social science.[19]

In conclusion, and contra the aggression and intolerance of positivism, we need to accept that the business of science, its philosophical foundations, are philosophically debatable, and will continue thus. We also need to see the correspondence theory of truth as far too simple an account of the relationship between theories and the world. Remember, too, and despite the emphasis placed on it by much of the philosophy of science, that much of the work of science is not directly concerned with explanation, and that physics is not the only model of science that we can have. In all of these respects, and among others, the 'internalist' views have much to commend them. But, note, such a view does not commit us to any particular theory, approach or method. What determines the effectiveness, the value, the fruitfulness of all of these is their ability to resolve, and rigorously, the problems that they set themselves by their own standards in pursuing their own inquiries. What of philosophy is all of this? Well, and to be blunt, philosophy can more than adequately take care of itself.

If all of this is read as suggesting that there is no place for philosophy in social science, this would be quite wrong. The aim is not to dismiss philosophy as totally irrelevant so much as to find a place for it given that, as social scientists, we need to give priority to social scientific problems rather than philosophical ones. As, hopefully, should be clear, resolving epistemological problems is difficult enough; just as difficult as resolving the problems set by the respective social science disciplines. The point is that we do not need to accept a juridical status for philosophy. We do have a choice in these matters. Nor do we have to accept that there can be only one all-encompassing relationship between philosophy and other disciplines that is unchanging. One can think of a number of areas where the engagement with and the deployment of philosophically derived arguments is an important step in trying to clarify just what the issues might be. The sociology of mind is a case in point as was the new sociology of science before it. There are other areas where, at least for now, there is no such imperative. Philosophical arguments will go on, as will social science arguments, and the two will connect in so many varied places.

One of the more interesting ways in which philosophy could be used is by deliberately choosing to treat philosophical doctrines as methodological recommendations, or agendas, rather than treat them as juridical reflections on a discipline. By this is meant converting philosophical or metaphysical doctrines into proposals for constituting programmes of researchable problems.[20] Not all philosophical doctrines will, of course, be amenable to such treatments or, even if they might look promising initially, will in the end bear much fruit. Seen in this way we can, perhaps, make better sense of, for example, Marx, Weber and Durkheim, and perhaps Lazarsfeld, too, all of whom could be seen as trying to work out programmes of research based upon their more philosophical ruminations. Garfinkel, too, explicitly treats Schutz's philosophy as the starting point for his programme of ethnomethodological work.[21] It is a strategy which emphasises differences by taking philosphically derived premises as prescriptive for the specification of researchable phenomena about which one hopes to produce findings. Of course, to be effective such a strategy needs to be rigorously deployed by refusing to dilute the initial prescriptions. Thus, Garfinkel, in pursuing his inquiries, took Schutz's philosophy, *and only that of Schutz,* as a set of methodological recommendations to see how far they would go. There is no attempt to produce bland syntheses by incorporating other perspectives into some so-called overarching one to make the ideas more 'plausible', more palatable, or to conform to some external standard to do with what a sociological theory, say, ought to look like as a bit of this and a bit of that, so that it is required to deal with both micro and macro orders of social life as if these were self-evidently the conditions for an adequate sociological theory. Rather, the aim is to push the ideas as far as they will go in order to see what they will and will not do. And, though all of this may take some time, it is consistent with the way in which much of natural science goes about testing its theories and exploring their ranges. Nor does it matter overmuch whether or not the doctrines chosen are philosophically 'correct' in order to make them interesting as methodological recommendations; what will count is whether, by making them so, they result in fruitful investigations which tell us something new.

Of course, none of the above implies an end to argument; rather it is a way of directing social scientific argument. As I said earlier, epistemological problems are difficult enough, as are those of designing satisfactory social scientific studies which work out. Behaviourism, to take one example, is a philosophical as well as an established research tradition, especially in psychology. As an ontology it tells us that the only legitimate entities are those publicly observable physical and physiological facts about human beings. In this sense it is a metaphysical picture and one that generates endless philosophical dispute. But, as social scientists, we do not have to become embroiled in this in order to make behaviourism interesting. We can choose to treat it as a proposal, an agenda, for research and just see how far the prescriptions, if rigorously followed, will take us in solving the empirical and theoretical problems, the objectives, the agenda sets. It may or may not take us far but this is not to be decided in advance. What will determine, or otherwise, the fruitfulness of behaviourism as a research programme, is how well it satisfies its own criteria, what problems it cannot solve, and how well it stands up in argument with those against it. Getting rid of the 'one-story' view – the 'one method/theory that will take us forward' view – means that we have to accept both a pluralism of theories, albeit a shifting one, and the patience to see how things work themselves out. This, after all, and as many of the new philosophies of science recognise, is the pattern of scientific discovery.

However, it could be said, surely that such an 'internalist' posture does just this; it ramifies the plurality of theories, competing points of view, when what it should be about is finding *the* theory, *the* method, *the* approach that will work the best? Even accepting this as an ambition, there remains the choice of how to achieve it and, if nothing else, it would seem that there is as much to commend the proposals outlined as there is in trying to seek the solution in other ways, including the philosophical. A unified theory, or a correct method, are not to be had for the wishing. If they are to be had at all, it will be the patient, steady, rigorous and imaginative investigation of the world.

REFERENCES

1. See, on this, Zaner, R. M., 'The phenomenology of epistemic claims: and its bearing on the essence of philosophy' in Natanson, M. (ed.), *Phenomenology and Social Reality,* The Hague, Nijhoff, 1970, pp. 17–34; also Blum, A. F., 'The corpus of knowledge as a normative order' in McKinney, J. C. and Tiryakian, E. A. (eds), *Theoretical Sociology,* New York, Appleton-Century-Crofts, 1970, pp. 319–16.
2. Anderson, R. J. *et al., The Sociology Game,* London, Longman, 1984.
3. Popper, K., *Objective Knowledge: An Evolutionary Approach,* London, Oxford University Press, 1972, p. 32.
4. Marx, K., 'Theses on Feuerbach' in *Marx and Engels: Selected Works,* Lawrence and Wishart, 1968, p. 30. Italic in original.
5. Note that there may be very good reasons to doubt particular theories, but not science *in toto.* Of course, we may still not want to subscribe to science as the be-all and end-all of all knowledge.
6. The notion of charitable interpretation is owed, though in a different context, to Davidson, D., *Inquiries into Truth and Interpretation,* Oxford, Oxford University Press, 1984; see also Anderson *et al., op. cit.* Much of this section is owed to ideas first aired, and at greater length, in that book.
7. This example is somewhat forced since I would have to agree with Doreen!

8. Anderson *et al.*, *op. cit.*, p. 37.
9. Garfinkel, A., *Forms of Explanation*, Cambridge, Cambridge University Press, 1981; also Anderson *et al.*, *ibid.*, pp. 43–4, for a fuller account.
10. Trepidation because this might be construed as an espousal of relativist doctrines of a metaphysical kind. Ordinarily, something is relative to something else, in this case, explanations relative to the question being asked. No more than this is intended.
11. Wittgenstein, L., *Philosophical Investigations*, Oxford, Blackwell, 1952.
12. Coulter, J., *Mind in Action*, New Jersey, Humanities Press, 1989, pp. 19–20.
13. Particular findings, theories, etc., might be false but not because they are social. Of course, particular scientists might cheat, lie, be overly influenced by self-interest, etc., but these possibilities do not vitiate science as a whole. This would be like condemning language because it can be used for lying.
14. A characteristic which is often notably absent from proponents of particular viewpoints.
15. It should be noted that the notion of 'grammar' that Wittgenstein uses is not to be confused with the grammar taught at school or when learning a foreign language. It can be glossed as what can sensibly be said within a language.
16. The literature on Wittgenstein and social science is now respectably large but variable in quality. For example, see Phillips, D. L., *Wittgenstein and Scientific Knowledge*, London, Macmillan, 1977; Bloor, D., *Wittgenstein: A Social Theory of Knowledge*, London, Macmillan, 1983; Hughes, J. A., 'Wittgenstein and social science: some matters of interpretation', *Sociological Review*, 25, 1977, pp. 721–41.
17. Anderson *et al.*, pp. 40–3.
18. See, for example, Barnes, B., *Interests and the Growth of Knowledge*, London, Routledge and Kegan Paul, 1977, and earlier citations.
19. I do stress that this is neither a criticism of philosophy nor a suggestion that if the social sciences abandon philosophy then their troubles will cease.
20. Anderson *et al.*, *op. cit.*
21. For a good account of Garfinkel's approach see Anderson, R. J. and Sharrock, W. W., *The Ethnomethodologists*, London, Tavistock, 1986.

INDEX

abstractive connection, 59-61
action,
    concepts, 97, 97-108, 126-36
    description of, 101-8, 110-11,
        129, 130-1
    interpretative nature of, 96-7
    meaning and, 94-7, 97-108,
        108-112, 115-27
    as moral appraisal, 129-30
    rules and motives in, 97-108,
        108-112, 115-26
agent, 103-8, 110
analytic propositions, 37, 81
anthropology,
    and understanding other
        cultures, 127-37
attitudes, 98, 115
        scales, 11, 42, 118-21, 124
Austin, J.L., 117

Bacon, F., 17, 18, 48
behaviour
    overt, 40, 130-31
behaviourism, 16, 162-3
beliefs, 16, 162-3
bureaucracy, 138

cause, causation, 28, 49-58, 85-6,
        90
    in sociology of knowledge, 76-9
    versus reasons, 100-7, 108-112
ceteris paribus, 57, 85
certainty, 80
Cicourel, A.V., 121
collectivity, 45
comparative method, 19
Comte, A., 18-19, 29, 41
    influence of Durkheim, 23, 30,
        31
concepts,
    dispositional, 97-108

'first order', 118
    lay versus scientific, 126-36,
        142-4, 149
consciousness, 39
    knowledge as act of, 140-4
Copernican revolution, 78
correlation, 28, 32, 53
culture,
    understanding another, 127-37
    relativism, 127-8

data,
    and meanings, 97
    'brute', 36, 115-116, 122
    social origins of, 118
Darwin, C., 19, 38, 48, 72
deduction, 51-8, 99-100, 143
Descartes, R., 8, 9, 11, 17, 18, 37
description,
    of actions, 97-108, 123
    literal, 100, 108
    'open textured' quality of,
        105-8, 119
    as social act, 106-7, 123
Dilthey, W., 89-90, 91, 138
documentary interpretation,
Durkheim, E., 1, 19, 44-5, 47, 98
    lessons of, 30-2, 64
    his positivism, 23-30, 44-5, 47,
        98
    his relational realism, 25, 31
    his study of suicide, 29-30, 55,
        118, 121

empirical
    indicators, 42-3
    regularities, 50
empiricism,
    differences between science
        and, 69-71
    'two dogmas of', 81

and interpretation of natural
  laws, 50-8, 59-64
redefining, 79-86
and theory, 50-8, 69-70, 85,
  96-7
Enlightenment, 17, 18, 138
epistemology,
  'evolutionary', 71
  and postivism, 16, 36-41,
    115-26, 148-9
  Quine's views on, 79-80, 84
  and scientific method, 10-11,
    40, 70-9, 84, 142, 155
ethnography, 144
ethnomethodology, 143, 144
Evans-Pritchard, E.E., 128-36
everyday life, 141-4
experiment, 10, 17, 28
  ceteris paribus conditions of,
    57-8, 85
explanation, 35, 99, 157
  causal, 28, 52-3, 59-60, 69
  Durkheim's views on, 26-7
  relativity of, 157
  teleological, 26
  in terms of meaning, 95-6,
    143-4

facts,
  'brute', 36, 115-16, 122
  social construction of, 75-9
  'social', 26-7
falsification, 35, 53, 70-2
free will problem, 112-13
functionalism, 63
Feyerabend, P., 78-9, 80, 83, 84

Gadamer, H-G., 138-9
Garfinkel, H., 107, 143, 144, 162
generalisation,
  'accidental', 56
  'empirical', 48-58
  'nomological', 55

Habermas, J., 139, 148
hermeneutics, 89-90, 138-9, 149,
  152
historicity, 138
history, 89-91
holism, 44-58, 72
humanistic, 94

Hume, D., 18, 20, 37, 49-50, 59,
  110
Husserl, E., 12, 140-1, 143
hypothesis, 15, 43, 77
  conjectural, 71
hypothesis-testing, 10, 156
hypothetico-deductive method,
  51-8, 62-3, 69-70, 72-3, 108

idealism, 20, 89
ideal type, 93, 137-8, 142-4
ideographic, 91
'imaginative reconstruction', 92-4
incommensurability, 74-9, 80,
  82, 128-9, 157
indexicality, 107, 122
individual
  and collective, 44-57
induction, 50-8, 70, 72-3, 78-9,
  148
intellectual authority, 5-10, 11,
  12, 62, 84, 124, 148, 161
interests,
  in scientific knowledge, 75-9
interpretation,
  charity of, 154, 158
  documentary method of, 108
  subjective, 140-4
interpretavism,
  some intellectual forerunners,
    89-94
  in hermeneutics, 138-9
  and meaning, 94-7
  and understanding, 92-4, 135,
    143-4
intersubjective,
  as character of social life, 107,
    117
  in hermeneutics, 138-9
interview method, 123-4
intuitionism, 92

knowledge,
  a priori, 21, 37, 50, 80
  as act of consciousness, 140-4
  common sense, 27, 121, 123,
    141-4
  foundations of, 7-9, 40, 90-1,
    92-4, 124-5, 137, 148-9, 152,
    161
  historical basis of, 8-9

incommensurability of, 74, 79, 80, 82, 128-9, 157
relativity of, 73, 128, 136, 149-50
social construction of, 64, 75-9, 124, 136-7, 142-4, 143, 149, 153-63
social dimensions of, 73-9
as trial and error, 72-3
Kuhn, T., 11, 35, 73-9, 80, 82, 84, 123

Lakatos, I., 72-9
language,
in hermeneutics, 139
lay versus scientific, 126-36, 149
and meaning, 116-27
observational and theoretical, 36-41, 52, 63, 124-5, 134, 149
ordinary, 110-112, 118
protocol, 38-41
and social reality, 117
of variables, 41-3
laws of nature, 19, 41, 85, 91, 93
'phenomenological', 83-4
and theoretical generalisations, 48-58, 59-64, 69-70
Lazarsfeld, P.F., 41-3, 56, 58, 143, 144, 162
life world, 140-4
Locke, J., 8, 12, 18
logic, 21, 37, 59
logical positivism, 12, 36-41, 70

Marx, K., 1, 2, 70, 72, 77, 137, 139, 148, 151, 162
materialism, 85-6, 89
historical, 139, 149
mathematics, 21, 37, 51, 53, 59, 149
meaning,
and causal explanation, 95-7
equivalence, 119-20
intersubjective, 117
and social action, 94-7, 108-12, 115-27
and social research, 136-44, 149
measurement, 53-4, 61-2, 90, 107
mental events, 39-41, 100-1
metaphysics, 20, 21, 31, 37, 70, 129, 150, 155, 159-60

methodology,
unity of, 19-20, 89-94
methodological individualism, 44-58
methodological reductionism, 47
motives, and action descriptions, 97-108, 110-12
Mill, J.S., 19, 23, 28, 30, 37, 48, 50, 52, 54
mind, 90

'natural attitude', 141-4
natural science,
and Enlightenment, 17, 18, 138
philosophical interpretations of, 35
and social science, 2, 13, 85-6, 91-2, 137
unity of method with social science, 19-20, 84, 89-94, 148
nomothetic, 91
'normal science', 11, 33, 73-4
normative order, 98

objectivity, 124, 136, 142
observation,
language of, 36-41, 53, 63, 124-5, 136, 148
ontology, 5-10, 36-41, 82, 84, 94, 96, 117, 140, 144
-ical realism, 42-3
multiple, 84
operationalism, 54, 130

paradigm, 73-5, 127
participant observation, 144
Pearson, K., 53
philosophy,
and intellectual authority, 5-10, 11, 12, 62, 84, 161
as methodological recommendations, 144, 161-2
nature of, 3-5, 12, 80, 150-61
and the research process, 10-14, 143
of science, 12-13, 36, 72, 84, 85, 149, 152
of social science, 1-2, 143, 148-9, 150-61
as therapy, 159-60

underlabourer conception of, 12, 13
Phenomenology, 12, 89, 136, 139-44
Popper, K., 70-9, 151, 158
Positivism,
    Durkheim's, 23-30
    elements of, 20-3, 148-9
    intellectual background to, 17-20
    interpretativist critique of, 115-26, 136-6, 142, 148
    methods of, 81, 84, 85, 90, 94, 107, 124
    and theory, 59-64
probability, 51
psychoanalysis, 139
Putnam, H., 82-3, 84

quantification, 42, 54
questionnaires, 11, 42
Quine, W.V.O., 79-86, 134

rationality,
    of methods of science, 73-9
realism,
    for theories, 83-4, 84
reasons,
    in action description, 97-108, 115-27
    ontological status of, 96
    versus causes, 95-7, 108-12
reductionism,
    methodological, 47
    psychological, 46-7
reification, 45, 46
relativism,
    cultural, 128-9, 149
    of scientific knowledge, 73-4, 78-9, 149-50, 152, 155-6
research,
    and philosophy, 10-14
    as practical activity, 123
    'programme', 77-9
'revolutionary' science, 73
Rikert, R., 91-3
Romanticism, 20
rules,
    and action description, 97-108
    constitutive, 103-8, 117

sceptic, -ism, 7, 80, 150
scientific method,
    as conventional, 124-6, 157-8
    as form of knowledge, 13, 69-70, 72-9, 84, 107, 124, 148, 152
    in Popper, 70-9
    as social construction, 75-9, 124, 136, 149
    as social practice, 78, 124, 149
scaling, 118-21
Schutz, A., 96-7, 128, 136, 140-4, 162
social science,
    and language of observation, 38-41
    and natural science, 2, 13, 89-94, 126, 152
    philosophical foundations of, 2, 153-4
    realist conception of, 85-6
    unity of method with natural science, 19-20, 36-41, 84, 89-94
social wholes, 44-58, 149
society,
    as level of reality, 23, 44
    as moral order, 23, 98
    'open', 72
    as subjective experience, 90-1
sociology,
    Durkheim's conception of, 24-5, 64
    formal, 143
    of knowledge, 75-9
    and philosophy, 151-2
    of science, 70-9, 123
    as science of subjective meanings, 142-4
Smith, A., 22
Spencer, H., 19, 23, 29
Strong Programme, 75-9, 155-6
structuralism,
    epistemology of, 112-3
subjectivity
    and meaning, 95, 115-27
survey, 11
Symbolic Interactionism, 144
synthetic propositions, 37, 50, 81

'theoretic attitude', 92-3, 136-7, 140-4

theory,
    common sense, 121, 123
    externalist versus internalist
        views of, 80-1, 148, 154, 61
    and nature of generalisations,
        48-58, 59-64
    realism for, 83-4, 85, 144
    and social science, 35, 148
    underdetermination of, 58, 74,
        79, 81, 82
translation,
    between cultures, 132-3
    between theories, 82
    'radical', 134
truth,
    correspondence theory of, 71-2,
        74, 153-6, 161
    as intersubjective agreement,
        124, 143
typifications, 121-2, 141

universal statements, 51-2

values, 115, 137-8
value neutrality, 93, 137-8
variables,
    language of, 41-4, 48
verification, 35, 37
versions, 116
verstehen, 92-4, 137
Vico, G.B., 89-90

Weber, M., 1, 2, 92-4, 98, 136-8,
        139, 140, 162
    definition of social action, 94
Winch, P., 109-12, 126-36
Wittgenstein, L., 12, 158-60